Mar 27/00 Happy 80th
love Dee, Steve & boys

GHOST STORIES

of

ONTARIO

D1553391

JOHN ROBERT COLOMBO

HOUNSLOW

Ghost Stories of Ontario

Copyright © 1995 by John Robert Colombo

1996 - 2nd Printing

All Rights Reserved. No part of this publication may be reproduced, stored in a retrieval system, or transmitted in any form or by any means, electronic, mechanical, photocopying, recording, or otherwise (except brief passages for purposes of review) without the prior permission of Hounslow Press. Permission to photocopy should be requested from the Canadian Reprography Collective.

Hounslow Press
A member of the Dundurn Group

Publisher: Anthony Hawke
Editor: Liedewy Hawke
Printer: Best Book Manufacturers

Canadian Cataloguing in Publication Data

Colombo, John Robert, 1936-
  Ghost stories of Ontario

ISBN 0-88882-176-X

1. Ghosts - Ontario. I. Title

BF1472.C3C6 1995   133.1'09713   C95-930614-5

Publication was assisted by the Canada Council, the Book Publishing Industry Development Program of the Department of Canadian Heritage, the Ontario Arts Council, and the Ontario Publishing Centre of the Ministry of Culture, Tourism and Recreation.

Care has been taken to trace the ownership of copyright material used in this book. The author and the publisher welcome any information enabling them to rectify any references or credit in subsequent editions.

Printed and bound in Canada

Hounslow Press	Hounslow Press	Hounslow Press
2181 Queen Street East	73 Lime Walk	1823 Maryland Avenue
Suite 301	Headington, Oxford	P.O. Box 1000
Toronto, Ontario, Canada	England	Niagara Falls, NY
M4E 1E5	OX3 7AD	U.S.A. 14302-1000

THE "PERSONAL ACCOUNTS" SERIES

*"They are the best collections of their kind being
produced by anyone, anywhere, so far as I can see."*
(Hilary Evans)

EXTRAORDINARY EXPERIENCES
Personal Accounts of the Paranormal in Canada

MYSTERIOUS ENCOUNTERS
Personal Accounts of the Supernatural in Canada

MACKENZIE KING'S GHOST
And Other Personal Accounts of Canadian Hauntings

UFOS OVER CANADA
Personal Accounts of Sightings and Close Encounters

DARK VISIONS
Personal Accounts of the Mysterious in Canada

Published by Hounslow Press, Toronto

Contents

Introduction

Ghosts of the past and of another country are recalled with affection by Noel Coward in the following lyrics:

The Stately Homes of England,
Tho' rather in the lurch,
Provide a lot of chances
For Psychical Research —
There's the ghost of a crazy younger son
Who murdered, in thirteen fifty-one,
An extremely rowdy Nun
Who resented it,
And people who come to call
Meet her in the hall.

The lively lines come from "The Stately Homes of England," an immensely popular song written in 1938 by Noel Coward. Had Coward decided to write about "The Older Homes of Ontario," instead of "The Stately Homes of England," the lyrics might not have been such a great hit, but there would have been ghosts aplenty about which to write.

When one thinks of Ontario in the 1990s, ghosts do not immediately come to mind. Perhaps what comes to mind is "ghost towns" because the province is suffering the ill effects of a serious recession, as it has suffered serious recessions in the past. There are more than one hundred "ghost towns" in the province, relics of cycles of boom and bust. But "ghost town" and ghost stories have little if anything in common.

No definition will be offered of what constitutes an apparition, a ghost, a haunting, a phantom, a poltergeist, a revenant, a spectre, a spirit, a spook, a vision, or a wraith. (*Roget's Thesaurus* will supply a dozen more synonyms.) Whatever terms are used, there is considerable overlap. Everything depends on definition, and it is difficult to define what cannot be seen, weighed, heard, etc.

The term "apparition" appeals to the author of *Harper's Encyclopedia of Mystical & Paranormal Experience* (1991), and according to that work there are seven types of "apparitions."

- Crisis apparitions (the dying acquaint the living with their plight);
- Apparitions of the dead (the spirits of the dead comfort the grieving, communicate information, conclude unfinished business, or announce their roles as guardian spirits);
- Collective apparitions (manifestations of the living or the dead, with multiple witnesses);
- Reciprocal apparitions (simultaneous communication of agent and percipient, a special condition rather like out-of-body experiences);
- Veridical apparitions (appearances that may be corroborated by fact);
- Deathbed apparitions (visual images of divine beings, loved ones, etc.);
- Apparitions suggestive of reincarnation ("announcing dreams" in which the deceased appear in dreams to members of the families into which they will be reborn, reported by the Tlingit and other Northwest Coast native groups).

To this list of apparitions could be added an eighth type, the poltergeist. While apparitions are principally visual, poltergeists are generally invisible, "noisy spirits" that go unseen but not unheard, for they are known by the noises and the disturbances that they create. Most visitors to haunted houses report sensations (footfalls, creaking doors, blasts of air, etc.) that are suggestive of poltergeists, not ghosts.

Arguments about the nature of ghosts and poltergeists and discourses on events and experiences of a psychical or a parapsychological nature are as old as the hills. Dr. Johnson summarized the opinions about ghosts when he said that all argument is against them, but all experience is for them. It seems silly to affirm that spirits exist in the same way that material objects exist, or that spirits are either subjective experiences or objective events, when it is apparent that by their very nature spirits partake of both levels of reality. The phenomenon exists on many levels of sophistication.

Short of having ghosts to study, we must content ourselves with studying reports of ghosts. We are lucky that reports are so numerous, even in Ontario. The reports that we have make remarkable reading, if nothing more; but if more, they attest to borderline states of consciousness that are intimately connected with the lesser-known human functions of intuition and imagination. It is possible that a mind, which is in some borderline state, may be intimately connected with another mind or even with a greater state of consciousness. All this is speculation. Speculation asks but does not answer the question "Do ghosts exist?" The regularly asked question is "Do *you* believe in ghosts?" The responsible answer to that query is "Ghosts do not belong to the category of belief, but to the the the category of experience."

It is probably safe to say about the views of the men and women whose ghost stories are included in the pages of this collection that they do not believe or disbelieve in ghosts; they have experienced ghosts. When read carefully, their personal accounts (technically known to folklorists and psychologists as "memorates") are seen to share features. For all their variety, for the varied incidents that they describe, the accounts seem to begin in the same way ("I know this sounds strange, but here's what happened to me"). They seem to end in the same way ("I know this sounds strange, but I do not know what to make of it"). Here are some other characteristic features of the accounts: the use of a chronological narrative, the sharing of information subsequently acquired, the charting of the emotional and physical effects of the experience, and (quite often) the witnesses' resolve to be a finer and more sensitive person in the future. Not all these characteristics are found in all these memorates, but many are there in full figure whereas others are there only in embryo. It is safe to conclude that ghost stories record transformative experiences that suggest that "ghosts are good for us."

This is the first collection of the province's ghost stories. The stories have a number of characteristics in common. Here they are:

The sixty-odd stories included in these pages come from the past as well as the present. They are Canadian and specifically Ontario stories. They were selected to represent the range of responses to the supernatural and the paranormal. A few of the stories recall well-known hauntings, but most of them deal with unknown hauntings, private affairs that are shared with members of the families of the affected or afflicted.

These are true, real-life stories. They are not works of the imagination. They should not be confused with literary short stories about ghosts, works of the imagination by well-known writers of fiction. Some of these stories are excellent. There are some quite good ones, and they may be found in a number of anthologies, including *Not to be Taken at Night* (1981), which I compiled with Michael Richardson, and Alberto Manguel's *The Oxford Book of Canadian Ghost Stories* (1990).

The stories in the present collection are products of human experience, not works of the human imagination. They are "told as true."

The stories from the past are reprinted from their original sources, and as their authors are dead, no one but a medium could vouch for their authenticity. Yet the themes of these accounts are consistent with those collected from living witnesses in recent years. The current stories are the products of my own researches. Nothing guarantees veracity, yet for each story specially collected for this volume, each living contributor has signed a statement that asserts its authenticity. Specifically, the statement signed by each author states that the incidents, the events and experiences, are complete in themselves, nothing relevant has been omitted, nothing irrelevant has been introduced, and the incidents were described with future publication in mind.

That brings us to the most characteristic feature of the present collection. These are first-person accounts. The witnesses themselves are the informants. There are no "as told to" stories included in this collection. These stories consist of the words of the men and women who have experienced ghosts or poltergeists or hauntings first-hand. Whenever we read a real-life ghost story, we are always moved and sometimes frightened. What scares us is not the description by the witness of the action so much as the description of the reaction of the witness. The non-human action — the luminous figure, the unaccountable cold air — is interesting in itself; it is the human reaction that is gripping, unusual, and convincing.

Collections of ghost stories are a fairly recent publishing phenomenon, but the person principally responsible for their present-day popularity was Elliott O'Donnell, the Anglo-Irish journalist and writer who in the early twentieth century published a series of ghost books, rather the way Andrew Lang a generation earlier established reading texts of the popular tales with his series *The Blue Fairy Book, The Red Fairy Book*, etc. Like Lang, O'Donnell was a tireless researcher of British lore and a high stylist, yet reading his tales one is always aware that one is being carried along by the sheer force of the words rather than by the force of the experiences. The reader often rubs his eyes and asks, "Could these things have really happened?" Perhaps the English ghost-story tradition reached its apogee in *Lord Halifax's Ghost Book* (1936). This influential collection has nothing to do with the city of Halifax, of course, but it was widely read across Canada. Lord Halifax even included the story of the Mackenzie River Ghost of the 1850s. It too is highly readable, rather literary.

Unlike the books written by O'Donnell and Lord Halifax, the present collection offers accounts of events and experiences in the very words of the witnesses. These are all first-hand accounts. In my researches, I turned up some lively, second-hand descriptions of ghosts and poltergeists, and I was tempted to reprint some of them because it would have given representation to mysteries that are more supernatural than paranormal in nature — that is, legends or superstitions rather than events and experiences *per se*. (I have in mind such "tall tales" as the ghost of Tom Thomson at Canoe Lake, the spectre that appeared in the foyer of Eldon House in London, and the University College Ghost in Toronto, tales for which there exists no documentation — at least not in the words of witnesses themselves.) Some accounts were written — but not witnessed — by news reporters and feature writers, but I find their accounts to be somewhat heartless. Such accounts abound, but they lack authenticity. So the present work is a collection of personal experiences of ghosts and poltergeists reported in Ontario by the witnesses themselves between 1764 and the early 1990s.

The Province of Ontario is an oddly shaped place with a number of peculiar features. For instance, Southern Ontario (the region of the province south of Barrie) is shaped like an elephant. (Turn the map upside down to see the image of the trumpeting Ontario Elephant.) Northern Ontario is the region of the province that extends from Barrie all the way to Hudson Bay. Part of the northern region suggests the image of the Windigo, the spirit of cannibalism of the Algonkian-speaking Indians. (To see the dreaded Windigo, turn the map upside-down; its head is outlined by James Bay; its eye corresponds to Akimski Island.) Readers unfamiliar with the Windigo may substitute for it the head and shoulders of a terrorist wearing a balaclava, an international image of contemporary horror.

Ontario is an unusual name; it means "beautiful water" in the language of the Iroquois. Indeed, innumerable lakes and rivers, large and small, are found throughout the province. Sightings of "lake monsters" are regularly reported in the spring and fall. (As someone noted about Ogopogo of British Columbia's Lake Okanagan and Scotland's Loch Ness Monster, sightings tend to occur at the opening of the tourist season.) But the name of the province is interesting in another way; it is an anagram. The letters of ONTARIO may be rearranged to spell the word ORATION. There is something magical about anagrams. Is any other province or territory distinguished with a name that is an anagram?

Ontario, with all its 10 million inhabitants, its relative affluence, its big cities that include the federal capital of Ottawa and the provincial capital, the city of Toronto, does not immediately appear to be the most mysterious part of the Dominion of Canada. Indeed, other parts of the country are pretty mysterious places in their own right. For instance, the Maritime provinces boast about the mysteries of the sea.

The coasts of Nova Scotia, New Brunswick, and Prince Edward Island, not to mention Newfoundland, teem with Grey Ladies who haunt their forlorn shores. Ancient curses protect pirate treasures. Fire Ships glow eerily on the horizon at dawn and at dusk.

After the Maritime provinces, the Prairie provinces might seem flat and dispiriting places. Yet there is the romance of the prairies and the woodlands, home of the ranging Ojibwa and Cree and other Algonkian-speaking Indians with their traditions of the Windigo and the rite of the Shaking Tent. Early explorers and rugged prospectors told tales of buried treasure, and everyone knows about haunted farmhouses exposed to the elements or to the elemental spirits of the land.

More than any other region, the Province of Quebec relishes its own, distinct traditions. Before the *terroir* became a province, *habitants* spent winter evenings huddled before hearths, recalling the legends of the *ancien régime.* They spoke and sang of the *loup-garou,* the Girl Who Danced with the Devil, and the Flying Canoe. Modern Quebecers still talk about miracle cures at historic shrines, bleeding statues, and outlines in tree-trunks of images of members of the Holy Family.

Then there is British Columbia, the province on the left. Its waters sustain strange creatures, like Cadborosaurus and Ogopogo; its foothills and deep forests are the stomping ground of the Sasquatch, the original Big Foot. The legends of the native people of the West Coast abound with strange beings, among them D'Sonoqua, the Kwakiutl giantess who carries off children in her great basket, all the while crying out, "OO-oo-oo-oeo."

The most mysterious part of the country may well be the Far North. The Polar Regions have their tales, as the balladeer Robert Service noted: "There are strange things done in the Midnight Sun ... the Arctic trails have their secret tales that would make your blood run cold ... the Northern Lights have seen queer sights ...." The disappearing Eskimo village of Angikuni (a discredited newspaper story that refuses to go away because it appeals to the imagination) and the occult speculation about the role of the North Pole and the North Magnetic Pole are ever current. The Arctic is not a body of land but a frozen sea; the Inuit tell stories of their sea-goddess Sedna who rules its abyssal depths.

If the Maritimes, the Prairies, Quebec, the West Coast, and the Far North are all mysterious places, what about Ontario? The province is surprisingly diverse. The Ottawa Valley is rich in the often-mysterious lore of its Franco-Irish settlers. Waterloo County carries on a German tradition of hex signs on barns and of farmers using charms from the tattered pages of *The Sixth and Seventh Books of Moses*. The Niagara Peninsula, settled by the English, includes not only the powerful Niagara Falls, the source of hydro-electric power as well as local traditions, but also the historic town of Niagara-on-the-Lake. This picturesque town has the distinction of having more ghosts (or at least reports of ghosts) per capita than has any other community in the country. Older cities like Ottawa, Kingston, Toronto, Hamilton, and London have ghostly tales that include forts and castles, churches and manses, even housing developments and highrise apartment buildings. Is there an Ontario hamlet, town, or city that lacks its "haunted house" or "cursed roadway"? One could write a short book on the subject of Toronto's ghostly past; one could do that, if one could find a publisher for it, sympathetic publishers being scarcer than ghosts in the 1990s! The native traditions range from strange doings on Walpole Island in the St. Clair River, past Dreamer's Rock on Manitoulin Island, all the way to the isolated communities with their Old Ways on the shores of Hudson Bay.

I will not argue that Ontario is the most mysterious of the provinces. But if the index of strange events and experiences is population pure and simple — the more people, the more numerous the reports of strange events and experiences — Ontario wins out. Because it is the most populous province, with ten million inhabitants, more reports of supernatural and paranormal incidents originate in Ontario communities than in any other province or territory.

There are two approaches to take to "the mysterious." One approach is the supernatural; the other is the paranormal. The word "supernatural" is shorthand for mysteries that offend logic and will forever remain miracles that defy reason. The word "paranormal" is a short form for occurrences that are mysterious but not miraculous because they will some day be rationally and scientifically explained. The reader is free to decide on the nature of the incidents in this book. Some may be supernatural; some may be paranormal. Indeed, some readers may decide that all of them are (in the words of the Bard) "much ado about nothing." Yet the incidents are intriguing all the same.

Whether supernatural or paranormal, Ontario comes by its traditions honourably for historical reasons. First there is the land and then there are the people. The landforms are varied and range from lush farmland to rugged Precambrian shield, the oldest rock in the world. If there is a "genius of place," it is certain to be found in places like Niagara Falls and Manitoulin Island. Throughout the provinces there are Indian pictographs that identify hundreds of "sacred sites." The "genius of place" is also found in abandoned fortifications and two-hundred-year-old public buildings that have weathered the storms of history. Castles, churches, and graveyards abound, not to mention modern apartment complexes.

Ontario's early history of occupation is suggestive. For perhaps ten thousand years both Northern and Southern Ontario have been inhabited by the so-called aboriginal people, distant ancestors of today's native people. The French explorers and missionaries called the Indians *sauvages*, meaning that they were indigenous to the land and that they held heathen beliefs and engaged in pagan practices. In the reports written by the Jesuit missionaries of the seventeenth century, there are descriptions of rites both gruesome and graceful that were ritually performed with enthusiasm by the Indians. Many of these rites involved the supernatural.

Few accounts of native practices are reported in the words of the native people. Some Indians who became missionaries gave their impressions of performances of the rite of the Shaking Tent in lands that are part of present-day Ontario, but these are far from what one expects to read when one hears the words "ghost story." The traditional tales are gripping, whether they were gathered at the Six Nations Reserve near Brantford, the Rama Reserve near Orillia, or the Cape Croker Reserve near Wiarton, but they are traditional accounts rather than personal accounts.

A little over two hundred years ago, the countryside was settled by the French and the English. It would be more exact to say it was settled by the French and the British; the English are numerous in Ontario, but so are the Celts, the Irish, Scotch, and Welsh. The Celtic strain is one that responds to mystery and to wonder, to mists and to harp-music! Delve into an early Ontario haunting and you will as like as not find a Celt lurking in the wings.

It was the English strain that was predominant; its dominance in society, commerce, and the arts gave the province its characteristic cast of thought. Northrop Frye caricatured that mindset as the "garrison mentality." The resourceful farmer, the hard-working labourer, the busy merchant, and the careful accounts-keeper were besieged on all sides. Nature itself was the besieger: the frigidity of winter, the swelter of summer, the rawness of the elements. One had to be cautious, especially with the boom-or-bust economy of mining. One had to accept the inevitable. Religion was a consolation; temperance was a safeguard; sanity lay in eschewing flights of fancy and imagination.

No one expressed this sense of caution with greater care and concern than the settlers who undertook to farm in the woods around Peterborough in the 1830s. Catharine Parr Traill came from England with few expectations and she found little here to please her. This is what she wrote about life in her book *The Backwoods of Canada* (1836):

> As to ghosts or spirits they appear totally banished from Canada. This is too matter-of-fact a country for such supernaturals to visit. Here there are no historical associations, no legendary tales of those that came before us. Fancy would starve for lack of marvellous food to keep her alive in the backwoods. We have neither fay or fairy, ghost nor bogle, satyr nor woodnymph; our very forests disdain to shelter dryad or hamadryad. No naiad haunts the rushy margin of our lakes, or hallows with her presence our forest-rills. No Druid claims our oaks; and instead of pouring with mysterious awe among our curious limestone rocks, that are often singularly grouped together, we refer them to the geologist to exercise his skill in accounting for their appearance; instead of investing them with the solemn characters of ancient temples or heathen altars, we look upon them with the curious eye of natural philosophy alone.

Mrs. Traill was describing absences rather than presences. In her books she shows no knowledge of native lore and little love of nature, although in later years her knowledge of the natural world increased. Her brother was another pioneer author. Major Samuel Strickland went even further in dismissing the mysterious in his book *Twenty-Seven Years in Canada West* (1853):

> Reader, did you ever see a ghost? A tall spectral-looking figure, with large saucer eyes, glides before you; and ere you summon courage to address it, vanishes from your astonished sight? Well, Canada is no place for ghosts. The country is too new for such gentry. We have no fine, old, ruined castles, crumbling monastic walls, or ivy-clad churches — no shelter here but the wild, wild wood.

Had he the inclination to explore, even imaginatively, the possibilities in the "wild wood," he would have been surprised. There may be no "ruined castles," but today there are "ivy clad churches," including a picturesque one that the Major himself helped the settlers to erect in Lakefield. Alas, there are no reports to suggest that this church or its graveyard is haunted.

Any references to Mrs. Traill and Major Strickland would be incomplete without a mention of their sister, Susanna Moodie. A pioneer settler and writer, the author of such classics as *Roughing It in the Bush* (1852) and *Life in the Clearings* (1853), she found herself critical of all aspects of life in Upper Canada and Canada West. (The largely uninhabited region became Upper Canada in 1791, Canada West in 1841, and Ontario in 1867.) She was even more matter-of-fact than they were about ghosts. From time to time she wrote about the consolations of religion, but she would have neither truck nor trade with the world of spirits. Or so it seemed. What has come to light in recent years is that she was a closet Spiritualist, as was her husband, the half-pay officer Dunbar Moodie. And so was her sister, Mrs. Traill.

Mrs. Moodie and many other people besides were caught up in the Spiritualist movement. In the 1850s in North America, it was as popular as are New Age practices in the 1990s. Spiritualists practised mediumship; New Agers practise channelling. The New Age movement grew out of the Spiritualist movement. As a social movement, the latter traces its origins back to the "spirit-rappings" that took place in the Fox Family cottage in Hydesville in upstate New York, just across Lake Ontario from the Bay of Quinte. Consecon is a farming community in the Bay of Quinte area, and it was from here that the Fox Family, which included the two young sisters Katie and Maggie, had some months earlier departed for greener pastures in the State of New York. At Hydesville, on 31 April 1848, rappings on a table were first identified as communications with the spirit of a dead pedlar whose body was lying undiscovered in the cellar of the cottage.

Mrs. Moodie and her husband Dunbar left the farming life in the Peterborough area far behind and by 1855 had re-established themselves in a lovely old house in Belleville, not far from Consecon. (The house is still standing today.) That summer Katie Fox, on the verge of becoming one of the world's most famous (or infamous) Spiritualists, was visiting family friends in Belleville. She met Mrs. Moodie and accepted her invitation for a visit. The account of that visit, which "converted" Mrs. Moodie to Spiritualism, appears elsewhere in these pages. It offers a rare glimpse of the private feelings behind the public face. After Mrs. Moodie watched with amazement as Katie Fox performed her unusual feats, she allowed herself to ask the following question, not in public but in a personal letter to her publisher in England, about trafficking with the supernatural: "Can such a thing as witchcraft really exist? Or possession by evil spirits? I am bewildered and know not what to answer ...."

Observing Katie Fox led Mrs. Moodie to try her own hand at "spirit-writing." This activity brought results far beyond her expectations. She was impressed, and so was her sister, Mrs. Traill, who then tried her hand at "spirit-writing" with equally strong and strange results:

> My sister, Mrs. Traill, is a very powerful Medium for these communications, and gets them in foreign languages. Her spirits often abuse, and call her very ugly names. Had I time, I could surprise you with some that she has received, but could not surprise you so much as she has been surprised herself. She, who was quite as sceptical as me, has been rendered very happy by the intercourse of her dear children, which has quite overcome the fears of death that she till lately entertained. Now, do not think me mad or possessed by evil spirits .... I could wish you altogether possessed by such a glorious madness.

Mrs. Moodie died in 1885, thirty years after being introduced to Spiritualism, yet she never proclaimed her interest in the principles or practises of the movement. During her lifetime she never identified herself as a Spiritualist, probably because in the public mind there was something sinister or shady about its practitioners if not its principles.

The founding of the Society for Psychical Research in London in 1882, and two years later that of the American Society for Psychical Research in Boston, lent the mantle of respectability to the field of research. Membership in the early SPR and ASPR included many of the leading scientists of the day. Sir Arthur Conan Doyle travelled widely and delivered well-attended lectures on the subject of "spirit-return" in which he emphasized the usefulness of psychical research. He found a friendly sparing partner in Harry Houdini, the magician and psychic debunker who was so fascinated with all aspects of mediumship and seances that he devoted much of his time to ridding the world of fradulent practitioners, which in his eyes meant all practitioners.

There was no shortage of Spiritualists in Ontario in the last half of the nineteenth century and the first half of the twentieth century. The British Spiritualist Mrs. Emma Hardinge-Britten visited the Queen City and so impressed were Torontonians that they named a congregation after her which is in existence to this day. The lectures of Sir Arthur bolstered the cause. Not all the proponents and practitioners were imported. There were home-grown psychics like the "trumpet-medium" Thomas Lacey. Alfred Durrant Watson, a prominent physician in Toronto, established the Canadian Association for Psychical

Research in 1908. It flourished briefly. Then he went on to explore mediumship, publishing three volumes of writings dictated by "the Humble Ones of the Twentieth Plane."

Today it is known that William Lyon Mackenzie King, who served as the Prime Minister, embraced spiritualistic principles and practices. He was born in Waterloo County in 1874. Until his death in Ottawa in 1950, he kept his spiritualistic leanings to himself. Only his closest friends knew that "table-rapping" was practised in the parlour at Laurier House in Ottawa and also at his estate Kingsmere in the Gatineau. Mackenzie King was exceptionally lucky that word did not leak out that he frequented mediums in London on his trips abroad and that he attended seances in cities across Canada. He attended seances in parlours in Ottawa, Brockville, Doon, Winnipeg, and elsewhere in the country. C.P. Stacey, the historian who studied King's deep and long-time interest in Spiritualism, found no evidence that mediumistic messages in any way influenced or affected King's political thoughts or actions. But Stacey came to a striking conclusion, after examining the detailed records that King kept of these sittings. The records noted the personal details of King's life that the mediums were conveying to him. Stacey had no real explanation for this. In *A Very Double Life* (1976), he wrote, "The only explanation I can offer is that thought-transference in some form took place between King and the medium. It is much easier to believe in this happening between living people than to believe in communication between the dead and the living."

The term "psychical research" gradually gave way to the term "parapsychology," largely as the result of the scientific and statistical studies of psychic phenomena that the psychologist J.B. Rhine conducted in the Psychology laboratory at Duke University. Rhine moved psychical research from the dark of the seance chamber into the well-lit research laboratory. He did this in the late 1920s after he became disenchanted with the mediumship that involved trickery associated with Mina Crandon, a psychic and socialite who was playfully known as Margery the Medium. She lived in Boston but was born, as was her brother Walter, in Princeton, Ont. Walter died there in a railway accident, but apparently his spirit acted as Margery's "spirit-guide" in Boston. So in a sense Walter was the catalyst behind the transformation of psychical research into parapsychological research.

Ideal for laboratory study is PK or psychokinesis, that is, movement of objects at a distance by immaterial means. This and thought-transference or telepathy were for many years the mainstay of Rhine's work. Most hauntings whether by ghosts or poltergeists involve PK in one form or another. One of the landmark studies of PK was conducted under the aegis of the New Horizons Research Foundation, established in Toronto in 1970. For seventeen years the group was led by biologist and statistician A.R.G. Owen and Iris M. Owen who conducted studies and published their findings. Their landmark study, known as the Philip Phenomenon, involved a circle of friends who acted *as if* they were in contact with a ghost or spirit, the entity (or non-entity) being an English Cavalier at the time of Cromwell named Philip of Diddington Manor. The group was surprised when seance-like results followed: table-rapping, table-tipping, etc. Then came results that were completely unexpected. Through a series of raps, Philip began to revise the cover story and offer a fresher version of his past and present. Elsewhere in these pages a small part of this interesting story is told through a passage from *Conjuring Up Philip* (1976) by Iris M. Owen and Margaret Sparrow. What is specially interesting is the notion that a ghost could be imagined, created out of whole cloth so to speak, and that the act of imagination could generate new notions, thereby acquiring an individuality and some form of life of its own. The Philip Phenomenon is assuredly a landmark case in the history of PK. The Owens added one more entry to Ontario's ghostly gazetteer, albeit an English one!

This brief survey of ghosts, poltergeists, Spiritualism, psychical research, and parapsychology, with special reference to Ontario, may seem far removed from the straight-forward appreciation of "ghost stories." Yet that is not the case. Knowledge about the traditions of hauntings increases one's interest in contemporary hauntings. Stories of ghosts and spirits should be told or read on dark and stormy nights. They should send shivers up and down the spine. They should seize the stomach and befuddle the brain. They should stop us in our tracks.

And they do all of that! But they also do more. They give us an occasion to pause to wonder, to wonder about the imponderables around us ... life, death, time, mortality, immortality, fate, and destiny.

Now all that we are waiting for is another Noel Coward who will write the lyrics for a song to celebrate the ghostly traditions of "The Older Homes of Ontario"!

Acknowledgements

I am grateful to the following people who contributed to the present work: Alice Neal, Dwight Whalen, Edith Fowke, Philip Singer, Anthony R. Hawke, Liedewy Hawke, Cyril Greenland, and David Gotlib. Important items appear here through the courtesy of Jeanne Hopkins of the North York Public Library, Rick Schofield of the Scarborough Historical Society, Najla Mady of St. Catharines, Ontario, and Jack Kapica of Toronto. Notable contributions to the present book as well as to previous books were made by Ontarians who later moved to other provinces: R.S. Lambert who retired to British Columbia; George and Iris M. Owen who relocated to Alberta. I wish to express gratitude to my wife Ruth.

But for the book's contributors who agreed to share their experiences with me there would have been no book. Some of the memorates which appear here have never before appeared in print; others are reprinted from earlier books in the Personal Accounts series published by Hounslow Press. Excerpts from the book *Boo!! Ghosts I Have(n't) Loved as Encountered by Najla Mady* are copyright 1993, appear courtesy NC Press Limited of Toronto, and are reproduced with permission.

There is a small but swelling literature that studies psychical research and parapsychology in Canada. Here are some germane contributions: Carl Ballstadt, Michael Peterman, and Elizabeth Hopkins: "'A Glorious Madness': Susanna Moodie and the Spiritualist Movement," *Journal of Canadian Studies*, Winter 1982-83. Eleanor Margaret Glenn: "Superstition and the Supernatural in Nineteenth Century Upper Canada," *Families*, Vol. 32, No. 3, 1993. Ramsay Cook examines Spiritualism in *The Regenerators: Social Criticism in Late Victorian English Canada* (Toronto: University of Toronto Press, 1985). C.P. Stacey examines Mackenzie King's Spiritualism in *A Very Double Life: The Private World of Mackenzie King* (Toronto: Macmillan, 1976).

There are three basic books in the field: R.S. Lambert's *Exploring the Supernatural: The Weird in Canadian Folklore* (Toronto: McClelland & Stewart, 1955). A.R.G. Owen's *Psychic Mysteries of Canada: Discoveries from the Maritime Provinces and Beyond* (New York: Harper & Row, 1975). Edith Fowke's *Tales Told in Canada* (Toronto: Doubleday Canada Ltd., 1986). A bibliography that is limited to 123 significant titles appears at the end of John Robert Colombo's *Mysterious Canada* (Toronto: Doubleday Canada Ltd., 1988).

Readers of this book who have unusual experiences are invited to set them down on paper and send them to the present author care of the publisher.

The Great Turtle

Let us begin with a turtle, the spirit of the Great Turtle, which the native peoples of North America maintain is the foundation of the known world.

Travels and Adventures in Canada and the Indian Territories between the Years 1760 and 1776 (Boston, 1809) is a classic of travel and observation written by Alexander Henry (1739-1824). The writer is called Alexander Henry the Elder so that he may be distinguished from his nephew, Alexander Henry the Younger. Both the Henrys were fur traders who kept journals of their experiences in the Northwest.

Alexander Henry the Elder was especially knowledgeable about native ways. In 1764 he witnessed a performance of the rite of the Shaking Tent by the Ojibways in the vicinity of Sault Ste. Marie in present-day Ontario. The spirit of the Great Turtle, held in special awe by the Ojibway, was invoked by the shamans who operated the oracle. They interpreted the answers to the questions directed their way. Henry was impressed with its operation, for the oracle was able to answer two of his questions. They referred to the disposition of the troops under the command of the British leader Sir William Johnson in faraway Fort Niagara and also whether or not Henry would ever return to live among his own people. Apparently the answers were correctly given though Henry was not in a position to assess them at the time.

The earliest references to performances of the rite occur in the journal of Samuel de Champlain in 1604. The rite of the Shaking Tent has been remarkably influential to the present day in surprising ways. It is felt that the birchbark tent-form led directly to the draped "spirit cabinet" employed by professional spiritual-mediums during seances in the nineteenth century. Present-day performances of the rite are regularly held in connection with native healing ceremonies at Kenora, Ontario.

Here are the words of Alexander Henry on the oracular turtle.

⚜

This was a project highly interesting to me, since it offered me the means of leaving the country. I intimated this to the chief of the village, and received his promise that I should accompany the deputation.

Very little time was proposed to be lost, in setting forward on the voyage; but, the occasion was of too much magnitude not to call for more than human knowledge and discretion; and preparations were accordingly made for solemnly invoking and consulting the GREAT TURTLE.

For invoking and consulting the GREAT TURTLE the first thing to be done was the building of a large house or wigwam, within which was placed a species of tent, for the use of the priest, and reception of the spirit. The tent was formed of moose-skins, hung over a framework of wood. Five poles, or rather pillars, of five different species of timber, about ten feet in height, and eight inches in diameter were set in a circle of about four feet in diameter. The holes made to receive them were about two feet deep; and the pillars being set, the holes were filled up again, with the earth which had been dug out. At top, the pillars were bound together by a circular hoop, or girder. Over the whole of this edifice were spread the moose-skins, covering it at top and round the sides, and made fast with thongs of the same; except that on one side a part was left unfastened to admit of the entrance of the priest.

The ceremonies did not commence but with the approach of night. To give light within the house, several fires were kindled round the tent. Nearly the whole village assembled in the house, and myself among the rest. It was not long before the priest appeared, almost in a state of nakedness. As he approached the tent the skins were lifted up, as much as was necessary to allow of his creeping under them, on his hands and knees. His head was scarcely within side, when the edifice, massy as it has been described, began to shake; and the skins were no sooner let fall, than the sounds of numerous voices were heard beneath them; some yelling; some barking as dogs; some howling like wolves; and in this horrible concert were mingled screams and sobs, as of despair, anguish and the sharpest pain. Articulate speech was also uttered, as if from human lips: but in a tongue unknown to any of the audience.

After some time, these confused and frightful noises were succeeded by a perfect silence; and now a voice, not heard before, seemed to manifest the arrival of a new character in the tent. This was a low and feeble voice, resembling the cry of a young puppy. The sound was no sooner distinguished, than all the Indians clapped their hands for joy, exclaiming, that this was the Chief Spirit, the TURTLE, the spirit that never lied! Other voices, which they had discriminated from time to time, they had previously hissed, as recognising them to belong to evil and lying spirits, which deceive mankind.

New sounds came from the tent. During the space of half an hour, a succession of songs were heard, in which a diversity of voices met the ear. From his first entrance, till these songs were finished, we heard nothing in the proper voice of the priest; but, now, he addressed the multitude, declaring the presence of the GREAT TURTLE, and the spirit's readiness to answer such questions as should be proposed.

The questions were to come from the chief of the village, who was silent, however, till after he had put a large quantity of tobacco into the tent, introducing it to the aperture. This was a sacrifice, offered to the spirit; for spirits are supposed by the Indians to be as fond of tobacco as themselves. The tobacco accepted, he desired the priest to inquire, whether or not the English were preparing to make war upon the Indians? and, Whether or not there were at Fort Niagara a large number of English troops?

These questions having been put by the priest, the tent instantly shook; and for some seconds after, it continued to rock so violently, that I expected to see it levelled with the ground. All that was a prelude, as I supposed, to the answers to be given; but, a terrific cry announced, with sufficient intelligibility, the departure of the TURTLE.

A quarter of an hour elapsed in silence, and I waited impatiently to discover what was to be the next incident, in this scene of imposture. It consisted in the return of the spirit, whose voice was again heard, and who now delivered a continued speech. The language of the GREAT TURTLE, like that which we had heard before, was wholly unintelligible to every ear, that of his priest excepted; and it was, therefore, that not till the latter gave us an interpretation, which did not commence before the spirit had finished, that we learned the purport of this extraordinary communication.

The spirit, as we were now informed by the priest, had, during his short absence, crossed Lake Huron, and even proceeded as far as Fort Niagara, which is at the head of Lake Ontario, and thence to Montreal. At Fort Niagara, he had seen no great number of soldiers; but, on descending the Saint Lawrence, as low as Montreal, he had found the river covered with boats, and the boats filled with soldiers, in number like the leaves of the trees. He had met them on their way up the river, coming to make war upon the Indians.

The chief had a third question to propose, and the spirit, without a fresh journey to Fort Niagara, was able to give it an instant and most favourable answer: "If," said the chief, "the Indians visit Sir William Johnson, will they be received as friends?"

"Sir William Johnson," said the spirit (and after the spirit, the priest), "Sir William Johnson will fill their canoes with presents; with blankets, kettles, guns, gun-powder and shot, and large barrels of rum, such as the stoutest of the Indians will not be able to lift; and every man will return in safety to his family."

At this, the transport was universal; and, amid the clapping of hands, a hundred voices exclaimed, "I will go, too! I will go, too!"

The questions of public interest being resolved, individuals were now permitted to seize the opportunity of inquiring into the condition of their absent friends, and the fate of such as were sick. I observed that the answers, given to these questions, allowed of much latitude of interpretation.

Amid this general inquisitiveness, I yielded to the solicitations of my own anxiety for the future; and having first, like the rest, made my offering of tobacco, I inquired, whether or not I should ever revisit my native country? The question being put by the priest, the tent shook as usual; after which I received this answer: "That I should take courage, and fear no danger, for that nothing would happen to hurt me; and that I should, in the end, reach my friends and country in safety." These assurances wrought so strongly on my gratitude, that I presented an additional and extra offering of tobacco.

The GREAT TURTLE continued to be consulted till near midnight, when all the crowd dispersed to their respective lodges. I was on the watch, through the scene I have described, to detect the particular contrivances by which the fraud was carried on; but, such was the skill displayed in the performance, or such my deficiency of penetration, that I made no discoveries, but came away as I went, with no more than those general surmises which will naturally be entertained by every reader.

The Baldoon Mystery

The earliest and eeriest haunting in the history of Upper Canada (as early Ontario was known) is the Baldoon Mystery.

The haunting took place in a farmhouse in the ill-fated colony of Baldoon. The colony was established in 1804, when Lord Selkirk resettled over one hundred dispossessed Highland Scots on the swampy land on the north shore of Lake St. Clair, between the present-day cities of Wallaceburg and Chatham. He held out hope that the frugal but hardworking Scots would become prosperous sheep farmers. But the settlement fell into decline and the settlers dispersed even before the War of 1812 dealt it a death blow. Thus did Baldoon became a ghost colony.

Today an official plaque marks the historic Baldoon Settlement. But its inscription makes no mention of the Baldoon Mystery, the sole event of continuing interest in the short history of Lord Selkirk's ill-conceived colonization scheme.

What happened at Baldoon was this. The large frame farmhouse of John McDonald and his family became the focus of a three-year haunting by a poltergeist. The haunting took place between the years 1829 and 1831. Over this three-year period, curiosity-seekers came from far and wide to witness the strange and inexplicable events. No ghosts were ever seen; instead dozens of witnesses reported hearing, seeing, and feeling typical poltergeist disturbances: hails of bullets, stones, and lead pellets; water and fire descending upon the house as if from the heavens. No one was ever hurt, yet on at least one occasion the house heaved from its foundations. The disturbances ended only with the house catching fire and burning to the ground.

Was the McDonald farmhouse being haunted by the devil? Was the cause of the commotion a poltergeist, a "noisy spirit"? Students of such matters point out that the Baldoon Mystery follows the worldwide poltergeist pattern, right down to the fact that the McDonald family included a pubescent girl whose name was Dinah. Skeptics have always maintained that the disturbances were, pure and simple, the product of hysteria, gossip, fear, superstition, and possibly revenge.

Whatever the cause or causes of the disturbances, there were many witnesses to the eerie events that took place at the McDonald farmhouse. Close to forty years after the disturbances, Neil T. McDonald, the younger son of the original owner, returned to the community where he was able to locate twenty-six of the older residents. They were willing to speak to him and he collected their statements and published them serially in the *Wallaceburg News*. The testimonials were then collected and printed in the form of a booklet titled *The Baldoon Mystery*. The booklet appeared in 1871 and has been reprinted from time to time.

One of the witnesses was William S. Fleury, an original member of the community whose farmhouse was just up the road from the McDonald's. Here is what he had to say about the Baldoon Mystery.

It was rumoured that there was a great mystery going on at McDonald's, and I, like a great many others, went to see for myself. I saw stones and brick bats coming through the doors and windows, making the hole whatever size the article was that came in. Parties would take these same things and throw them into the river, and in a few minutes they would come back again. I saw a child lying in a little cradle, when the cradle began to rock fearfully and no one was near it. They thought it would throw the child out, so two men undertook to stop it, but could not, still a third took hold, but stop it they could not. Some of the party said, "Let's test this," so they put a Bible in the cradle and it stopped instantly. They said that was a fair test.

The gun balls would come in through the windows and we would take them and throw them into the river, which is about thirty-six feet deep, and in a few minutes they would come back through the windows, so we were satisfied that the evil one was at the helm. I saw the house take fire upstairs in ten different places at once. There were plenty to watch the fires, as people came from all parts of the United States and Canada to see for themselves. No less than from twenty to fifty men were there all the time. The bed steads would move from one side of the room to the other, and the chairs would move when someone was sitting on them and they could not get off. They thought the devil was going to take them, chair and all. I saw the pot, full of boiling water, come off the fireplace and sail about the room over our heads and never spill a drop, and then return to its starting place. I saw a large black dog sitting on the milk house while it was burning, and thinking it would burn we threw sticks at it, but it would not stir, but, all at once, he disappeared. I saw the mush pot chase the dog that happened to come with one of the neighbours, through a crowd, and the people thought the devil was in the pot. It chased the dog all over the house and out of doors, and the mush stick would strike it first on one side and then on the other. The dog showed fight, and turning round caught hold of the ring in the stick, which swinging, would strike him first on one side of the face and then on the other. It finally let go of the dog's teeth and went back to the pot. I was acquainted with Mr. McDonald and knew him to be an upright man and in good standing in the Baptist Church.

This is my true statement of what I saw.

William S. Fleury

A Lumber Merchant's Story

Although hauntings usually take place indoors, some do occur outdoors. The crypts of crumbling churches and the cramped bedrooms in frame farmhouses may be ideal settings for spirits and wraiths, but fine locales are found in deep forests and on the vast tundras of the North, especially during summer storms or winter blizzards.

The events in the following story took place during a snowstorm. The setting is the Ottawa Valley, the picturesque region along the Ottawa River so fabled for its tall tales. The farming and lumbering region was settled by families that boast they are half-Irish and half-French.

In the present story, recorded in 1891, a lumber merchant recalls how almost forty years earlier, when he was a young shanty man or logger, a mysterious figure appeared in the blizzard to urge him on and thus to save his life. The merchant's name is not included in the account, but it seems he was an English-speaking logger working for an English boss. The locales that are mentioned are all on the Quebec side of the Ottawa River, but the shanty man's experience follows the pattern of apparitions known in Britain and on the European continent.

"My Ghostly Guide — A Lumber Merchant's Story" is reprinted from the columns of the *Ottawa Free Press*, 15 Jan. 1891.

⚜

In January 1853 I was engaged as assistant clerk in a large lumbering camp in the woods about a hundred miles north of the Ottawa River. Our main shanty was by the side of an outlet of Red Pine Lake about two miles from the south side of the lake itself, a sheet of water of oblong shape, about a mile and a half wide and five miles long. There was a fairly good road from the edge of the lake to the shanty, and from the north or opposite side of the lake, a road had been made for some miles through the forest, to a point where a smaller camp had been established, and where a number of our men were engaged in making timber. From the main shanty to the smaller one was probably twenty miles. One day my chief, Mr. Simpson, sent me off with some instructions to the foreman in charge of what we called the Crooked Creek camp. I started with my snowshoes on my back and moccasins on my feet, at a brisk pace. It was a bright clear day. The road to the lake had been well worn by teams, and as there had been a thaw covered with frost, the ice on the lake was hard and smooth. The road from the lake to the Crooked Creek camp was rather rough and narrow, and a stranger might have difficulty in following it. However, I knew the route well, and arrived at my destination in good time, just as the men were returning from their work, with axes on their shoulders. I spent the night in the camp, being asked innumerable questions, and hearing all the petty gossip the men had to relate. It must be remembered that these shanty men go into the woods in October or November and excepting in rare instances hear nothing whatever from the outside world until they come out in the spring. Next morning I executed my commission and about ten o'clock started back for the main camp. I had not travelled more than half the distance when a snowstorm set in. In the woods the flakes fell down steadily, and I had no difficulty in keeping the road. It was about sundown when I reached the edge of the lake. The snow had covered the track across the ice and there was nothing to guide me to the entrance to the road to our main camp on the opposite shore. Out on the lake the storm was blinding, but I did not doubt my ability to reach the other side and find the road. So I started across the lake. When less than half a mile from the edge of the woods, the snow was so thick that I could see neither shore. Moreover it was getting dark and exceedingly cold. If I should lose my way on the lake and have to spend the night there I would certainly perish. What was to be done? I turned in my tracks and managed to reach the North Shore again, stopping in the shelter of some bushes to recover my breath. Should I stay there all night? To tramp back to Crooked Lake camp was my first decision, but on reflection I remembered that any person travelling that road at night was liable to be attacked and eaten by wolves. Moreover, I was hungry and fatigued. While I was thus communing with myself, jumping up and down and slapping my hands to keep myself warm, I saw a man dressed in a grey suit with a toque on his head and a scarf around his waist, about 200 yards out on the lake, beckoning to me to follow him. I at once jumped to the conclusion that Mr. Simpson had sent one of the axe-men to meet me and guide me across the lake. So I ran with all my might towards him, calling to him at the same time. When I came close to the spot where he had stood, I looked around. He was not there, but a lull in the drift showed him some distance farther on, still beckoning me to follow. No reply came to my calls to the man to wait for me, but every few moments he would appear some distance ahead beckoning me towards him. I could not tell what to make of the man's eccentric behaviour, but thought possibly he was angry over being sent to look me up, and was taking this method of evincing his displeasure. At last I saw him on the shore, pointing towards the woods, and reaching the spot where he had been standing I found myself at the point where the road to our camp left the lake. The road was easy to follow, and I hurried forward, still somewhat puzzled over the refusal of my guide to wait for me; and wondering also why he had not brought a horse, and sled. I reached the camp just as the men had finished their supper, and everybody was surprised at my return. Mr. Simpson said he supposed that even if I had started from Crooked Creep camp in the morning I would have turned back when the snow storm came on. Somewhat bewildered I asked which of the men it was that guided me across the lake and pointed out the road to the camp. "Why did he not wait for me?" I asked in a rather injured tone. The men looked at one another in amazement. Not a man had been out of the camp that evening. Every man had returned from work at the usual time and remained in camp until my arrival. We were nearly seventy miles from the nearest settlement and there was no camp nearer than the one at Crooked Creek. Every person in the camp became restless and nervous. That man who guided me across Red Pine Lake was not a being of flesh and blood, was the general conclusion of the shanty men and my description of his disappearances and reappearances tended to strengthen their theory. The experience was such an inexplicable one that very few of the inmates of our camp slept that night. I was grateful for my rescue, and it was evident that whoever my guide was it was not my destiny to be eaten by wolves or frozen to death in attempting to cross Red Pine Lake in a snow storm.

The Spirit-Rapper

It is a quantum leap from the poltergeist of the Baldoon Mystery and the apparition of the Lumber Merchant's Story to the Spirit-Rapper. There are descriptions of poltergeists and apparitions throughout human history; Spirit-Rapping is a modern invention. Spirit-Rapping is concerned with the spirits of the dead and with establishing not one-way communication with those spirits but two-way communication with them.

In time Spirit-Rapping came to be called Spiritualism and forms of spiritualistic principles or practice are found in all the world's religions and spiritual traditions. There are churches that practice Spiritualism and offer their congregations readings and healings in most Canadian and American cities. The practices are called Spiritism throughout the Latin American countries. The rites of Spiritualists are found in those shamanistic practices of the indigenous peoples of the world that have survived since prehistoric times to the present day. The 1960s saw the birth of the so-called New Age. The experience of "channelling" is but a variety of spiritualistic practice.

The birth of the modern Spiritualism Movement, which may be seen as a rebirth of an inchoate desire of mankind to establish personal contact and responsive communication with superior powers in the universe, may be conveniently dated. The date is 31 March 1848. The place where two-way communication with the spirits of the dead was inaugurated was an isolated cottage in Hydesville, a small farming community in upstate New York. Anyone interested in visiting the birthplace of the movement will find that Hydesville is usually described as lying east of Rochester. In fact it lies north of the city of Newark, N.Y., and it is due east of Palmyra which boasts Hill Cumorah, a sacred site of the Mormons that is described in the pages of the *Book of Mormon*.

The Fox family was living in the Hydesville cottage in 1848. The family included two sisters, Margaretta (Maggie) Fox (1833-1893) and Catherine (Katie) Fox (1837-1892). They had been born not in New York State but in the farming community of Consecon in Ontario's Bay of Quinte region.

Late in 1847 the Fox family was finding it hard to make ends meet. Subsistence farming was not very profitable, so the family simply moved from Consecon, across Lake Ontario, to Hydesville, north of Newark. It was here the following year, on 31 March 1848, that Maggie and Katie's "spirit-rappings" were heard for the first time. The teenage Spiritualists were quick to attract rural, state, national, and finally international attention. They profited from it and became in time the best-known Spiritualists in the world. It is their Hydesville "rappings" that mark the birth of modern Spiritualism which includes the practice of mediumship, spirit communication, and what since the 1960s has been called "channelling."

Today there are no historical markers in Consecon to draw attention to the birth of Maggie and Katie Fox, yet the Fox Sisters were among the most famous Canadians of their time. They conducted seances throughout the United States and Great Britain, and they moved on all levels of society. In later years they were praised by fellow Spiritualists and disparaged by free-thinkers and church-goers alike on two continents.

The Fox Sisters did not forget the Bay of Quinte area. On one of their visits to Belleville in 1855, Katie paid a social visit to the pioneer author Susanna Moodie (1803-1885). Mrs. Moodie was a no-nonsense sort of person. She scoffed at the suggestion that the backwoods of Canada might be inhabited by spirits. If there are spirits at all, she argued, they haunt the castles of Old England, certainly not the pioneer homesteads on the old Ontario strand. Yet in her own living-room, Mrs. Moodie experienced the effects of "spirit communication."

Her memorable encounter with Katie Fox is described in much detail in the letter she addressed to her British publisher Richard Bentley in the autumn of 1855. She makes references to Mr. Moodie, her husband Dunbar, a half-pay officer. The letter was first published in *Susanna Moodie: Letters of a Lifetime* (1985) edited by Carl Ballstadt, Elizabeth Hopkins, and Michael Peterman.In a subsequent letter to Bentley, Mrs. Moodie described how she was inspired to experiment with automatic writing and with an early form of the Ouija board devised by Mr. Moodie. The Moodies took a quantum leap, from skeptics to "closet Spiritualists."

Since I last wrote you, I have had several visits from Miss Kate Fox the celebrated Spirit Rapper, who is a very lovely intellectual looking girl, with the most beautiful eyes I ever saw in a human head. Not black, but a sort of dark purple. She is certainly a witch, for you cannot help looking into the dreamy depths of those sweet violet eyes till you feel magnetized by them. The expression on her face is sad even to melancholy, but sweetly feminine. I do not believe that the raps are produced by spirits that have been of this world, but I cannot believe that she, with her pure spiritual face is capable of deceiving. She certainly does not procure these mysterious sounds by foot or hand, and though I cannot help thinking that they emanate from her mind and that she is herself the spirit, I believe she is perfectly unconscious of it herself. But to make you understand more about it, I had better describe the scene first, prefacing it with my being a great sceptic on the subject, and therefore as a consequence of my doubts anxious to investigate it to the bottom.

Miss Fox has near relatives in this place to whom Mr. Moodie had expressed a wish to see the fair Kate should she again visit our town.

One morning about three weeks since, I was alone in the drawing room, when my servant girl announced Miss F. and her cousin. I had seen her the summer before for a few minutes in the street, and was so much charmed with her face and her manners that it was with pleasure I met her again. After some conversation on the subject of the raps, she said, "Would you like to hear them?"

I said, "Yes, very much indeed, as it would confirm to do away with my doubts."

She then asked the spirits if they would communicate with Mrs. M. which being replied to, by three loud raps upon the table, which in *spirit language* means yes, I was fairly introduced to these mysterious visitors.

Miss F. told me to write a list of names of dead and living friends, but neither to read them to her, nor to allow her to see them. I did this upon one side of a quire of paper, the whole thickness being between her and me; writing with her back to me.

She told me to run my pen along the list, and as a test the spirits would rap five times for every dead, and three times for every living, friend.

I inwardly smiled at this. Yet strange to say, they never once missed. I then wrote under the name of poor Anna Laura Harral, a daughter of Mr. Thomas Harral who was for several years Editor of *La Belle*

Assemblée who had been one of my friends of my girlhood, "Why did you not keep your promise?"

This promise having been a solemn compact made between us in the days of youth and romance, that the one who died first would appear if possible to the other. The answer to my unseen written question was immediately rapped out, "I have often tried to make my presence known to you." I was startled, but wrote again, "If so rap out your name." It was instantly done. Perhaps no one but myself on the whole American continent knew that such a person had ever existed.

I did not then ask more questions, nor did Miss Fox know what I had asked. She told me to lay my hand upon the table and ask the spirit to rap under it. This I did. The table vibrated under my hand as if it was endowed with life. We then went to the door. Miss Fox told me to open the door and stand so that I could see both sides at once. The raps were on the opposite side to my hand. The door shook and vibrated. Miss F. had one hand laid by mine on the door. I am certain that the sounds were not made by hands or feet. We then went into the garden. She made me stand on the earth. The raps were under my feet, distinct and loud. I then stood on a stone pavement under me. Her hand slightly pressed my arm. The strange vibration of the knocks was to me the most unaccountable. It seemed as if a mysterious life was infused into the object from which the knocks proceeded. "Are you still unbelieving?" "I think these knocks are made by your spirit, and not by the dead."

"You attribute more power to me than I possess. Would you believe if you heard that piano, closed as it is, play a tune?"

"I should like to hear it — " I did not, however, hear it that morning, but two nights after, in the same room. I heard the strings of that piano accompany Mr. Moodie upon the flute, Miss Fox and I, standing by the piano, with a hand of each resting upon it. Now it is certain, that she could not have got within the case of the piano.

Mr. Moodie had on a mourning ring with his grandmother's hair. On the inside of the ring was engraved her birth, death, etc. He asked the spirits to tell him what was inside that ring, and the date of birth and death were rapped out, he had to take off the ring, having forgotten the date himself, to see if it was correct and found it so ...

I thought I would puzzle them, and asked for them to rap out my father's name, the date of his birth and death, which was rather a singular one from the constant recurrence of one figure. He was born Dec. 8th. I did not know myself in what year, was 58 when he died, which happened the 18th of May 1818. To my astonishment all this was rapped out. His name. The disease of which he died (gout in the stomach) and the city (Norwich), where he died. The question being mental could not have been guessed by any person of common powers. But she may be Clairvoyant, and able to read unwritten thoughts. I have not time just now to give you more on this subject, and though still a great sceptic as to the spiritual nature of the thing, the intelligence conveyed is unaccountable.

Can such a thing as witchcraft really exist? Or possession by evil spirits? I am bewildered and know not what to answer.

A Human Magnet

While the focus of this book is on ghosts in Ontario, from time to time the book's peripheral vision will catch sight of some related oddity or prodigy. Here is a genuine oddity: a human magnet.

In the early nineteenth century, with scientists like Kelvin and Faraday conducting experiments in the generation of electrical power, the lay public was concerned about the possibly beneficial effects of magnetism and mesmerism and other forms of "fluid energy." Health products employing magnetic principles were offered for sale in classified columns of newspapers and magazines. There were reports that some people, particularly young girls, were able to direct electrical currents at will.

Caroline Clare of London was such a human magnet, and her name appears in books about the paranormal by such authors as Colin Wilson as proof of this strange ability. The idea seems to be that human beings swim in ether rippling in various magnetic-electrical-mental currents and that some people are able to manipulate these currents — or be manipulated by them.

The information on Caroline Clare to date has come from a popular article titled "Electrically Charged People" contributed by Henry Winfred Splitter to *Fate*, Aug. 1955. Where did Splitter find his information? Did it flow to him from the ether? He did not bother to give his source.

Caroline Clare and her purported abilities are subjects that have long been of interest to me. One would think that the Ontario Medical Association would take an interest in such an oddity. There is no mention of her in its reports for 1879 or contiguous years, nor do references to her appear in other Ontario or Canadian medical journals of the day. Yet the reference to "a certain Doctor Tye" is verifiable. William Henry Tye was a physician from Chatham, Ontario., and an examiner in

Histology and Physiology for the College of Physicians and Surgeons of Ontario from 1881 to 1885. There is no such address as No. 25, Second Rodney Concession. The 1871 Census of London lists neither Caroline Clare nor her six brothers and sisters. In short, there is no proof that Caroline Clare existed, not to mention her purported abilities.

I was therefore pleased when W. Ritchie Benedict, a fellow researcher, sent me a newspaper account that is obviously the source of Splitter's information. The account titled "A Human Electric Battery" appeared in the *Daily Sun* (Saint John, N.B.) on 23 June 1879 and is reproduced here. Apparently the editors of the *Daily Sun* reprinted the article from the columns of the *Spectator* (Hamilton, Ontario.). Perhaps some diligent researcher will find the original article in a back issue of the *Spectator*. It is always possible that the original article includes further information about poor Miss Clare.

About two years since a daughter of Mr. Richard Clare, Caroline by name, and then seventeen years of age, living on Lot 25, on the 2nd con. of Rodney, was taken ill. Her disease could not be correctly diagnosed, and had many peculiar features. Her appetite fell off, and she lost flesh till from a strapping girl of 130 pounds weight, she barely weighed 87 pounds. There did not seem to be any organic complaint. The bodily functions were not impaired, the falling off in this respect was not such as in itself would alarm her friends. After a lapse of a few months she took to her bed. Then it was that a change occurred in her mental condition. Formerly she was noted rather for lack of conversational powers, but now fits or spasms would come over her, on the passing away of which, her eyes would become set and glazed, her body almost rigid, and while in that state she would discourse eloquently and give vivid descriptions of far-off scenes, far exceeding in their beauty anything which she had ever seen or presumably ever read of. On the passing away of this state she exhibited a great degree of lassitude and indisposition to move, and was taciturn and surly in reply to any questions. This continued till about a month since, when an extraordinary change occurred. The girl, although still not gaining flesh, appeared to rally. She became light-hearted and gay, and her friends anticipated an early release for her from the room to which she had been confined so long. Their expectations were not vain, for she is now about the house apparently as well bodily as ever. But a most remarkable development has taken place: She is constantly giving off electrical discharges, and seems to be a perfect battery. A person, unless possessed of the very strongest nerves, cannot shake hands with her, nor can anyone place his hand in a pail of water with hers. By joining hands she can send a sharp shock through fifteen or twenty people in a room, and she possesses all the attraction of a magnet. If she attempts to pick up a knife the blade will jump into her hand, and a paper of needles will hang suspended from one of her fingers. So strongly developed is this electrical power that she cannot release from her touch any article of steel which she may have taken up. The only method yet found is for a second party to take hold of the article and pull while the girl strokes her own arm vigorously, from the wrist upward. On her entering a room a perceptible influence seizes hold of all others, and while some are affected with sleepiness, others are ill and fidgety till they leave, and even for a considerable time afterwards. A sleeping babe will wake up with a start at her approach, but with a stroke of her hand she can at once coax it to slumber again. Animals also are subject to her influence, and a pet dog of the household will be for hours at her feet motionless as in death. A curious part of the phenomena is the fact that the electricity can be imparted by her to any article with which she habitually comes in contact. The other day a younger sister, while doing the house work, took up a pair of corsets belonging to Caroline, and on her hand touching the steel she was compelled to drop them with a loud cry and an exclamation to the effect that she had run a needle into her finger. Wooden spoons have had to be made for her, as she cannot touch metal. Altogether the case is a most remarkable one, and attracts scores of visitors to the house of Mr. Clare. Medical men are especially interested themselves, and it has been stated that Dr. Tye, of Thamesville, will read a paper on the subject at the meeting of the Provincial Medical Association which is to be held in London in the course of this summer. Mr. Clare is the father of a family of seven children, none of whom, except Caroline, show any abnormal qualities.

The Humberstone Poltergeist

An air of innocent charm accompanies these accounts of the outbreak of poltergeistery. The outbreak took place in a farmhouse in the Township of Humberstone in the Niagara Peninsula. The infectious charm is that of an earlier era that held that mystery, imagination, humour, and romance (rather than incredulity or commercialism) surrounded hauntings or alleged hauntings by spirits and poltergeists.

The first account originally appeared in the news column of the 15 June 1887 issue of the *Welland Tribune*. Subsequent mentions come from miscellaneous columns in the same newspaper for 22 July 1887.

The explanation offered for the outbreak of poltergeistery is so oblique — what with the reticence of the correspondent and the passage of years — that it obscures rather than offers an explanation for the details of the outbreak.

1. Ghostly

Humberstone has enjoyed a big "spiritualistic" sensation the past week, stirring society to its very core. Every evening, between 8 and 9 o'clock, stones kept falling upon the roof of Mr. Elihu Neff's residence, in this township, and there was no accounting for the whenceness of their coming. The stones could be seen descending, were heard to strike the roof, seen to roll upon the ground, and were picked up. That was all. Where they came from and what power sent them was the mystery. Watchmen were stationed in the house and about the house in all directions, but no light was thrown upon the stone-throwing. The excitement became intense and the crowd of watchers increased nightly. On Friday night the watchers were numerous, and on Saturday evening the number of ghost-hunters had swelled to between two and three hundred people. On the Friday evening, when the stones began raining down, an adjournment was made and the party entered the house determined to try and lure the "spirits" into a conversation. A circle was formed about a large extension table. Landlord McNeal acted as interpreter between the spirits and those of the flesh and demanded silence. During fifteen minutes one could have heard an ear-drop; then Mac said, "Let us repeat the Lord's prayer; and you may depend upon it, the spirits will trouble the house no more." With solemn dignity Mac began, and the responses from the twenty who composed the circle were clear and impressive. Everything passed smoothly along until half the prayer had been spoken, when Mac hesitated, and then whispered for a prompter. He had forgotten his early training in the excitement of the situation. His right and left supporters were in the same fix, and this beautiful supplication was brought to a hurried close. From that moment the stones ceased to fall, and excitement is slowly subsiding. Our illustrative artist was unable to get even an instantaneous photo of the ghost; but our special poet, who was also present at a great expense, read the following minutes of the seance, and the meeting dispersed:

(By Doc. W.)

'Twas on the 8th of July, '87,
A crowd went to Elihu Neff's to see the stones fall from heaven.

About thirty in number; Ah, how jolly we did feel,
And they chose for their captain bold Mr. McNeal.

We arrived at the place between seven and eight,
And the throwing of stones we patiently did wait.

Captain McNeal and his friend in their carriage sat,
The rest were enjoying a ghost-story chat.

When a thud and a far, and down came a stone,
Which made some of the boys begin to groan.

The stones kept falling helter-skelter,
When Mac crawled out of his carriage and got under shelter.

We surrounded the house by a dozen or more,
When Mac went in and then took the floor.

"A new idea," says Mac, "I now would suggest,
Which I think, perhaps, will be for the best."

Then around the table we quietly sat,
All joining hands, conducted by Mac.

"Keep quiet," says Mac, "those stones that are thrown,
Is done by a spirit that will make itself known."

Then very quietly we sat, not a word nor a sound,
Waiting very patiently for the spirits to come round.
About fifteen minutes then had elapsed,
When Mac thought at the time he had heard a few raps.

"If there is a spirit," says Mac, "that wishes to make itself known,"
We would like to hear from the one who does the stone throwing."

We listened a while, then at each other we did stare
When Mac struck out repeating the Lord's prayer.

We then all adjourned, and shook hands with Mr. Mac,
Who had banished the spirit and it never will come back.

2. Explanation

Mack [sic] was so successful at the Humberstone ghost matinee that his services were in demand at the gas well during the crisis this week.

*

The "ghost" is played.

*

Editor Tribune: — It seems surprising that in this enlightend age and country there should still be found those who "take stock" in such humbugs as witches, ghosts, spiritualism, &c. That we have a few such in our midst is evident from the "ghostly" story in your columns last week. The "stones descending," &c., was a mystery to those only who are believers in such humbugs — who always look for something weird and mysterious instead of natural and rational causes to explain anything that seems unusual and strange. When those stones, &c., were seen descending, it was evident to all except such as alluded to, that they were caused to do so by human hands, instead of the "spirits," as mentioned last week. This version is clearly established. *An individual well known in these parts,* from a concealed position threw the stones, pieces of brick, coke, &c. His object is also well known. As there are good reasons for believing that he and a few others are heartily ashamed of their conduct in this connection, their names will charitably be omitted — at least for the present. No reasonable person can object to a repetition of the Lord's prayer, or even part of it if the whole is not remembered, so long as it does not form part of a mixture of the sublime and ridiculous, as it did on the occasion referred to. The idea of a supernatural power being given to any person to enable him to *lure the spirits into conversation!* Nonsense. As long as persons are willing to be duped there will be those ready to dupe them.

An Eye-witness.

The Dagg Poltergeist

The Dagg Poltergeist was one of the wonders of the Ottawa Valley in the late nineteenth century. The focus of the disturbances caused by the poltergeist (an unseen but noisy spirit) was the farmhouse of George and Susan Dagg in the village of Clarendon on the north side of the Ottawa River, near Shawville, Québec. The Daggs were a typical farming family. They had two children of their own, four-year-old Susan and two-year-old John. The family was increased by one member when they adopted Dinah Burden McLean, an eleven-year-old Scottish orphan.

John Dagg and sixteen of his fellow farmers described some of the manifestations that took place on his farm in a short Report which was prepared by them at the request of Percy Woodcock, a journalist who covered the exciting events for the *Brockville Recorder and Times*. The manifestations extended over a period of about three months. The events were observed by Woodcock and by the witnesses who signed this statement, as well as by numerous spectators who were attracted to the little community from far and wide by reports of wondrous happenings. So close was Woodcock to the action, that many observers (especially rival reporters and correspondents) felt that he was somehow orchestrating it.

R.S. Lambert devoted a chapter to the Dagg Poltergeist in *Exploring the Supernatural* (1955). He called his account "The Ghost that Talked." The chapter concludes with these words:

> Most readers of this chapter will feel inclined to set the affair down to fraud, or hallucination. If so, one would like to know the answers to a few supplementary questions. What benefit did the Daggs, or the girl Dinah, get out of it? If it was a mere case of hysterical exhibitionism, why did it suddenly stop in

the early hours of November 18th, and never repeat itself? What degree of skill in ventriloquism was necessary to trick such a large crowd of people? Did Dinah (if she was the agent) ever display such skill in later life?

Alas, to these questions history gives us no answer!

Report

To whom it may concern:

We, the undersigned, solemnly declare that the following curious proceedings, which began on the 15th day of September, 1889, and are still going on, on the 17th day of November, 1889, in the home of Mr. George Dagg, a farmer living seven miles from Shawville, Clarendon Township, Pontiac County, Province of Quebec, actually occurred as below described.

1st, That fires have broken out spontaneously through the house, as many as eight occurring on one day, six being in the house and two outside; that the window curtains were burned whilst on the windows, this happening in broad daylight whilst the family and neighbours were in the house.

2nd, That stones were thrown by invisible hands through the windows, as many as eight panes of glass being broken; that articles such as water jug, milk pitcher, a wash basin, cream jug, butter tub and other articles were thrown about the house by the same invisible agency; a jar of water being thrown in the face of Mrs. John Dagg, also in the face of Mrs. George Dagg, whilst they were busy about their household duties, Mrs. George Dagg being alone in the house at the time it was thrown in her face; that a large shelf was heard distinctly to be played and was seen to move across the room on to the floor; immediately after, a rocking chair began rocking furiously. That a washboard was sent flying down the stairs from the garret, no one being in the garret at the time. That when the child Dinah is present, a deep gruff voice like that of an aged man has been heard at various times, both in the house and outdoors, and when asked questions answered so as to be distinctly heard, showing that he is cognizant of all that has taken place, not only in Mr. Dagg's family but also in the families of the surrounding neighbourhood. That he claims to be a discarnated being who died twenty years ago, aged eighty years; that he gave his name to Mr. George Dagg and to Mr. Willie Dagg, forbidding them to tell it. That this intelligence is able to make himself visible to Dinah, little Mary and Johnnie, who have seen him under different forms at different times, at one time as a tall thin man with a cow's head, horns and cloven foot, at another time as a big black dog, and finally as a man with a beautiful face and long white hair, dressed in white, wearing a crown with stars in it.

John Dagg, Portage du Fort, P.Q.; George Dagg, Portage du Fort, P.Q.; William Eddes, Radsford, P.Q.; William H. Dagg, Port. du Fort; Arthur Smart, Port. du Fort; Charles A. Dagg, Port. du Fort; Bruno Morrow, Port. du Fort; Benjamin Smart, Shawville, P.Q.; William J. Dagg, Shawville, P.Q.; Robert J. Peever, Cobden, Ontario.; Robert H. Lockhart, Port. du Fort; John Fulford, Port. du Fort; George H. Hodgins, Shawville; Richard E. Dagg, Shawville; George Blackwell, Haley's, Ontario.; William Smart, Portage du Fort; John J. Dagg, Portage du Fort.

Sir John A. Macdonald's
Advice from the Dead

As every school child knows (or should know) Sir John A. Macdonald became the first Prime Minister of Canada in 1867. Every Canadian history graduate should know that he died in office on 6 June 1891 and that he was affectionately dubbed Old Tomorrow for his habit of procrastination. He resided in Earnscliffe with his handicapped daughter Mary; the stately building is now the residence of the British High Commissioner. The most colourful character ever to hold that high office, he was knowledgeable about spirits — the potable kind. Not much is known about his religious or spiritual beliefs, but he was certainly no "closet Spiritualist."

Upon his death he was succeeded by Sir John S. Thompson who served as Prime Minister for only two years (from 1892 to 1894). Thompson also died in office, but whereas Macdonald died in an Ottawa hospital, Thompson died unexpectedly while on an official visit to Windsor Castle, 12 Dec. 1894.

Did Old Tomorrow try to communicate with Thompson, his successor as Prime Minister? Thompson had reason to think that it might be so. Thompson himself is responsible for the currency given this political anecdote. The anecdote is undated in its original source, but he related it to friends in Muskoka, Ontario's cottage country, in the summer of 1893 or 1894.

It is not a matter of historical record that Old Tomorrow attempted to communicate his views about private matters and affairs of state to his successor as Prime Minister through "a young man." Indeed, it is not a matter of record that dominant personalities are able to survive bodily death. But the story made the rounds in Ottawa at the time. "Anecdote of Sir John Thompson — A Curious Experience Related by

Faith Fenton" is the title the Spiritualist Benjamin Fish Austin gave this curious anecdote in *Glimpses of the Unseen* (1898). It is attributed to a woman named Faith Fenton. Nothing is immediately known about Fenton, but it seems that she contributed the second half of the anecdote about the newly deceased Sir John S. Thompson; the first half likely flowed from Austin's pen.

⁂

Sir John Thompson was never given to much speaking. He lacked the small coin of gossip and light badinage in a marked degree. His words were few and thoughtful. His attitude was that of the onlooker rather than the participant. Yet when time for speech arrived he was always ready.

This was noticeable in the House. When one of those breezes of disagreement so common in parliamentary debate sprang up between member and member, or party and party, Sir John — who usually sat in that atmosphere of absolute quietism which seemed in itself a strength to his followers — waited until the matter had gone far enough or threatened the dignity of the House, then he arose and spoke the few wise, judicial words that made instantly for peace.

In debate it was the same. His was always the final utterance upon any subject; not because of his official position, but because his few words summed up the entire matter. He was judicial always, and his impartial attitude won recognition and favour upon both sides of the House.

In private life he was much the same, speaking little but always a kindly observer; and nothing was more attractive to those privileged to meet him socially than his attitude of readiness to be interested and pleased.

"I know I am not a talker; but I am pleased to hear you talk, and ready to listen," his quiet look and bearing said to all who approached him. And because of these abiding qualities of strong sympathy, and a thoughtfulness that was not secretive, wrapped in an atmosphere of quietism, Sir John was a prince of listeners.

Yet he enjoyed fun, as most quiet people do, and when in the privacy of a friendly circle the merry talk went round, he — the usually silent listener — would frequently arouse himself to contribute something — an opinion, may hap, or an incident out of high official experience — that was well worth the hearing.

It was on such an occasion, and only a few months before his death, that he related in the presence of the writer one of those curious experiences that, doubtless, occur to all men of high official position, who become naturally a mark for cranks and faddists.

That it relates very closely to the Old Chieftain, and has hitherto been known only to some three or four of Sir John's associates, will render it of interest to Canadians everywhere:

It was an August afternoon that last summer of Sir John Thompson's life, and in the company of his family and two or three friends he sat on the deck of a certain pretty yacht as it rippled its way across the waters of Lake Rosseau. The Premier had been silent, as was his wont, lying back in his chair with closed eyes, with only an occasional smile, showing that he heard the conversation carried on about him.

Presently the talk turned on hypnotism. Sir Mackenzie Bowell, who was an adept at the art in his young days, related certain stirring experiences of his personal explorations into the misty land of psychology; and urged on by the joking skepticism of Senator Sandford, offered to give practical illustration of his power on the spot.

Sir John roused suddenly into a decisive veto against the half-jesting proposal.

"The thing is all nonsense, of course, but we mustn't have anyone tampered with," he said; and as the conversation drifted on naturally to the subject of clairvoyance and dreams, he related the following incident:

I had been premier something less than a year, and Sir John Macdonald had been dead, as you will remember, a year or so, when one morning my private secretary came into my office and said that a young man wanted to see me, but would give neither his name nor his business.

As on enquiry he appeared to be respectable and well-mannered, I gave orders that he should be admitted.

On finding himself alone with me, he told me frankly that he was afraid I would be surprised at his errand.

"What do you want?" I said.

"I have a message for you from Sir John Macdonald," he answered.

I looked him over keenly; but he was evidently in earnest, and moreover seemed conscious of his position.

I enquired quietly what the message was, and in what manner he received it.

Sir John Macdonald had appeared to him distinctly on several recent occasions, he said, urging him to bring a certain message directly to me; and so strong was the influence exerted, that he felt impelled to relieve himself of responsibility in the matter of complying with what he believed to be a request from a departed spirit.

The message related to certain private funds that belonged to Miss Mary Macdonald, and which her father — so the young man asserted — desired to be transferred and otherwise invested.

After the young man departed I made a few enquiries concerning him. He came from Nova Scotia, and was engaged in temporary work at Ottawa in the Buildings. He belonged to a thoroughly respectable family, and up to the present bore no reputation for erraticism of any kind.

I mentioned the matter to the lawyer entrusted with the Earnscliffe investments, and he confessed himself at a loss to understand how the private affairs involved in the "message" could have come to the young man's knowledge since they were known only to himself. But he admitted that the course indicated concerning the funds in question might be sound business advice.

The matter had almost passed from my memory, when one day, several months later, the young man presented himself again with a second "message" from the same source, this time for myself. Sir John Macdonald was earnestly desirous that certainly changes should be made in the Cabinet.

I took the young fellow in hand and questioned him closely. As far as I could discover he was honest, and apparently an unwilling bearer of these peremptory messages.

Why they were given to him, he said, he did not know; but after they were given he had no peace with the nightly appearance of Sir John Macdonald reiterating his commands until they were filled.

Sir John Thompson's quiet face broke into a smile of amused remembrance at this point in his story.

"You would need to understand Sir John's well-known penchant for planning Cabinet changes," he said, "in order to appreciate the effect of this last 'message' upon my colleagues, whom I took into confidence in the matter."

They listened in silence; but it was Sir Adolphe Caron who voiced their thought in one expressive sentence:

"Good Lord!" he exclaimed, "is the old man at it again?"

"What were the proposed changes, Sir John?" queried one of his listeners when the laugh subsided.

"Ah, that is another story," he said, smiling. "But again the curious fact is that they were excellent suggestions, and just such changes as I should like to have made myself had it been practicable. Yet this young man knew nothing of politics — much less of the inner workings of the Cabinet."

Appearance of the Lake Steamer

So much of Ontario is coastline it is surprising there are not more marine mysteries in the province's past. Yet one striking "mystery of the seas" is the appearance of the lake steamer on Lake Ontario off Etobicoke, west of Toronto.

The vision was witnessed by Rowley W. Murphy, former seaman and marine historian. According to Murphy, the event or experience took place in August of 1910. At the time Murphy was a youth, but he was not alone in experiencing the vision or apparition, for it was simultaneously observed by at least ten other experienced sailors and seamen.

Murphy recalled the appearance in considerable detail in his two-part article "Ghosts of the Great Lakes," published in *Inland Seas*, Summer 1961. Even a half-century after the experience, he was still of two minds as to the nature of the ghostly lake steamer.

⚓≈⚓

Experienced Great Lakes seamen have, like the writer, seen curious and extraordinary sights which remain clear in the memory. Could not some of these members record impressions of strange or wonderful occurrences which they have seen afloat, and yet appeared to be outside the boundaries of fact?

*

Another appearance from the past was seen by the crews of three yachts one beautiful night with full moon (like cool daylight) in August, 1910. My father, a cousin, and I were on a holiday cruise around the west end of Lake Ontario, and as we were late getting underway from Toronto Island, and were running before a light easterly, decided to spend the night in the quiet, sheltered and beautiful basin at the mouth of the creek, spelled "Etobicoke" — but always pronounced "Tobyco" by old timers. (This seems hard for present residents of that area to tolerate, as they insist on trying to pronounce each syllable.)

In 1910, the Tobyco Creek was really a small river which made an abrupt turn westward and widened into a small lake, with a good beach held by poplar trees, between this harbour and the Lake. There was perfect shelter in this excellent harbour from wind from any direction, though in a hard easterly, it was not easy to reach Lake Ontario through the narrow harbour entrance.

At the date of this cruise, there was one brick farm house westward of the harbour entrance and no buildings at all among the walnuts and oaks on the lovely grassy banks of the creek, except one ancient landmark, known as "The Old House," from the veranda of which Lieutenant Governor Simcoe is said to have shot a deer in 1794. This house was in good condition, when a few years ago it was torn down to increase parking space for a supermarket! The whole area is now completely built up, but in 1910 the beautiful grassy plains contained no buildings from Lake Ontario to the Lakeshore Road, except the landmark mentioned.

Our cruising yawl, with a larger sister of the same rig and a still larger Mackinaw (one of several "fish boats" converted to cruising yachts with great success), were the only occupants of the harbour this perfect night. The crews of the three yachts numbered eleven in all, and as is generally the case, after dinner was over and dishes done, gathered on deck in the moonlight to engage in the best conversation known to man.

All hands turned in earlier than usual, there being no distractions ashore, and by midnight were deep in happy dreams, helped by the quiet ripple alongside. At what was about 1:30 a.m., the writer was wakened by four blasts on a steamer's whistle. After waiting for a repetition — to be sure it was not part of a dream — he put his head out of the companionway.

There, flooded by moonlight, was a steamer heading about WSW — at about half speed, and approximately half a mile off shore. She had a good chime whistle but not much steam — like *Noronic* on that awful night of September 17, 1949, who also repeated her four blasts many times.

But who was she? On this amazingly beautiful night, with memory strained to the utmost, it was difficult to do more than think of who she was not! She was considerably smaller than the three famous Upper Lakers, *China, India,* and *Japan* (about this date under Canadian registry, known as *City of Montreal, City of Ottawa,* and *City of Hamilton*). She was not as small as *Lake Michigan,* but like her, did not appear to be of all wooden construction. However, there were many in the past, of quite related design and size. The vessel seen had white topsides and deckhouses, and appeared to be grey below her main deck, like the Welland Canal-sized freighters (at this date, the big wooden steamers of the Ogdensburg Line of the Rutland Transporation Company). *Persia* and *Ocean* were like her in size and arrangement, but were all white and came to known ends, and of course *Arabiana* was of iron, and was black.

In this appearance off "Toby Coke" (a variant of spelling), the starboard light, deck lights and some other lights seen through cabin windows, had the quality of oil lamps; and her tall mast, with fitted topmast, carried gaff and brailed-up hain-sail. Her smokestack was all black, and she had no hog beams — but appeared to have four white boats. Her chime whistle was a good one, but was reduced in volume as previously mentioned, and was sounded continuously for perhaps ten minutes. Very soon all hands now watching on the beach decided that something would be done. So a dinghy was quickly hauled over from the basin, and, with a crew of four made up from some of those aboard the three yachts, started to row out with all speed to the vessel in distress, to give her what assistance might be possible.

As the boys in the dinghy reached the area where something definite should have been seen, there was nothing there beyond clear and powerful moonlight, a few gulls wakened from sleep — but something else, impossible to ignore. This was a succession of long curving ripples in a more or less circular pattern, which just might have been the last appearance of those caused by the foundering of a steamer many years before on a night of similar beauty. In any case, the four in the dinghy returned in about an hour, reporting also small scraps of wreckage which were probably just old driftwood, seldom seen with any fresh breezes blowing.

But something more there was. This was the appearance to the visual and audible memory, which those on the beach and those afloat had seen and heard, of something which had occurred in the more or less distant past, and which had returned to the consciousness of living men after a long absence.

Whatever the cause, the experienced crews of the three yachts mentioned were of one mind as to what had been seen and heard. At least eleven lake sailors would be unlikely to agree on the character of this reappearance without good reason! And the reason was certainly not firewater working on the mass imagination, as no one of the three yachts had any aboard. So, reader, what is the answer?

The Bluish Light

Rochelle M. Wallis lives in retirement in Ridgeway, Ontario. She read in the *Fort Erie Review* that I was collecting accounts of odd and unusual experiences for one of my publications. She mislaid the notice, but a year or so later she came across the clipping and resolved to write out an experience that had occurred to her many years earlier.

On Nov. 1, 1991 she sent me the following account. It is interesting how the incident of "the bluish light" has remained so vivid in her memory — for close to eight decades! It is also intriguing that the memory of an event or experience that occurred to an eight-year-old child way back in 1913 should be independently confirmed to the satisfaction of an adult in 1965.

⚜

I remember well when I was eight years old. We lived in a log house by Georgian Bay, at Pine Point, or Pointe aux Pins as the place was then called. My two brothers and I slept upstairs and our parents downstairs. The stairway was behind a pantry, and there was a door one step up. Also, the stove pipe went through the floor and up, so we could get some warmth. One side of the house had no windows, as there was a long shed located there.

During the night, I woke thinking someone was coming up the stairs. I heard the sound of shoe packs or moccasins, yet no sound approached the bed. I heard this sound again. I was scared and woke one of my brothers. He said, "Just pull the covers over your head and go to sleep. It will soon be morning."

A short time later I heard my mother say to my father, "Ed, wake up! There's something or someone here."

He got up and answered, "It looks like a lantern. Someone is going past on the road."

She said, "No! Take a look. There's a light with a bluish colour and flame over the rocking chair."

There was a light above the trivet on the stove, where the teapot stood. Then it played over the baby's cradle in the corner. My father could see it too.

Then it appeared at the foot of their bed. I heard my mother say there was a heavy weight on her legs. Dad said, "Whoever you are, speak, and say what you want, or get out!" His actual words were, "Get the hell out!" I remember well. This bluish light hovered, then moved toward the window by the stove, and finally disappeared.

My brothers slept through it all. But I was awake.

When we were called to get up and to go to school, Dad had already gone out. In those days, children were seen but not heard. But instead of going to work, Dad had gone to the post office to send money for a Mass for the Dead to be said. This was at my mother's request. She had lost a sister a short while before, and being Catholic, my mother thought she needed prayers to be said for the spirit to be at rest.

My parents never spoke of this incident to us. My mother died two years later, in 1915. A week before my father died in 1965, he related this incident to me. He likely never knew that I had heard it, and that I had been scared nearly out of my wits.

I'm now in my eighty-sixth year. The past is vivid in my memory.

The Vision of Walt Whitman

Old Walt is an immense ridge of precambrian rock in Lake Mazinaw in Bon Echo Provincial Park. The rock acquired its name or nickname in 1919 when it was dedicated to the "democratic ideals" of the great American poet Walt Whitman. Responsible for the dedication was a stalwart band of Canadian Whitmanites led by Flora Macdonald Denison, pioneer feminist and mother of the writer Merrill Denison.

Horace L. Traubel (1858-1919) was the guest of honour at the dedication ceremony at Bon Echo on 23 Aug. 1919. This was only appropriate; Traubel was Whitman's closest friend in life and his devoted biographer in death. Traubel had kept vigil at Whitman's bedside and was present at the poet's death in 1892 at Camden, N.J. Whitman valued loyalty and friendship, and Traubel was nothing if not a loyal friend.

Traubel informed the other guests at the lodge that he had experienced visions of Whitman. Traubel was very close to death. Indeed, he died at Bon Echo on 6 Sept. 1919. He said Whitman had appeared to him on two occasions. Whitman appeared to Traubel the third and final time when Traubel was on his deathbed. Traubel died two days later. The curious thing is that the vision was witnessed not only by the dying Traubel but also by his very healthy friend, Lt. Col. L. Moore Cosgrave, one of the Canadian Whitmanites. As Cosgrave later explained, he and Traubel saw "the likeness of Walt Whitman, standing upright beside the bed ...."

Cosgrave's testimony took the form of a letter written from his residence in Toronto in late May 1920. It was addressed to Walter Franklin Prince, the well-known psychologist and psychical researcher, and Prince reproduced the letter in his important book *Noted Witnesses for Psychic Occurrences* (1928). The statement of Whitman's "likeness" rests not only on Cosgrave's statement but also, as Prince shows, on corroborative evidence from Flora Macdonald Denison and others who were present at Bon Echo that fateful summer.

❧❧❧

With reference to your communication of May 25, in connection with the psychical occurrences connected with the passing of Horace Traubel, I hereby state as follows:

During the months of August and September, 1919, I was in close touch with Mr. Horace Traubel, well known for his numerous writings and spiritual plane of thought; previous to that time I had not known him personally, nor had I a deep knowledge of the works and ideals of Whitman; this I state to show that my mind, conscious or subconscious, had not been engrossed in their works or belief, in addition, my long service in France with the Canadian forces, practically continually in the advanced lines from January, 1915, to the Armistice, had, naturally, made me familiar with the presence of death and the atmosphere around the dying, and though imbuing me with natural reverence, created no unusual tension or emotional excitement such as is common to those unfamiliar with death; this is also stated to indicate that I was in a normal condition when the occurrence took place to which Mrs. Denison alludes, and I beg to corroborate in toto the statements made by her in reference to myself. Briefly, it was as follows: During the three nights previous to the passing of Horace Traubel, I had remained at his bedside, throughout the latter hours of darkness, momentarily expecting the end; my thoughts at all time were very clear and spiritual, owing to the quietude of the surroundings, the close touch of nature and the peculiar clean magnetism that seemed to surround this remarkable selfless man, who had given his whole life to the service of humanity; I had felt this curious spirituality surrounding but few great people, and never with ordinary beings.

During this long watch, Horace Traubel, who was suffering from paralysis and debility, was without visible pain, and semi-conscious, unable to articulate owing to paralysis of the tongue. His eyes, however, which were remarkably brilliant and expressive, gave us the clue to the majority of his needs. On the last night, about 3 A.M., he grew perceptibly weaker, breathing almost without visible movement, eyes closed and seemingly comatose; he stirred restlessly after a long period, and his eyes opened, staring towards the further side of the bed; his lips moved, endeavoring to speak; I moved his head back, thinking he needed more air, but again it moved away, and his eyes remained riveted on a point some three feet above the bed; my eyes were at last drawn irresistibly to the same point in the darkness, as there was but a small shaded night

56

lamp behind a curtain on the further side of the room. Slowly the point at which we were both looking grew gradually brighter, a light haze appeared, spread until it assumed bodily form, and took the likeness of Walt Whitman, standing upright beside the bed, a rough tweed jacket on, an old felt hat upon his head and his right hand in his pocket, similar to a number of his portraits; he was gazing down at Traubel, a kindly, reassuring smile upon his face; he nodded twice as though reassuringly, the features quite distinct for at least a full minute, then gradually faded from sight. My eyes turned back to Traubel, who remained staring for almost another minute, when he also turned away, his features remarkably clear of the strained expression they had worn all evening, and he did not move again until his death, two hours later. I reported the occurrence to Mrs. Denison, who entered the facts in her diary at once, as she had records of several other psychic phenomena to date. I am thoroughly convinced of the exactness of the above statements, and did not regard it as extraordinary, owing to the fact that I had experienced similar phenomena at crucial movements during heavy casualties in France.

An Early Morning Visitor

Here is a creepy tale. It recalls an event that occurred almost fifty years earlier. It originally appeared as "An Early Morning Visitor to the Abandoned Hotel" on a page reserved for true-life ghost stories published in the *Edmonton Journal*, 30 Oct. 1988. The writer is F.D. Blackley, Professor Emeritus of History, University of Alberta, Edmonton. The narrative recalls a scary episode in the life of the author while still a student in Southern Ontario in 1939. It conveys some of the enthusiasm of youth!

❧❧❧

In the summer before the outbreak of the Second World War, my girl-friend had a summer job in a small town on Lake Ontario.

One afternoon I hitchhiked from Toronto to see her. We had a pleasant evening, including a walk along the beach. I noticed an abandoned building, presumably an old hotel, a little distance from the water, in a grove of trees. Eventually, I parted with the young lady and had to decide what I should do for the night, as it was now dark.

A university student, I had very little money. I considered the town hotel but it was very close to the chiming town clock, which I knew would bother me. I recalled the abandoned building and thought that I might find a dry spot there on which to curl up until morning.

I went back to the beach and had no problem entering the building. I went to the second floor. This had a long, central hall with many rooms opening from it on either side. I took a room at the far end of the hall with a window that overlooked the roof of a porch. I lay down on a raincoat that I had brought with me.

About 4:00 a.m., while it was still dark, I awakened with a jump. It was as if I had been startled by a loud noise, although I am convinced that this had not been so. I stood up and looked down the hall, lit by a bit of moonlight from a window over the stair. Coming towards me was an indistinct figure with a softly burning lantern.

It was entering each room in turn as if it was looking for someone, or something. As it neared my end of the hall, I saw its face, a horrible one that seemed to drip evil. Worse, perhaps, I could see some of the details of the hall through its body. I did not wait for the lantern-carrier to enter my room. I went out the window onto the porch roof. As I jumped to the ground, I could see the lantern flashing in my "bed-room."

I went uptown and found an all-night truck stop, where I had coffee to calm my nerves, and some breakfast. The café wasn't very busy and I was able to ask the proprietor about the abandoned building by the beach. It had been a hotel, he said, but it had not been successful. Some locals, he added, said that it was haunted by an old man with a lantern! He didn't believe the story. I did not tell him that I did.

That Light that Night Saved My Life

On 7 March 1989, I was the guest of David Carr on his ninety-minute, open-line show on radio station CFOS in Owen Sound, Ontario. We talked for some time on psychical and other matters, then we listened as callers shared their paranormal experiences with us and the show's radio listeners.

One of the listeners was Mary O'Donnell of Port Elgin who, later that day, wrote out an account of her own experience and sent it to me. In her letter she recalled a Lindsay family tradition of the forerunner, the forewarning of death ...

March 7, 1989
Dear Mr. Colombo:

This morning I listened to the radio program from Owen Sound and found it fascinating. I'd like to tell you something that happened in our family, the Lindsay family, a long time ago (in the 1940s).

My grandmother was dying, and all the members of her family had come to our house in Timmins where she stayed. They had been there a few weeks when my Uncle Len, who worked on the railway out of North Bay, decided that he would return to work the next day.

That night a strange light played up and down the door of my grandmother's bedroom. It was like the headlight of a train engine. I was not there at the time but later, when I came home, I heard them all talking about it. They all believed it was a sign that my grandmother would die the next day. They felt that my Uncle Len should not return to North Bay the next day but should remain in Timmins for the funeral.

Well, Grandmother did not die the next day, but she did die a few days later. Uncle Len remained in Timmins, and it is a good thing that he did. If he had returned to North Bay, as planned, he would have joined one of two crews that worked out of North Bay. All the men on those crews were killed in a head-on collision east of North Bay. I believe the crash took place at Rutherglen.

When we took Grandmother's body by train for burial in Mattawa, we passed the scene of the crash. The engines were lying down the slope and were still smoking.

My Uncle Len lived for many years after that, but I'm sure of one thing: That light that night saved his life.

I hope you find this interesting.

Sincerely,
(Mrs.) Mary O'Donnell

I Saw the Outline of the Head

Carol Goodger-Hill, a resident of Waterloo, Ontario., sent me the following account of an extremely vivid childhood memory on 24 June 1990. She sent it after reading my request for "ghost stories" carried in the correspondence columns of the *Guelph Mercury*.

Ms. Goodger-Hill added, "I tried to set it down a few years ago and you may find the telling somewhat dramatic for your purposes. At any rate, here it is. I should add that we left the house when I was fifteen and it is now, I understand, a sort of half-way house for people who are trying to recover from drugs. I rather wonder what they make of the place."

❦

When I was a child we always went away on Labour Day weekend. The trip was in some ways an ordeal. My parents were always nervous to be far from home and longed to be back. I could not bear to be cooped up for hours in a car with nothing to do, and after dark, nothing to see. It would be late when we finally drove into the back yard. We would gather up our things and without saying much, go into the house, happy to be away from each other.

The year before, when I had been nine, I had bounded up the darkened staircase towards my room at the back of the second floor. I had to go through an upstairs hall and my parents' room to reach my small back bedroom. I discovered that while I had been away part of the ceiling above my bed had fallen. It lay in heavy chunks on the pillow and the blanket. I had been frightened, but my mother had reminded me that the house was very old. The ceiling had been cracked. She felt it was a lucky chance that had kept me from home when it fell.

Now, a year later, I again ran up the hairpin staircase. The moonlight lay cold and white across the upstairs hall. I hesitated a moment in the hall, but went on into my parents' room. I was part way across the room before I became aware that I was not alone. By the window, in the moonlight, someone sat in the chair and watched me. I saw the outline of the head and a glow; I saw the eyes and I felt a dread that gripped the back of my neck and froze my hair.

Without a thought, I turned in mid-step and tore back the way I had come, clattering and calling down the staircase. I met my mother in the downstairs hall and tried to make her understand that something was in her bedroom. Compressing her lips, my mother made me retrace my steps and go back upstairs with her. Swiftly she crossed the hall and flipped on the light. In the sudden glare, the room was neat and empty. The window was black. The chair had nothing worse on it than a cast-off housecoat.

Together we went over to my room and turned on the light. After its collapse, a year earlier, the ceiling had been repaired and my bed had been moved. In horror, I saw that once again the ceiling was down. Once again my bed was littered with large, heavy chunks of plaster. Above it the lathes were bare. There was no other damage in the house.

After many years I still have no explanation for that night. My mother, unrelenting, matter-of-fact, believed it was all a coincidence. She still believes that. All the time we lived in that house, she found it comfortable. She could walk through it from cellar to attic without a light, if she thought she heard a strange noise in the night. She never had a bad experience. The rest of the family were not so brave.

The back bedroom remained mine for two more years. Usually, it was peaceful, but some nights I lay awake in terror for something that I could not name. After two years, I inherited the west bedroom. For some reason the atmosphere on that side of the house was more benign. In the years that followed, that bedroom was my island of peace. Often, when the rest of the family was out, I would sit behind the closed door, listening to the house live around me. I knew that so long as I stayed there quietly, I would be safe.

The Forerunner

Hazel L. Mack is a researcher and writer, based in Guelph, Ontario., who has contributed accounts of some of her other unusual experiences to *Fate Magazine*.

Mrs. Mack prepared the present account and sent it to me along with a covering letter dated 15 March 1990. In the letter Mrs. Mack wrote as follows:

> I remember being very "keyed" up that day and I was driving much faster than I usually did. My late husband paid little attention to any ideas I had. He had no belief either in psychic matters. I don't believe now that Mrs. Ware would have paid any attention to me either. She was originally from London, England, and had far different ideas to those that I have. In Canada, she became a farmer's wife. She may secretly not have liked her position. It was "something" to see this all-black figure walking down the farm laneway. I wish I understood better such things.

Mrs. Mack expressed a desire that is no doubt shared by every reader of her account.

Here we have a description of the appearance of a forerunner, a figure that forebodes tragedy. It is written in a straightforward manner about an incident that took place some forty years ago. How vivid it remains in the correspondent's memory!

※⁇⊕⁇⫏

It happened in the late autumn of 1952, a Saturday. My husband and I had been doing the various errands in preparation for the coming weekend.

We lived then in a forty-acre section of rich swamp land that bordered the narrow Eramosa River. It was also a good farming area, one of the best in Wellington County. Our particularly well-treed area was always cool in summer and warm in winter. My husband cared for a large number of peafowl and ornamental pheasants. He did not drive a car, so I did many of the errands, often driving him where he wished to go.

On this particular day we had finished the shopping and were making good time, headed homeward, taking a short cut off No. 7 Highway on the 4th Line. Often a rough surface to drive on, there seemed to be more ruts than usual. The road went down to the edge of the Eramosa River, across a narrow bridge, and then we were climbing again.

I was driving fast despite the rough roads, for I knew my husband had an appointment awaiting him. We began to climb out of the valley. We were approaching the Ware farm on the left-hand side of the road. Looking up as we approached the driveway, I saw Mrs. Barbara Ware walking down towards the roadway, probably to their mailbox. To my amazement she appeared entirely black. I at once began to slow the car, for I intended to turn around when I saw a suitable place to turn and tell her how she had appeared to me. I had never spoken to Mrs. Ware, for in a way I was a newcomer to the area some four years previously. Not being involved with farming in any way, we had never met.

"Keep going," my husband said impatiently. "We're already late."

Regretfully, I stepped up the speed of the car, for I knew someone was waiting for him at home.

The afternoon work in my home kept me busy for some time, but I kept thinking of Mrs. Ware. I had never met her. I had almost become acquainted with her sister a while previously when in Acton, but both girls were from England and did not seem to want to get acquainted.

I wanted to tell Mrs. Ware how she had appeared to me, although I had never seen anything like it previously. It seemed to me to be a warning, but finally I gave up on it, not being sure what all the blackness portended. I had become tired and it was too far to walk to her home. We had no telephone then so I couldn't warn her that way. Finally it all slipped out of my mind.

The next morning a relative arrived with the dreadful news. Mrs. Ware had been killed the evening before, seven hours after I had seen her.

There was nothing I could say to my husband. I felt he should not have minded that day if we were but a few minutes late. The distance was, of course, several miles by road.

Several years later I attended a meeting at the home of Dr. A.R.G. Owen, a well-known writer on matters pertaining to heredity, biometrics, nature, and parapsychology. His fairly recent book, *Psychic Mysteries of Canada,* is a fund of psychic knowledge. "What a shame you didn't go back and warn Mrs. Ware," Dr. Owen remarked.

Indeed it was, and I have never ceased to regret it.

Mackenzie King, Spiritualist

W.L. Mackenzie King (1874-1950) was Prime Minister of Canada for close to twenty-two years — one-third of the enigmatic man's life. The first knowledge that he was a closet Spiritualist came to light a year and a half after his death, when the journalist Blair Fraser published a well-researched article in *Maclean's*, 15 Dec. 1951, titled "Mackenzie King's Search for Survival."

The public at large had to wait a quarter-century for the complete revelation of Mackenzie King's spiritualistic activities. The revelation came in the form of a scholar's study of the immense and highly detailed diary that Mackenzie King had kept throughout his public life. The study was called *A Very Double Life: The Private World of Mackenzie King* (1976) and it was written by the military historian C.P. Stacey.

As the diaries reveal, King was most active as a Spiritualist in his latter years when he was between periods of leadership. But as early as 1925, he attended a seance in Kingston, and in the 1930s he sat with mediums in Brockville, Ottawa, Kingston, Winnipeg, Toronto, etc. The attractions of the subject never paled. At Laurier House in Ottawa, he conducted innumerable sittings with "the little table." On a visit to London, England, he was given an introduction to the London Spiritualist Alliance (later called the College of Psychic Science) by the Marchioness of Aberdeen. There he sat on numerous visits with such well-known psychics and mediums as Helen Hughes, Hester Dowden, Geraldine Cummins, and Mercy Phillimore.

At the time none of this was known to the public at large. Many of Mackenzie King's personal friends were frightened lest knowledge leak out that the Prime Minister was consorting with mediums and consulting with the spirits. Yet there is no evidence that messages from the spirit-world influenced any affairs of state or even that in his private or public capacity he acted on any information he received from "the beyond." During his lifetime many members of the public felt that Mackenzie King had a strange, spiritual streak. After all, he was born in Waterloo County, a region in Ontario noted for its traditions of the soul and the soil that are both mystical and material. But he was as sly as he was superstitious, and he was the beneficiary of immense good luck, so it is not surprising that his secret went with him to the grave — but not beyond.

The well-kept secret of Mackenzie King was well known during his lifetime to Nandor Fodor, the Hungarian-born psychoanalyst and psychical researcher. In 1935-38, Fodor was director of research for the International Institute for Psychical Research, London. In his book of studies of paranormal phenomena called *Between Two Worlds* (1964), Fodor recalled meeting Mackenzie King in the 1920s and corresponding with him in the 1930s and 1940s. The correspondence commenced when King posted a letter to the Institute requesting a copy of one of its publications, Baron Palmstierna's *Horizons of Immortality*.

Mackenzie King and Fodor each exchanged three letters. Here are some excerpts from King's letters which are dated 19 April 1938, 8 Aug. 1938, and 21 Sept. 1942. They shed a little light on one man's long and lingering interest in the world of the spirit.

❧☙

I much appreciate your kindness in suggesting that I might become a member of the International Institute for Psychical Research. At some later time, I would much appreciate this opportunity. For reasons which you will appreciate, it has seemed to me inadvisable to become too actively identified with Psychical Research work, pending the time that I may continue to hold my present position.

... I have read with quite an expression of interest Baron Palmstierna's book. Reincarnation is still a good deal of a mystery to me, and the part of Baron Palmstierna's book, which had to do with reincarnation, seems to relate to a subject which I have still to come to believe. The parts of the book which had to do with evidences of personal survival, also of teachings, appealed very strongly to me, and were in the nature of confirmation of experiences of my own concern, of which there can be no doubt whatever.

Psychic study affords me considerable relaxation. It is a field of research to which I would devote much time, had I the time to spare.

I Talked with Mackenzie King's Ghost

Did Percy J. Philip engage in a conversation at Kingsmere with the ghost of the late William Lyon Mackenzie King?

During his lifetime it was a closely guarded secret, shared only with intimate friends and associates, that William Lyon Mackenzie King was a closet Spiritualist. No one knows whether or not the late Prime Minister believed in the tenets of Spiritualism. What is known for certain is that he practised the methods of Spiritualism. He consulted mediums, he practised table-wrapping, and he believed in omens. Following his death, the closely guarded secret of his spiritualistic interests became common knowledge.

Mackenzie King played favourites among the newspapermen who covered political events on Parliament Hill. One of his favourite scribes was Percy J. Philip, well-known war correspondent and veteran Ottawa correspondent for the *New York Times*. Two years after the Prime Minister's death, Philip paid a sentimental visit to Kingsmere, King's stamping-ground in the Gatineau Hills north of Ottawa, and sat down at a bench ... and proceeded to converse with the late Mackenzie King.

"I Talked with Mackenzie King's Ghost" is reprinted from the Dec. 1955 issue of *Fate* Magazine. Here is the strange but true story of how one man was affected by the legacy ... the spirit, if you wish ... of William Lyon Mackenzie King.

❦

On a June evening in 1954 I had a long conversation with the former Canadian Prime Minister William L. Mackenzie King as we sat on a bench in the grounds of his old summer home at Kingsmere, 12 miles from Ottawa. It seemed to me an entirely normal thing although I knew perfectly well that Mr. King had been dead for four years.

Of course, when I returned to Ottawa and told my story nobody quite believed me. I myself became just the least bit uncertain as to whether it really had happened, or at least as to how it had happened. Did I fall asleep and dream? Was this due to paranormal circumstances which cannot be explained?

Of one thing I am sure. Mr. King himself would believe me. He once held similar conversations — almost daily in some cases — with persons who had left this world. He talked with his father and mother regularly and with great men and women of the past. His diary, in which he recorded his spiritual experiences, as well as his political activities and contacts, gives detailed accounts of these conversations. Unfortunately it is not likely to be published in full because his will provided that certain parts should be destroyed. His literary executors feel bound to carry out these instructions.

It was not until after his death that the Canadian people learned that their bachelor, liberal Prime Minister communed with the dead both directly and, occasionally, through mediums. When it did become known — in a rather sensational way — it shocked many.

Yet the Prime Minister made no secret of his beliefs and practices. To friends who had lost dear ones he wrote in this manner: "I know how you feel. It seems as though you cannot bear to go on without that wonderful companionship and affection. But let me assure you that love still exists. A bond as strong as that is not broken by death or anything else. Your father is still near you. If you can be still and listen and feel, you will realize he is close to you all your life. I know that because it is so with my mother and me."

That quotation is from one of the many hundreds of letters of condolence which Mr. King wrote with his own hand for he was punctilious in such matters. At funerals he always spoke similar words of comfort to those bereaved. Otherwise, although he made no secret of his beliefs, he did not parade them.

Once, at Government House, about Christmas time in 1945, he told the Governor General, the Earl of Athlone, that he had spoken with President Roosevelt the previous night. "President Truman, you mean," said the Governor. The Earl saw that some of his staff were making signs from behind Mr. King's back, evidently trying to convey some message. He was puzzled but, being a good constitutional Governor General, he kept quiet and did not again correct the Prime Minister when he repeated, "Oh, no, I mean the late President Roosevelt."

The occasion of the incident was the showing of the Noel Coward film, "Blithe Spirit," which Mr. King found "most interesting."

"It is difficult to imagine the life after death," he said, chatting gaily. "Probably the best thing to do is to regard it as a continuation of the one we know with the same processes of growth and change until, eventually, we forget our life and associations on this earth, just as old people tend to forget their childhood experiences."

His Excellency who was a brother of the late Queen Mary and a soldier by profession muttered, "Yes, yes, probably." He obviously was shaken. He had been chosen by Mr. King to be Governor General of Canada and it made him nervous to learn that his Prime Minister was receiving advice from extra-mundane sources.

"Good God," he exclaimed when his staff explained why they had tried to shush him, "is that where the man gets his policies?"

Having an open mind about the occult and being inquisitive by nature, I later managed to turn several conversations with Mr. King to this subject. Once, especially, when we were crossing the Atlantic to Europe, he talked freely about his beliefs and experiences as we walked the deck.

"If one believes in God and a life after death," he said, "it is inevitable that one must believe that the spirits of those who have gone take an interest in the people and places they loved during their lives on earth. It is the matter of communication that is difficult. For myself I have found that the method of solitary, direct, communion is best. After my father and mother died I felt terribly alone. But I also felt that they were near me. Almost accidentally I established contact by talking to them as if they were present and soon I began to get replies."

These and other things that the Prime Minister said to me at different times came back to my mind as, on that June evening, I drove up the Kingsmere road and was reminded by a sign that the estate of Moorside, which Mr. King had left to the Canadian people in his will, lay just ahead.

It is a beautiful place. There are 550 acres of woodland and clearings, through most of which everyone is free to wander at will. A little stream with a waterfall flows through it down to the valley below. Mr. King accumulated it almost acre by acre, adding steadily in his methodical way, to the original lot he had bought when he first came to Ottawa at the beginning of the century. His quick temper seldom flashed more hotly than when he discovered that some neighbour had sold a parcel of land without giving him a chance to buy. Adding to his estate became a passion with the future Prime Minister. There he loved to receive visitors and also to be alone.

In buying the land Mr. King showed his Scottish shrewdness. But the building of the "ruins" was a perfect example of that romantic daftness that sometimes bewitches the supposedly hard-headed Scot. The direction sign now set up for tourists calls them "ruins" but the uninformed must wonder what they once were. There were doorways and windows, a fireplace, a row of columns, which Mr. King called the cloisters, coats of arms carved in stone, bits and pieces of the old Parliament Buildings, the mint, banks and private houses all built into an artistic enough wholly whimsical suggestion of a ruined castle. Somehow, perhaps because the surroundings with outcrop rock and pine are so fitting, they escape being silly.

On that evening there were no other visitors. The air was clear and cool. I sat down on a bench beside the ruins and thought about the strange little man who loved his hill-top home so dearly. I suppose I was in what I called a receptive mood. Although I had not then read it, I was following the instructions in that letter from which I already have quoted, to "be still and listen and feel."

I became conscious that I was not alone. Someone sat on the park bench beside me.

There were no sighs, groans and lightning flashes such as mark a spirit's arrival on the Shakespearian stage. There was, if anything, a deeper peace. Through a fold in the hills I could see a stretch of the broad Ottawa Valley. I tried to concentrate on it and keep contact with the normal but the presence on the bench would not be denied.

Without turning my head, for somehow I feared to look, I said as naturally as I could, "Good evening, Mr. King."

In that warm tone which always marked his conversation the voice of Mr. King replied, "Good evening, Philip. I am so glad you spoke to me."

That surprised me. "I was thinking of you," I muttered.

"Oh, yes," he replied. "I knew that. But one of the rules which govern our conduct on this side is that we are like the children and must not speak unless we are spoken to. I suppose it is a good rule because it would be very disturbing if we went around talking to people. The sad thing is that so few of them ever talk to us."

Here I think I should say that the reader must decide for himself whether or not he believes this story. It puzzles me greatly.

"I suppose," I said, or I think I said, resuming the conversation, "that we are just a bit scared. You know how hard it is to speak into a dark, empty room."

"That certainly is a difficulty for many people," Mr. King said. "But the room is never really empty. It is often filled with lonely ones who would like to be spoken to. They must, however, be called by name, confidently, affectionately, now challenged to declare themselves."

"Your name," I said, "must often be so mentioned in this lovely place you bequeathed to the Canadian people."

"Oh, yes, mentioned," he said. I glanced at him and seemed to see his eyes sparkle as they did in life, for he had a great deal of puckish humor. "But between being mentioned and being addressed by name, as you addressed me, there is a great deal of difference. I have heard things about my character, motives, political actions and even my personal appearance and habits that have made me laugh so loudly I thought I must break the sound barrier. And I have heard things about myself, too, that have made me shrink."

In the evening silence I had the sensation of being suspended in time and space as the quiet voice went on. "There are things that I said and did that I could regret but, on this side, we soon learn to have no regrets. Life would be meaningless if we did not all make mistakes, and eternity intolerable if we spent it regretting them."

He paused and I thought he looked at me quizzically. "By the way," he said, "Do you still write for the *New York Times?*"

When I said that I had retired, he chuckled. "But still," he said, "I think I had better not give indiscreet answers to your questions."

I asked several but he answered with the same skill as marked his replies to questions in the House of Commons and at meetings with the press, divulging nothing. It was I who was the interviewed. He was eager for news and it surprised me then, as it does now, that he seemed not to know fully what was happening in the world. The dead, I discovered, are not omniscient. Or perhaps what we think important is not important to them.

We talked of the development of Canada, of housing and new enterprises like the St. Lawrence Seaway. "My successor has been lucky," Mr. King said. That was as far as he went in any personal reference. "Canada has been very prosperous. I hope it will continue to be so. But you cannot expect good times always. It is adversity that proves the real value of men and nations."

The conversation drifted to the international scene, to philosophic discussion of forms of government, of the balance between Liberty and Authority, the growth and decay of nations and of systems. I cannot tell how long it lasted but I noticed that the sickle moon was getting brighter. I mentioned the time, fumbling for my watch.

"Time," said Mr. King, "I had almost forgotten about time. I suppose I spend a great deal of time up here. There is so much beauty and peace. I gave it to the Canadian people but in a way I have preserved it for myself. It is good to have some familiar, well-loved place to spend 'time' in, until one gets used to eternity."

We both rose from the bench — or at least I did. When I looked at him, as I then did for the first time directly, he seemed just as I had known him in life, just as when I had talked with him once at this very spot.

"I think you told me once that you are Scottish born and a wee bit 'fey,'" he said. "It's a good thing to be. We have two worlds. Those people who think their world is the only one, and who take it and themselves too seriously, have a very dull time. Do come back and talk with me again."

I muttered words of thanks and then, following the habit of a lifetime, stretched out my hand to bid goodbye. He was not there.

An Anecdote about Mackenzie King's Mediums

The anecdote which appears here is recorded by the newspaperman Richard Doyle in his memoirs *Hurly-Burly: A Time at The Globe* (Toronto: Macmillan of Canada, 1990). For many years Doyle was the influential editor-in-chief of the *Globe and Mail.* He was summoned to the Senate in 1985.

Doyle's anecdote concerns Leonard Brockington, another "power behind the throne" and "backroom" wielder of power and influence. Welsh blood flowed through his veins. He was an exceptional orator and anecdotist. Privately he was called upon to intercede in difficult situations on behalf of the Liberal Party of Canada.

In another version of this anecdote recorded by Doyle, "Brock" was requested by the Prime Minister's Office, while on a business trip to Great Britain, to meet with the two London Spiritualists whom King had on occasion consulted when in London on official government business. It seemed that the two mediums were threatening to release to the Fleet Street press some private letters about Spiritualistic matters that they had received from King. It was Brock's task to ensure their silence. He met with them, and when he returned to Ottawa, Brock was able to give assurances to the officials in the Prime Minister's Office that his mission had been one hundred percent successful. Hence the punchline of this version of the anecdote runs: "Never strike a happy medium."

⁂

King has retreated to the private life he had looked forward to. There would be so much to be done; papers and diaries to be edited, writing

75

to be started, people to see, advice to be given, honours to be received, attention to be accorded to the supernatural which had preoccupied him through his long career. But retirement wasn't like that amid the ruins that King had had his masons build to give character to his Kingsmere estate. People were too busy to pay him much attention or they bothered him with inconsequential things. One man he asked to pay a visit was Leonard W. Brockington, the first president of the CBC who was now the chief of Odeon's movie operations in Canada.

King was overjoyed to see him, Brockington recalled. Their earlier differences, when Brock wrote the PM's speeches, were described as misunderstandings and nobody's fault. King was ready to pick up where they had left off. He had writing to do and he would need Brockington's advice. Leonard was one of the few he could trust. Perhaps he could counsel him on the disposition of his estate.

"He was not a happy man," Brock said. He had been wounded by the spiteful things the newspapers had written about him. Not when he returned, but when he was carrying his dreadful burdens of the war years. Perhaps he had retired too soon. He had the greatest respect for Mr. St. Laurent, but there were things that needed doing in the govern-ment and in the party — risks that were being taken needlessly. "If only he was consulted or even listened to."

Did he say anything about counsel from beyond, anything about the supernatural? "Oh, no," said Brock. "He never talked about such things with colleagues." The question, however, prompted Brockington to tell one of the stories that were always on the tip of his tongue.

"It was while I was in Britain during the war and word had reached us that a Spiritualist, who had corresponded with King, was negotiating to publish his letters. I went down to London with another government lawyer and explained to her that Mr. King owned the copyright of every word that he had written and that if she ever attempted to sell his property, we'd have her in court faster than you could say Ellen Terry.

"As we came away into the blackout, I said to my companion, 'I think we have struck a happy medium.'"

It was one of Brockington's literary tricks to stand a cliché on its head and give it freshness or relevance. To have a young head on old shoulders could have been said of him.

The Crystal Ball at Laurier House

The editors of *Fate Magazine*, the well-established American monthly devoted to the unexplained, ran my call for strange Canadian experiences in the April 1991 issue. A number of readers from both countries responded with letters that set forth accounts of their experiences in Canada.

The account that follows was sent to me by Mrs. Irmgard Parrington, a resident of Hancock, located east of Binghampton, N.Y. It is dated 28 May 1991. It casts some light on the continuing relationship of Prime Minister William Lyon Mackenzie King, who died at Kingsmere in 1950, and his mother Isabel Baxter Mackenzie who died, also at Kingsmere, in 1917.

⚬⚬⚬

Three months ago, I took a trip to Ottawa and signed up for a bus tour of Canada's capital. I found the city interesting. It exudes Old World charm. A visit to the Parliament, a cruise on the Rideau Canal, dinner at Mother Tucker's, sightseeing past the houses of government officials and foreign diplomats ... it was great. And tulips, tulips everywhere.

Suddenly, I remembered that the first husband of Avis, my sister-in-law, had been the minister in charge of Indian Affairs following World War I. Avis, formerly Lady Darlington, died a few years ago, so there was no way I could ask her for particulars — where she had lived in Ottawa, etc.

When we visited Laurier House, a National Historic Site, I could not get Avis out of my mind. I was sure that she must have personally known its resident, William Lyon Mackenzie King, the Prime Minister of the day. The decor — thick drapes, flocked wallpaper, dark reds and purples, the almost black wood — it was Avis's style all over.

I was amused when the guide told us about Mackenzie King's interest in the supernatural. There was even a crystal ball on the top of the piano in his souvenir-crammed, upstairs living-room. Naturally I was fascinated with it. I stared into it and was puzzled to see, reflected in the crystal, the silhouette of a female figure in a long gown.

The figure was kind of triangular in shape. First, I thought, it must be the reflection of a nearby photograph or portrait. I looked around, but there was nothing resembling the shape anywhere around it. I made fun of myself and reasoned that my imagination had got the better of me. But the image reminded me somewhat of Avis, especially my sister-in-law's silvery hair. However, she didn't have her hair parted right through the middle as did the figure in the crystal. I blamed my preoccupation with her on my starting to see things.

To my surprise, the guard — a charming, very knowledgeable older gentleman — noticed my interest and unhooked the rope, inviting me to step closer and take a good look. I did.

Now, there definitely was nothing between me and the crystal ball. When I squinted, I still could see the figure in it. It was weird but fun. Finally, I saw something in the crystal ball!

Arlene Avery, the tour guide on our bus, joined me. I guess she was checking to see what was taking me so long on the second floor. She, too, was pleased to get a close-up look at the crystal ball and all the historical bric-à-brac. Then we continued on our tour of the remaining floors.

On the ground floor, a young, handsome Canadian soldier took over. He pointed out the importance of the furnishings and portraits and pictures. As we entered one room — I think it was the dining-room — he motioned to the first painting at the right: Mr. King's mother. I did a double-take.

"This is the woman I saw in the crystal ball!" I said. I was sorry the second I had said it. "He'll think I'm nuts!" I thought to myself.

Arlene, who had seen my fascination upstairs, uttered nervously, "Oh, you're giving me goose bumps!"

The young guard, eying me a bit peculiarly, explained that Prime Minister King had held nightly séances in the upstairs room, communicating with his dead mother. In later years he even concluded that her spirit had come back to him in the form of his dog.

Well, I don't believe that. But his dead mother was definitely in the crystal ball — I saw her!

The Haunting of
Mackenzie House

Mackenzie House is one of the most historic homes in Toronto. Since 1960 it has been maintained as a museum by the Toronto Historical Board. Despite the fact that Mackenzie House has been called the most haunted house in Toronto — and perhaps the most haunted house in all of Canada — it is the policy of the Board to maintain that Mackenzie House is not haunted. Guides dressed in period costume who escort visitors through its halls and rooms, which are furnished to recall the period of the 1860s, make no mention of reports of ghosts or poltergeists or mysterious happenings.

Today the residence bears the proud name of William Lyon Mackenzie (1795-1861). Mackenzie was the energetic publisher of the *Colonial Advocate*, first Mayor of the City of Toronto in 1834, the promoter of responsible government, and the leader of the Rebellion of 1837 in Upper Canada. When the rebellions were suppressed, Mackenzie fled (dressed as a woman) and found refuge in New York State. There he continued his agitation. With the amnesty he returned to Toronto in triumph. He is known to this day as "the firebrand."

The three-story brick residence at 82 Bond Street, erected in the 1850s, was acquired and presented to him by grateful friends in recognition of public service. He lived in the house from 1859 until his death in the second-floor bedroom on 28 Aug. 1861. Isabel Grace King, his youngest daughter, also lived and died in the residence. She was the wife of the lawyer John King and the mother of William Lyon Mackenzie King.

William Lyon Mackenzie King (1874-1950), the grandson of William Lyon Mackenzie, was born at "Woodside" in Berlin (now Kitchener), Ontario. The grandson took great pride in the grandfather's commitment to responsible government. He studied law and went on to became Canada's tenth Prime Minister and the country's most curious and long-lasting leader. It is now known that throughout his life Mackenzie King was fascinated with spiritualism and with the question of human survival after death. Indeed, one of his friends, the correspondent Percy J. Philip, claimed that in 1954 the ghost of Mackenzie King joined him and conversed with him for some time on a park bench at Kingsmere, Mackenzie King's country estate in the Gatineau region of Quebec. While Mackenzie King's spiritualistic beliefs and practices are well documented, the views of his grandfather, William Lyon Mackenzie, go unrecorded. Yet it is hard to believe that the grandfather, who was Scottish-born, was unfamiliar with the subject.

There are no reports of any psychical occurrences in Mackenzie House prior to 1956; there are none of substance later than 1966. The earliest accounts come from a responsible couple, Mrs. and Mrs. Charles Edmunds. They were the house's first live-in, caretaking couple. They occupied Mackenzie House from 13 Aug. 1956 to April 1960 and only left because of the disturbances. They were followed by Mr. and Mrs. Alex Dobban who arrived in April 1960. The Dobbans, complaining of the same disturbances as the Edmunds, left that June. Archdeacon John Frank of Holy Trinity Anglican Church was called to conduct an exorcism in the parlour, which he did in the presence of reporters on 2 July 1960. Since that time the house's caretakers have lived off the premises, but workmen on the premises and visitors have intermittently complained of disturbances.

The most intelligent discussion — and debunking — of the ghostly happenings at Mackenzie House was conducted by Joe Nickell in one chapter of his book *Secrets of the Supernatural: Investigating the World's Occult Mysteries* (Buffalo: Prometheus Books, 1988). Nickell is both a professional stage magician and a licensed private investigator. He has both prosaic and highly imaginative explanations for all the disturbances. Although he writes well, the story he has to tell is not as gripping as the stories that were told by members of the Edmunds family.

Mr. and Mrs. Charles Edmunds, the first caretaking couple, lived in the house for four years. Their reports are included here, as are the shorter reports of their son Robert and his wife Minnie who were guests in the house. The four reports first appeared in the *Toronto Telegram* on 28 June 1960 as part of a series of articles titled "The Ghosts that Live in Toronto" written by the paper's enterprising reporter Andrew MacFarlane. The series appeared following the refusal of the Dobbans to remain in the house. MacFarlane secured sworn affidavits from all four member of the Edmunds family. They are reproduced here in a slightly edited form.

1. Mrs. Charles Edmunds

From the first day my husband and I went to stay at the Mackenzie Homestead, we could hear footsteps on the stairs when there was nobody in the house but us.

The first day, when I was alone in the house, I could hear someone clearly, walking up the stairs from the second floor to the top. Nearly every day there were footsteps at times when there was no one there to make them.

One night I woke up at midnight. I couldn't sleep, although I am normally a good sleeper. I saw a Lady standing over my bed. She wasn't at the side, but at the head of the bed, leaning over me. There is no room for anyone to stand where she was. The bed is pushed up against the wall.

She was hanging down, like a shadow, but I could see her clearly. Something seemed to touch me on the shoulder to wake me up. She had long hair hanging down in front of her shoulders, not black or gray or white, but dark brown, I think. She had a long narrow face. Then it was gone.

Two years ago, early in March, I saw the Lady again. It was the same — except this time she reached out and hit me. When I woke up, my left eye was purple and bloodshot.

I also saw the man at night, a little bald man in a frock coat. I would just see him for a few seconds, and then he would vanish.

I often saw one or the other standing in the room — at least eight or nine times.

A year ago last April, I told my husband: "I have to get out of here." I had to get out of that house. If I didn't get out, I knew I'd be carried out in a box.

I think it was the strain all the time that made me feel this way. I went from 130 pounds to 90¹/2 pounds. I wasn't frightened, but it was getting my nerves down.

It was just like knowing there was someone watching you from behind all the time, from just over your shoulder.

Sometimes we'd sit watching the television. My husband might look up all of a sudden at the doorway. I knew what it was. You felt that someone had just come in.

My son and his wife heard the piano playing at night when they were staying with us. When my husband and my son went to look — it stopped.

We could feel the homestead shaking with a rumbling noise some nights. It must have been the press in the basement. We thought at first it might be the subway. But we were too far from the subway ...

I did not believe in ghosts when I went to stay at the Mackenzie Homestead. But I do now. It's the only explanation I can think of.

I wish to say that I would not say anything against the Mackenzies. They were hard-working people and so are we. They were not hard on us ... it's just that the house was a strain on the nerves.

2. *Mr. Charles Edmunds*

Certain happenings during the three years and eight months my wife and I served as caretakers of the Mackenzie Homestead have convinced me that there is something peculiar about the place.

On one occasion my wife and I were sleeping in the upstairs bedroom. She woke me up in the middle of the night and said that she had seen a man standing beside her bed.

My wife, to my certain knowledge, knew nothing of Mackenzie or his history. All of the pictures in the homestead show Mackenzie as a man with hair on his head. The man my wife saw and described to me was completely bald with side whiskers. I had read about Mackenzie. And I know that the man she described to me was Mackenzie. He wore a wig to cover his baldness. But she did not know this.

On another occasion, just after we moved in, my two grandchildren, Susan (then aged 4) and Ronnie (then aged 3) went from the upstairs bedroom down to the second-floor bathroom at night.

A few minutes later there were terrific screams. I went down and they were both huddled in the bathroom, terrified. They said there was a Lady in the bathroom. I asked where she was now and they said she just disappeared.

On another night my wife woke up screaming. She said: "There was a small man standing over my bed." She described Mackenzie.

Another night, a woman came up to the bed and looked at my missus. She was a little woman, about my wife's height. My wife said: "Dad — there was a woman here." I told her she was dreaming.

Another night my wife woke up and woke me. She was upset. She said the Lady had hit her. There were three red welts on the left side of her face. They were like finger marks. The next day her eye was bloodshot. Then it turned black and blue. Something hit her. It wasn't me. And I don't think she could have done it herself. And there wasn't anyone else in the house.

On another occasion something peculiar happened with some flowers we had in pots on a window ledge inside the house. This was in winter and we had the geraniums inside. We watered the plants twice a

82

week on Sundays and Wednesdays.

On a Saturday morning we found that they had all been watered, although we hadn't done it. There was water spilled all over the plants and the saucers they were standing in were full. There was mud on the curtains, and holes in the earth as someone had poked their fingers in the earth. There was water on the dressing table. Neither of us had watered the plants, and neither had anyone else.

We often heard footsteps on the stairs. Thumping footsteps like someone with heavy boots on. This happened frequently when there was no one in the house but us, when we were sitting together upstairs.

The whole house used to shake with a rumbling sound sometimes. My wife is convinced that this was Mackenzie's press.

I am not an imaginative man, and I do not believe in ghosts. But the fact is that the house was strange enough so that we had to leave.

We would have stayed if it had not been for these happenings. But my wife could not stand it any longer.

3. Robert Edmunds

One night my wife woke me up. She said she heard the piano playing downstairs. I heard it, too. I cannot remember what the music was like, but it was the piano downstairs playing.

Dad and I went downstairs. When we got to the last landing before the bottom, the piano stopped.

It was similar with the printing press in the basement. My wife heard it first and wakened me. I heard it, too. I identified the sound because it was the same as old presses I'd seen in movies and on television. A rumbling, clanking noise — not like modern presses. When Dad and I went downstairs to see about it, it stopped when we reached the same landing.

We heard the piano three or four times, the press just once.

I was not walking in my sleep. I heard them. I don't know what the explanation is. I am not prepared to say I saw any ghosts or apparitions. But I can say that I dreamt more in that house than I ever have before or since.

I do not believe in ghosts. But I find it hard to explain what we heard.

4. Mrs. Minnie Edmunds

When my husband and I were staying at Mackenzie Homestead I heard the piano playing downstairs at night three or four times.

We discovered that there was no one downstairs to play it these times, and yet I heard it distinctly. Each time, I woke my husband, and when he and his father went downstairs to investigate it, it stopped.

On one other occasion I heard the printing press running in the basement. I woke my husband, and he and his father went to investigate it. It stopped.

It is not possible to operate the press, because it is locked, and on the occasions when I heard the piano, there was no one downstairs to play it. I can find no natural explanation for these occurrences.

Out-of-Body Experience

The following account of an out-of-body experience was submitted to a survey of paranormal experiences that appeared in the *National Enquirer*. The call for material was made in the issue of 21 April 1978. The "Psychic Survey" was conducted by the well-known psychical researchers Iris M. Owen and A.R.G. Owen, and the psychiatrist Joel Whitton, all then living in Toronto.

Two thousand five hundred readers, mainly American but some Canadian, filled out questionnaires and described their experiences. No informants' names were published. The following contribution comes from M.F., St. Catharines, Ontario.; 64, female, 16 years schooling.

❧

Place: Southwest corner of Warden Avenue and St. Clair Avenue East, Scarborough, Ontario.
Date: Approximately spring 1955.
Time: Approximately 11:00 a.m. to 1:00 p.m.
Age: 41.
Medication: None.
Health: Excellent.
Mental State: Happy, excited by the occasion.
Others present: My five children; and a sprinkling of the populace of Scarborough.
Occasion: Queen Elizabeth was to pass by motorcade during her first visit to Canada as the reigning monarch.

I had a very busy morning getting myself and my children ready. Then the two youngest were put into the carriage and we all trudged the two miles. We were early enough to get a good front-row spot among those people waiting eagerly to see the Queen. My eldest daughter (fifteen years old) held up her one-year-old brother, while I held my two-year-old daughter in my arms. My nine and six-year-old daughters stood in front of us.

As the motorcade passed by at thirty miles per hour, the Queen appeared ethereal, exquisite in a grey, upturned hat, which allowed her delicate skin and fine features to be seen to best advantage. Just before the open limousine passed us, she turned and appeared to look directly at us with a kind, warm expression. It seemed as if she looked deep into my eyes. I floated up and away above my family as I felt a profound sensation of joy. I had been deeply moved to think that this young girl could be persuaded to come from her home in England to let her subjects in Canada see her. It was a profound and wonderful privilege for me to be able to take my children to see their Queen.

Three Ghostly Experiences

One Thursday morning I was the guest of Steve Madely on his phone-in show on CFRA Radio in Ottawa. We chatted for a while about real-life ghost stories, then Steve opened the lines to hear from callers. Thirteen callers shared their experiences with us on air. A good many listeners wanted to tell their stories but had no opportunity to do so. So they contacted me directly. Here is one letter from Joan E. Skidmore of Gloucester, Ontario. She was born in Ottawa in 1941. "I am a third-generation Canadian," she wrote. "My ancestors were German and British. I am a homemaker and mother of five grown sons, and we have two grandchildren. My husband and I will be celebrating our thirty-fifth anniversary this coming October. I sew, knit, crochet, garden, read, write poetry, and love camping."

February 18, 1994
Dear Mr. Colombo:

I am writing after hearing you on radio station CFRA this morning. The topic was ghost stories.

Here are three of my ghostly experiences:

The first experience occurred in 1955, when our family was living at 20 Chamberlain Avenue in Ottawa.

My Aunt Annie, my maternal grandmother's sister, had lived with us the previous year. Her health was not good but when it improved she moved to Pembroke, Ontario. Then she took ill again, and my grandmother travelled to Pembroke to stay with her.

My mother, my sister, and I were in the kitchen washing the dinner dishes when we heard footsteps on the back porch. The steps sounded as if someone was entering the room beyond the kitchen. We searched high and low but there was no one there.

A short while later my grandmother phoned us from Pembroke to say that Aunt Annie had passed away. Aunt Annie had always sat on the back porch.

In 1976 my husband was transferred to Kitchener, Ontario. We bought an old brick house at 100 Moore Avenue. The house was situated quite close to a cemetery.

Shortly after moving in we realized that we were not the only occupants of the house. We apparently had the company of several ghosts. The ghosts were seen or heard by all the members of our family. We had five sons who at the time ranged in ages from six to sixteen years. It was a fascinating experience.

The original owners of the house, the Beerwagon family, had spent their entire married lives in the house. The land had been given to Mr. Beerwagon by his father. Mr. Beerwagon was a stone mason and he built the house in 1911. He brought his bride to their new home. They raised seven children and departed the house in death. We were told that they had the services of a live-in housekeeper named Mary.

My first ghostly encounter in the house was with an older woman in the upstairs hallway. She seemed to float past me. I was sure she was carrying laundry over her arm. I saw her several times, but for some reason I did not mention her appearance to the other members of the family. One day my eldest son came and told me about a woman he had seen in the upstairs hall. He described the same women whom I had seen, and he said that she appeared to be carrying something.

Our next visitor was an older gentleman. My oldest son told me that this gentleman had sat on the edge of his bed. He also said that he had gotten into the car with him. My husband suffered a serious injury, so we set up a bed in our living room. A leather chair stood near his bed. My husband told me about an older gentleman sitting in the chair. He said he thought the gentleman was smoking. My son had also mentioned that the gentleman smoked.

My husband had renovated our attic, turning it into a large bedroom. We were startled to hear someone pacing back and forth in this room. The floor was carpeted yet we could hear the sound of footsteps on bare wood. One day, when I was the only one in the house, I was sitting in the room on the second floor near the stairway. I could hear footsteps come down the stairs. My hair felt as if it was standing on end.

Once the footsteps on the stairs started up, they were heard again and again by our family. Often the steps would be heard descending the stairs from the second to the first-floor landing. These stairs were carpeted; the stairs from the attic were not. However, all the footsteps sounded as if they were on bare boards.

Our third son slept in the attic bedroom. Every so often he complained that I was calling out his name to wake him. But I had not called him.

At times the window at the back of the attic room would open by itself. My husband had installed a new Pearson window that slid sideways and was difficult to open or shut. One day I closed the window and then sat down, only to watch the window open all by itself. There were no high winds and the room was electrically heated.

Our house was often filled with the delicious aroma of baking, usually chocolate. This occurred when I had not been baking. There were no baking odours coming in from outside. When my sister came from Ottawa to visit us, she also mentioned the smell of baking. While talking to the next-door neighbour one day, she began telling me about Mrs. Beerwagon's love of baking. After her children had grown up, she used to bake cupcakes full of nuts, which she placed outside for the squirrels.

We had a bathroom off the dining room. Originally the diningroom was the kitchen, and the bathroom was the summer kitchen. The bathroom door kept opening to the point that we had to install a chain lock on the door for privacy.

One evening my husband and sons were downstairs watching television. I was upstairs in bed reading, when a woman started sneezing. I searched the bedroom and the entire upstairs but found no one there. I was the only one upstairs.

We had decided to take out the dining-room windows and install patio doors and build a deck. We called for estimates. Three contractors came separately. The house seemed to come alive, especially upon the arrival of the third contractor. Lamps shook. There was banging in the basement. The house seemed so unsettled. This was the one time we felt nervous about our ghost. As a result, we decided against undertaking the renovation.

Once in a while we would hear things being moved about in the basement. When we checked, everything was always in place. I later learned that Mr. Beerwagon had placed a cot in the basement and he took naps behind the furnace. He also puttered around down there.

Our second son's girlfriend, who is now our daughter-in-law, maintained that our house made her feel nervous.

Before we bought 100 Moore Avenue, it had been rented to students. It was then purchased by a family of four and they undertook extensive renovations. After we sold the house, it apparently changed hands several times.

In all, we spent five years with ghosts from the past wandering through our rooms. This was the first home that I was glad to leave. On moving day, we never looked back, and never shed a tear.

Throughout all these ghostly experiences, for some reason or other, we never spoke about what was happening to anyone other than my sister and her husband.

My third ghostly experience came about in 1984. We were again living in Ottawa. Around 3:00 a.m., I was awakened by the sound of my great-aunt Myrtle calling out my name. At the time Aunt Myrtle was in the hospital in Pembroke. She was very close to us. She was ill with cancer. Later that day we learned that she had passed away. Upon talking to my sister that day, she told me that she too had heard Myrtle call out her name, around eight o'clock that morning.

My maternal grandmother had very strong intuition. She would always know when something was wrong. She would call me to say she had not slept all night because something was wrong at our house. She was usually right.

This gift was passed down to me. Sometimes it almost frightens me.

Possibly these stories will be of interest to you. It feels good to tell someone about them.

Sincerely,
Joan E. Skidmore

An Ottawa Apparition

Reg Hartt, a Toronto legend for his screenings of motion pictures, has been active in the city since the late 1960s, when he began showing his films out of Captain George Hendersen's Memory Lane Bookshop in Mirvish Village. Since then Hartt has become as well known for the talks he gives before the films as for the films themselves.

I Can't Believe You Are Still Alive?! is the title of Volume 1, Number 1, of Hartt's privately printed memoirs. Reading the memoirs I learned a lot about Hartt that I did not know. In fact, I came to realize that I really knew nothing about him: Because he is well-known, people like me think they know him well. In his memoirs he quotes a remark made by Carl Jung which goes like this: "The true path is the one we discover for ourselves and upon which we walk alone." It could well be Hartt's own maxim.

The short excerpt that follows comes from the memoirs and describes an incident with a ghost that occurred in Ottawa in the early 1960s.

While in Ottawa I had discovered the Bartonian Metaphysical Society. I had been browsing through an Anglican bookstore. I picked up a couple of books on the occult. The clerk told me that, if I was interested in that, there was a group that was studying it and they were having a meeting that night.

I went over and checked them out.

I sat at the back of the room where I could not only get a view of the speaker but also a view of everyone in the room. A woman, who introduced herself as Dr. Winnifred Barton, rose and spoke for one hour. While she was speaking I scanned the room. My eyes fell on a man in a red plaid shirt who, when he caught me watching him, pulled a Star Trek and faded away.

It was pretty far out.

I saw him do this a couple of times before the intermission. At the break I introduced myself to Dr. Barton and told her what I had seen. She left and returned with a photograph which I recognized as my phantom. "Yes, that's the man," I told her.

"That's the caretaker," she said. "That was his favourite spot. He died yesterday."

Needless to say they made me a member and I had a very interesting year.

Poltergeist in the Attic

I received the following letter from Gladys Ramsay, a resident of Dashwood, Ontario. Mrs. Ramsay saw my letter requesting "ghost stories" in the *London Free Press* and responded with this account of the haunted house she and her family owned in the 1960s.

There is no question that a house is like a person and has a personality and perhaps a spirit of its own. Often a house reflects the character of its occupants. In this account the house is inhabited by a "familiar spirit." What Mrs. Ramsay is describing is a poltergeist.

June 8, 1990
Dear Mr. Colombo:

In the late sixties we lived in an old farm house outside of London, Ontario. From the first week we used to hear unusual sounds in the attic. So my husband and son went up with flashlights to check it out, but they found no holes and no signs of squirrels.

The next evening the sounds from the attic were frightening, as though giant birds were bouncing off the walls. This was odd since one of the first things my husband did after we moved in was insulate the attic. Another trip up to the attic was to no avail.

A few weeks later, around 3:00 a.m., we were awakened with the sounds of cupboard doors opening and closing. We all woke up, except for our oldest son who is a heavy sleeper. We put the lights on and went downstairs to check. Everything was fine.

We had a German shepherd named Prince at that time. He slept on a mat by the kitchen door. He was terrified. His ears were flat to his head and he never made a move or even barked. This was our watchdog! We never even locked a door while we had this dog.

One day during the fall of the year, I was staining the old staircase. I decided to make a cup of tea and went downstairs. After one cup, I put the teapot back on the stove and climbed up the stairs and continued with my work. About an hour later I went back downstairs for another cup of tea but couldn't find the teapot. I wasn't going to let it get the better of me, so I decided I'd have a glass of milk. When I reached for the milk, there was the teapot!

After all these happenings, I talked to the man who had sold the house to us. He now lived across the road from us. I explained what had been going on and he said the previous tenants had told him pretty well the same thing had happened to them. He said the only explanation he had was that an elderly sister and brother had lived in the house for years. This was when his parents had owned it, and they told him the brother and sister had a quarrel and the sister told her brother she wouldn't speak to him for the rest of her life and when her mother and father visited them they spoke through them.

Our daughter always had the feeling of a man's presence in the house. Many a day and night we'd hear heavy footsteps on the staircase and along the upstairs hall. The minute anyone went up to see what was making the noise, it would stop.

I should mention our dog Prince always came upstairs at night to check us out. He visited our bedroom first. He would touch our hands with his nose to let us know he was there and then he went into the children's rooms. The night we heard the cupboard doors banging, he never moved. We were told animals are afraid of the unknown.

I hope you'll be able to make something out of it. Please let us know when your book will be published.

Yours truly,
Mrs. Gladys Ramsay

P.S. Sorry I couldn't mention names of previous owners and addresses. It would hurt a lot of people. The house stands empty to this day. It is so sad because my husband renovated this beautiful old home and we loved it. We sold it to a customs agent who sold it to a lawyer who rented it out. From there on we lost track of it. We heard through friends and old neighbours that it is vacant. As I said, it is a long way off the road and surrounded with trees.

Ghost in the Hallway

The sadness of the human condition is as much the subject of the experience that follows as is the supernatural.

Parapsychologists have long noted that times of grief are times productive of psychical phenomena. Indeed, for some people, the two seem to be inseparable.

Certainly it is a time of grief that is being recalled in this letter sent to me by Linda C. Marlok, a housewife for twenty years and a mother of three and now a resident of Val Caron, Ontario.

12 July, 1990
Dear Sir,

I read your letter in the *Northern Life* newspaper in Sudbury, Ontario, the one asking people to write to you about happenings and sightings of ghosts, UFOs, and strange creatures.

The story I'm writing to you about is true.

The incident was something that happened to me about six years after my father died. Members of my family and I decided to go to visit my mother for the weekend. At the time she was staying at the cottage that had been my father's favourite place. It was a log cabin up on a hill which overlooks a small lake called Bat Lake, at Minden, Ontario.

Our first night at the cottage I was awakened shortly after going to bed. I could hear footsteps pacing up and down the hallway. I thought it was my mother, so I got up to go and make sure. No one was there. Everyone was in bed sleeping. I found it strange, so when I went back to bed, I woke up my husband and told him of the strange sounds.

The following day I spoke with my mother about what had happened that night. She replied, "Oh, yes, I have a lady ghost who walks the hallway at nights. It's nothing unusual. You see, the lady who was the former owner had died in this cottage, and she walks the hallway at nights. It was her sister who sold us the cottage and who told us of this back then."

Later that day my mother and I exchanged harsh words, and I went to the washroom crying. I said the following words in my upset state: "Dad, I'm sorry, I can't reason with her, and I don't know what to do. I find it hard to hold my promise to you."

Just then, under my feet, there were three knocks on the floor boards. I could feel the vibration and so frightened was I that I left the cottage right away.

There is no basement to the cottage, just a crawl space, and the door to it is always padlocked. It was so when I went to check.

There are other incidents that have happened to my sister, my brother-in-law, and many other people who have stayed at this cottage.

Sincerely,
Linda C. Marlok

A Well-Loved Persian Cat

Joan Finch is a correspondent and cat lover who lives in Langley, B.C. She read of my interest in "the mysterious" in the *Langley Times* and sent me the following account of an unusual experience that involved her well-loved Persian cat, Sybby. The account is dated 24 July 1990.

A great deal of literature has been published that alludes to the special relationship, even the kinship, that seems to exist between animal beings and human beings. There is a good deal of writing that suggests that over years of association and friendship masters and pets establish a deep and psychic interrelationship.

Nothing in Mrs. Finch's letter proves or disproves the existence of any special or psychic relationship. But the experience she writes about certainly shows how deep and meaningful the special relationship may be.

⁂

I saw your letter in my local newspaper, asking if anyone had had any supernatural experiences. I wondered if you would be interested in a supernatural pet experience.

It happened in Toronto, in Willowdale to be exact, about twenty-eight years ago.

My husband and I were married in England four years before coming to Canada. We obtained a kitten the first year of our marriage, and after four years we were still childless. Consequently we treated our kitten, a long-haired Persian called Sybby, like a child.

I was especially attracted to Sybby, so much so that I could not come to Canada without her. We came by ship. It took us ten days to get here. The cat and I were in a cabin, sea-sick together for those ten days.

We moved a lot after arriving in Canada. We still had no children. Sybby was about fifteen years old when we adopted our first baby. Needless to say, Sybby was very jealous of the new baby, so much so that one morning she walked out the front door, never to return.

I couldn't think what had become of her. My husband toured the district every day for weeks, thinking she may have been the victim of a car accident. I had the local children looking for her, and we advertised in supermarkets, on the radio, etc., but to no avail. We even combed through a forest near us each evening, because one of the local children thought he had seen a cat in the woods that looked like the photo of Sybby.

I was very emotional about our loss and upset for about three months. If I had seen Sybby die, it wouldn't have been so bad. But I didn't know what had happened to her. Consequently, she was always on my mind.

One morning, as I was lying in bed, half-awake, thinking I must get up to feed our newly-adopted, four-month-old baby, I felt as though I was experiencing an electric shock. I couldn't move, my hair felt funny and all on end. Then I felt a weight jump on my stomach and the weight started to purr and kneed me.

I wanted to see and stroke the weight. But we had no cat at this time. I couldn't move. Then all at once the weight leapt off into mid-air. There was no noise of anything landing on the floor. I felt a delicious peace come over me, and in that instant somehow I knew that Sybby was dead, but very happy. And from that moment on, I have never worried about her any more.

We have had a dog and lots of cats since Sybby. At the time of writing, I have four cats, but I have never been as close to any of them as I was to Sybby or had any other similar experiences.

Thank you for looking into these things.

The Beautiful Lady in White

Mrs. M. Kirkpatrick is a resident of North Woodstock, Ontario. She was born in Chelsea, England. She read my request for true-life "ghost stories" in the Woodstock weekly newspaper *Sentinel-Review* and sent me her own account of the appearance of the Beautiful Lady in White in 1965 or 1966. I received the handwritten letter on 25 May 1990.

The account is interesting in two ways. Although the ghost was not seen by Mrs. Kirkpatrick, it was seen by both her young son and her adult house guest. She later learned that there was a local tradition about a wandering spirit which inhabits small stone houses or cottages, as well as the story of a suicide in her own house.

It seems that local lore buttresses local experiences. Or is it the other way round?

⚜

I once rented a stone house on a farm at R.R. 7, Woodstock. The house was later burnt down, but its remains are still to be seen.

I lived there with my two boys, then ten years old and twelve years old. They slept in separate bedrooms upstairs. We were in the house several years.

It was getting towards Christmas. One night, my younger son told me the next morning, that a beautiful lady in white came into his room and smiled at him. This happened for a few nights in a row.

Once I had some friends stay overnight. I put one of them in my younger son's room. Nobody had mentioned his story about the beautiful lady in white, especially not me, as nobody else had seen this lady.

Anyway, the next morning, our guest came down. He asked me if I had gone into his room. I said no, because I had no reason at all to go upstairs or into his room. Anyway, as he described it, this beautiful woman in white came into the room, looked at him, smiled, and then went away.

By this time I was getting "the willies." I decided to move back into town. I figured the house must be haunted and the ghost must be a beautiful lady.

By this time it was very near Xmas of the following year. I was about to have another child.

One day I picked up the *Sentinel Review* and read about a ghost. There was this story of "The Lady in White." Evidently she was about to marry and her future husband had built a little stone house for her. He got killed in a crash on the eve of their wedding. So she went around to all the stone houses looking for her husband. She was harmless, according to the article.

I never saw her, but my son, who is now forty-two years old, will swear to this day that he saw the Lady in White. My guest saw her, too, but unfortunately he is now deceased.

I found out afterwards that a man's wife left him and he hanged himself in the little stone house in which we lived.

I believe in ghosts, as I saw two myself in England. I saw the famous ghost of Dr. Phene, well known on King's Road in Chelsea, and I saw the spirit of a nun when I was a young girl. So I now believe in ghosts.

I only wish I had seen the Lady in White. I may have been able to console her. She only goes to stone houses, and whenever I see a stone house I always think of the Lady in White.

This is a true story.

Past Life Vision

Here is another account from the "Psychic Survey" conducted by the Owens and Dr. Joel Whitton for the *National Enquirier*. It concerns an informant who identified herself as L.M.B., Mt. Hope, Ontario; twenty-nine, female, clerk and housewife, twelve years schooling.

‎⚜‎

My first past life experience came with a bang.

I drove my girlfriend down to Niagara Falls to spend the day and part of the evening. I was nineteen and working, just starting to feel a little bit independent. We borrowed my parent's second car for the day. When we got there, we had a marvellous time shopping and sightseeing.

Rita suggested that we go into Madame Tussaud's and I was quite agreeable. Inside we were enjoying ourselves very much and Rita asked me to accompany her into the Torture Chamber or Chamber of Horrors because she was afraid to go alone. As I had been in that part of the exhibit some years previously and had not been impressed, I protested that heads with eyeballs hanging out of them and statues of infamous people weren't nearly as interesting — besides being very distasteful to look at — as some of the truly magnificent exhibits that could be seen upstairs.

Nothing would do but that we had to go into the horror chamber. I remember being dragged along disinterestedly and occasionally going into shouts of laughter at some of the more lurid exhibits. We began comparing some of the figures to people we worked with, saying the figures displayed some of their least attractive habits. With Rita a little way ahead of me, I turned a corner and came upon an exhibit labelled The Hook of Algiers.

The instant I clapped eyes on this exhibit, I froze on the spot. The contents of my stomach became lodged in my throat, and I experienced what I later termed a "flashback." The exhibit itself showed a man suspended by the abdomen from a giant meat-hook. A paragraph or two explained the method of torture and execution. I later forced myself to read the explanation, but all I can now remember of it is that if the victim was cut down within three days, he often survived.

What actually happened went like this. As soon as I saw the exhibit, Madame Tussaud's disappeared. I found myself outside a walled city. I was watching a person being suspended from a hook. Other people were around and I was terribly upset. I wasn't positive if the victim was a man or a woman, but I "knew" that this person was in some way connected to me and that I was involved with him/her. I felt that I was a woman and was dressed in the flowing garments of that period.

It was full daylight and the city walls seemed to be baked clay or very dusty stone. The ground was either dust or sand. I could hear what sounded like a large crowd going about its daily affairs. The other people around were all dressed in flowing robes of various colours. There seemed to be other people whom I felt to be like a "family" around me.

The victim was in a small cleared space in front of the wall and the rest of us in a semi-circle around him. It was a small crowd and I got the impression that this was no big deal — just a minor matter. There were two or three men who were inside the semi-circle and I felt them to be officials of some kind.

The most distinctive feature of this happening was the waves of feeling that engulfed me. I was horrified and terribly afraid. Before this happened, I could read about or see movies of people being hurt or mutilated and it never really affected me. After this incident anything like that makes me very sick and repulses me so strongly that I almost become ill at the thought.

Anyway, the whole experience must have taken less than a minute. Then I found myself in Madame Tussaud's again. I tried to rationalize the incident by forcing myself to look at the exhibit and read about it, but I was so upset that I simply had to leave — fast. I grabbed my girl-friend and we left.

I don't remember driving home. But when I got home, my mother, after one look at my face, asked, "What happened?" I told her, and it was she who suggested that the experience might have been that of a past life.

I agree with this theory because no one can shake my belief that I was actually there outside those city walls.

A Very Vivid Apparition

"There you go," wrote Donna Englund-Price. "If you think there is merit to this story, perhaps you'll want to use it."

Mrs. Englund-Price wrote to me on 17 June 1990. She sent me an account of a series of unusual — and heart-wrenching — experiences. There is much suffering here; also a sense of resolve or resolution. It is difficult to know what to make of the premonitions, birth, deaths, and apparitions. Yet one lesson is clear: One has to accept rather than reject anomalous experiences, and incorporate them into one's everyday life.

⁂

In the year of 1968, I was pregnant with our daughter Barbara Ann. My husband David's mother had been dead for several years, and the course of her life had never been smooth. It was for that express reason that we decided to make our about-to-be-born daughter her namesake, in the hope that we could provide her with a better life than her grandmother had enjoyed.

My husband had described in some detail how his mother had died. He also described the events leading up to the death of her father, my husband's grandfather. On that particular day, a clock struck twelve, only my husband insists that it struck thirteen. For some unexplained reason, my husband had experienced a premonition that his grandfather had succumbed to heart failure. That insight unfortunately proved to be correct, as, indeed, he had passed away.

Several years later, in the Summer of 1968, our beautiful daughter Barbara Ann was born. In an almost total repeat of his grandfather's death, my husband went to check our daughter after the clock struck 12:00 p.m., Thanksgiving Day, 1969. Our daughter had died of crib death.

No matter how much those around us tried to reason with me, I insisted that I would bear the same daughter again. Like some incredible coincidence, our daughter Sherrilee was born the following Thanksgiving Day.

There are pictures of my late mother-in-law and other pictures of my second daughter that show an uncanny resemblance. That, too, may be sheer coincidence, but there is more. I am not at all sure how what I am about to describe fits into this scenario. But I sense that it does.

Our son was four years old at the time of his sister's death. Some time later he told us that the night before our daughter died he had seen funny, frightening faces looking and laughing at him from outside the window. This may not be an unusual occurrence for a young child, but that was the first occasion on which we had ever had to reassure him that he must have been asleep. Until then he had never been afraid of the dark.

Also, during the time prior to our second daughter's birth, a very vivid apparition appeared before my eyes. It was the face of a beautiful man, typical of the way men are depicted in the pages of biblical texts. The most outstanding feature was that the apparition appeared to be standing sidewise, not straightforward.

The birth, death, and apparition all occurred during the period when we lived in St. Catharines, Ontario. Several years later, when we lived in Toronto, I was alone in our townhouse. I decided to lie on the couch to rest until my husband returned home. Suddenly, I felt almost a whisper of a touch. At first I thought that our cat had jumped up beside me and that I was feeling her tail. Then, without knowing why, I knew it wasn't our cat at all. I am not sure whether I said, "Can I turn over?" but through words or thoughts, I knew that I could. Upon turning, the same apparition appeared to me, but this time it lingered longer. I experienced the most sensual feeling I had ever known. The man smiled at me and, after perhaps thirty or forty seconds, faded.

I remember thinking how strange it was that I felt no fear, only amazement. Suddenly I felt completely drained and turned back around to face the couch. There was a swirling pattern of illumination all over the back of the couch and I literally passed out.

I've never seen that face again, but I often wonder what all of this was about.

Until these events took place, I'd never even heard about the theory of reincarnation, and I'd laughed at other people's ghost stories. Now I am convinced that I have had paranormal experiences. I rarely talk about them to anyone, except family members and close friends, and even then I find it a little embarrassing.

Haunted House on Pape Avenue

"Enclosed please find the story of Pape House," wrote Gertie Sequillion in her letter to me dated 23 Dec. 1988. "I hope that this story is all right, as I have not attempted to write for publication before."

The story is indeed all right. It is being published here in Mrs. Sequillion's own words. The account arrived in a carefully prepared, six-page typescript which I have minimally copy edited. Mrs. Sequillion originally phoned me in response to an invitation that I issued on an open-line radio programme. I had asked listeners and others to share with me any paranormal experience that they may have had.

Mrs. Sequillion contacted me by phone the following day. She had not heard the programme, but a friend of hers had, and the friend then encouraged her to relate to me this account of living in a haunted house at 557 Pape Avenue in Toronto's East End. The events occurred in 1969. I encouraged Mrs. Sequillion to write out an account of the episode and mail it to me. A week or so later, the six pages of typescript arrived. The reader is invited to make of it what he or she will!

⚜

It all started innocently enough. I was doing the dishes at the sink, like most new mothers-to-be, while waiting for my husband to come home for dinner, when there came a knock on the door and there descended on me my whole family from Newfoundland.

Well, you can imagine my surprise, and all the noise and inconvenience in a one-bedroom flat, with five more people in it! That, however, was not all, as they had news to relate. My mother had sold our family home, which my father had built. My father had had a heart attack over the idea of the move to Toronto. He was still in the hospital in St. John's. Annie, the youngest, was with Mom, waiting for news of his release. Then they too would descend on us, with Dad to follow thereafter.

To save time and confusion later, I will here introduce my family: Dad (Chesley), Mom (Annie Clara), Jessie, who was married and away with the Armed Forces (thank God!), Rod, Chesley Jr., also married and thus saved the ordeal, Ed, who could tell his own story of the place, and Rich, who decided to leave rather suddenly, myself (Gert), Marina, John, who was slightly retarded, Lily, Bernice, and Annie, named after my mother and the youngest since our baby sister Celeste had died at the age of two and a quarter years.

Thus we are a big family like steps and stairs. If it had not been so, my experience would have been of more fright, but as the human mind tends to rationalize things supernatural, so did I at the time.

However, I had no idea of this when Rod first said, "Gert, your flat just won't do. Mom wants us to find a place for all of us. That includes you and Fred." I thought, "My husband, poor man, this is something you aren't going to like!"

Most people would say "no" right then and there, but I must confess I was not the "no" kind. I had never said "no" to my mother about anything in my life, so true to form I said "no" in my heart but not in the open. So I found myself with the problem, which to everyone else was so simple. I just had to tell Fred, when he came home, that we were moving. But, oh, how unsimple it was to me!

You see, my husband was not a patient man by any means of the word. He was good-looking, and thus his appeal to me, but patient or understanding of anything but his own comforts he was not. Rather verbal he could be, but not, thank God, to a person's face. Thus I knew the brunt of it would be felt by me alone. Still, he wasn't home yet, so I had time to think just what I'd say. I decided food was my best bet, so dinner turned into something special and lots of it!

To say he was surprised to find a whole houseful of family, all of them mine, is to lighten an otherwise ghastly ordeal. I introduced them much the same as I have to you, with the exception of Dad, Mom, Jessie, Marina, Chesley Jr., and Annie.

"Gert, we don't have room for all these people," he said, and he was amazingly calm. But you just knew he was trying to figure a way of getting rid of them as quickly as possible.

"Honey," I said, as a way of softening the blow, "you can get a newspaper after dinner." Whereupon I was interrupted by Rod who said, "You mean supper, don't you, or have you turned into a bunch of Torontonians?"

This interjection lightened everyone's mood, and soon we were all laughing about the differences between being a Newfie and a Mainlander. This merriment was short-lived, however, when our landlord got wind of the matter and notice to leave was given. Fred, being a man to take care of his money, saw that it would be a profitable venture to move in with my family. Thus the difficult problem for me was solved without me having to tell him anything. And to this day he doesn't know that moving in with my family was already a foregone conclusion.

To us, then, the ad in the paper for the Pape Avenue house seemed a godsend at the time. It read something like this: "Three storey house for rent in the East End of the city. Kitchen, bath, living-room, and possible five bedrooms. Immediate occupancy. Phone — — ."

We called and made arrangements to see the place. It had really large rooms. Everything had been newly painted, and to us the price per month seemed like a steal. Once the first and last months' rents were paid, we still had a little left for more furniture, as ours alone wasn't enough. The packing and moving were done very swiftly. Still, we were not yet all moved in when Mother and Annie arrived.

"Happy birthday!" she shouted from behind us, as I was carrying a box out the door. It wasn't my birthday, of course, but she had bought me a gift and couldn't wait any longer to give it to me. It was only the first of May and my birthday was not till the eighth. When it did come, only my brother Rich and I remembered, as his birthday is the same as mine. By then I was in the new house already a week, and what a sleepless one it was!

The house was clean and nice, large enough for all. I don't think we've ever had so much room in our lives. But the noise was driving me crazy.

Let's see. The kids were in the middle bedroom, the one with that awful stain on the floor. Yes, that's right, and Dad and Mom had the larger bedroom across the hall. I just couldn't stand the noise from the kids' room anymore, and neither could Fred. I was going to kill the kids if they didn't go to sleep. We had tried to keep quiet about the racket they made, but Fred did have to work in the morning, and as a pregnant mother I needed my rest, didn't I? Mom and Dad would just have to be mad at me. Fred was very close to leaving me altogether. Living with relatives is bad enough, but the man couldn't get any sleep at all.

It was the same thing every night, always noises like people fighting, and then running up and down the stairs after one another like a herd of elephants, and then in their bedroom it was like they'd fight and even knock one another down. Sometimes it was as if one of them was seriously hurt. But as the noise kept up all night, I guess they weren't.

Well, tonight it was going to stop or else! That's just what I was thinking that night, but I was not prepared for what I found out. I went into their bedroom, prepared to kill, but like little angels they were sound asleep. In fact, I went all over the house, even up to the third floor, where my older brothers were sleeping. My, it was an eerie place! I felt like someone was watching me, but though I turned around two or three times, the only thing I saw was sleeping men. Still, I got out of there fast. I felt weird up there.

Upon returning to our bedroom, Fred was mad at me. "I thought you were going to quiet them down. Well?"

"Honey," I said, "you and I are the only people awake in this whole house."

"Gert, that's garbage. You can hear that racket," he said, waving towards the stairs.

"Fred, everyone is asleep," I nearly screamed at him. "I'm cold," I added, tucking myself back in bed. "If you don't believe me, you can check for yourself."

Fred grumbled under his breath, but he didn't do anything about getting up. I didn't know what time it was, but I do know I must have fallen asleep from exhaustion, for in the morning, when I awoke, it was nearly ten.

This was the routine, for routine it became, until Fred could take it no longer. He himself decided to go check on the kids. He was cold when he returned and quite determined to leave this house. He said it was the strangest place in the world, where people make a noise and no one is supposed to be doing it.

Telling my mother wasn't going to be an easy chore. But Fred was my husband, and a wife had to go along with her husband, didn't she? So the news was given and accepted with bad feelings all around.

It was about our last night. We all sat at the TV after supper. For that matter, the TV in our place never seemed to be off. Ed mentioned quite jokingly that he would return to the third floor to sleep up there with the other boys. Apparently for the last week he'd been sleeping on the sofa downstairs, because he didn't feel comfortable up there. Rod and Johnny were joking with him about it, and at first he didn't want to tell why, but afterward he did.

"I don't want you guys to think I'm afraid to be on my own or anything, but last night something woke me suddenly, and so I was getting up to see what it was, when my face turned to the window and I saw a hideous-looking face staring at me. Well, you know I'm not one to go crying about ghosts or anything, but I don't want some guy looking in at me sleeping either."

Well, what a shock it must have been for him. So it was decided, with a lot of good ribbing, that he'd return upstairs. Funny, no one had mentioned it to us.

Well, the noises never stopped. In fact, they just seemed to us more sinister than ever. So two days later, my husband and I moved out, amid Mother's groaning and reproaches.

My time came and I was finally delivered of a son, healthy, happy, and bawling. After leaving the hospital, my mom was the first to call with the news that they had moved into a new house and I was to come over and show her the baby. So to Mother's house we went, baby and all, that very night, and everyone loved Fred Jr.

It was while we were checking on the baby that Mom and I had a good chance to talk. She wasn't mad at us anymore, and she said so. She then showed us around her new house. "Isn't it marvellous, Gert, and there's no ghosts in it, either."

"What, Mom?" I asked.

"Oh, dear, your father told me not to tell you. But I suppose it is all right to tell you now that the baby's come an' all."

"Tell me what, Mom? What about the ghosts?" I was all questions, and my ears were ready to hear anything, but not what she said.

"Well," she began, "when you left, we took over yours and Fred's bedroom. Honey, we started hearing what you and Fred heard. We were not aware that you were going through so much and hearing so many noises. Your dad recognized it right off, as spirits living in the house. You see, our bedroom wasn't so noisy, but the third floor was terrible, and the boys couldn't stand it up there. Ed and Johnny saw all sorts of things, men mostly, and we tried to keep the knowledge from you, by making you think it was one of us who caused those noises. We were afraid you would be frightened and something would happen to the baby. We didn't want you to move out, though, as we were intending to get another place anyway, when the money situation was a little better for your father.

"Anyway, we didn't know all about the ghosts. Then we had our doubts, at least until we took over your bedroom. But then we were sure. Your father says there's no such thing as ghosts anyway. They had to be demons, because the living don't come back. Sometimes demons, whoever, try to make it appear as if they did. Realizing it was demons, your father opened our big Bible, but at night the demons seemed to be rustling the pages of it. You could hear them turning in the night.

"So we told one of the Brothers of the Church about it. You remember Mr. ——— ——. He lives down the street. Well, he told us about the house. He said that two brothers had lived there. They had had an argument on the third floor, and a fight broke out, one apparently knocking the other down the stairs, and then ran downstairs to his bedroom, that being the middle one where the children sleep. Well, the other got up and ran after him and found him at the sink, trying to wash or something, and struck him over the head from behind and killed him. There, that is why there's that big stain on the floor there in that room."

"Mom, that sounds just like what we heard," I said. "Are you sure?"

"Yes, dear, I am sure that there was something in that house. I was sure the second I came into this one and that eerie feeling was gone. I knew."

"Well, your father said it's so in the Bible, my dear."

"Yes, honey, we all know that."

Truth, they say, is stranger than fiction, and I know that my mind doesn't want to believe it, but that's just how it happened, and I know. That house is still there today, for anyone to visit and see. I'll show you where it is, and even if necessary take you to the spot, but there ain't no way I'm going back in there.

Someone Else in the House

David Peacock, the author of this letter, is a creative marketing consultant with a background in advertising. He and his wife Suzanne are collectors of old furniture and old houses, as the letter shows. He collaborated with his wife on a book called *Old Oakville: A Character Study of the Town's Early Buildings and the Men Who Built Them* (1979) which features photographs by Patrick Knox.

The Peacocks still live in the old Ontario community of Oakville where David has his office. But their first house, their dream home, was not as homey as it should have been. It seems they shared it with a spirit, perhaps a poltergeist ...

28 March, 1989
Dear John:

Attached is the story of our encounter. It is surely not as dramatic or as frightening as many of the stories you must have come upon, but it was and is very real to us.

We bought the house in question in Oakville, Ontario, in 1969. It is a three-storey, frame farmhouse, located on a wooded acre, surrounded by more recently built homes. We purchased the property from an elderly spinster who was the daughter of the original owner. Both of her parents had passed away in the house. Her father had grown quite senile, and her mother had been restricted to the first floor, as she was confined to a wheelchair for much of her later life.

My wife Suzanne and I thought the house would be perfect for us. It was far away from the city and it would be the ideal place in which to bring up our two young children. Fresh air. Tree houses. A creek. An attic. And a rambling old house. All the things that make for a story-book childhood. However, we had not counted on the presence that occupied the house.

We never actually saw a ghost, but we were all very much aware of there being someone else in the house. The children called the presence Grandpa — — — , after the original owner. Hundreds of times we would close a door, only to come back to find it open. Or we would open the curtains, only to return to find them drawn. Once we woke up to find a light fixture missing from the hall ceiling. Later we found it safely tucked into the corner of the cellar behind the furnace. I sup-pose this was just some sort of a prank.

One evening, after the children had been put to bed, Suzanne and I were sitting in the living room, reading the paper, when suddenly a cold chill ran over me, and the hair rose on the back of my neck. I looked up at my wife, who was sitting across the room, and I could see that she was experiencing a similar sensation. We felt as if the tempera-ture of the room had plummeted thirty degrees. Nothing appeared. But someone was there.

Perhaps the most startling and the most difficult event to explain away occurred during our last winter in the house. The previous owner had left a large pine cupboard in the cellar. It was so large, in fact, that it had been lowered into the cellar as the house was being built. It was a very early piece and it was in excellent condition. It had its original buttermilk stain, inside and out, but unfortunately its exterior had been splashed with whitewash every time the cellar had been repainted.

In my spare time I began to sand the exterior of the cabinet to reveal its natural red pine finish. Over the course of the many weeks that it took to do the sanding, sanding dust accumulated and covered the floor around it. Then, in the midst of refinishing the cabinet, the entire family came down with the flu. At the same time, one of the old lead pipes in the cellar chose to spring a leak. The plumber said that he could not get around to fix it until the next day, so I had no alternative but to shut off the water overnight. Too sick to care, I left the cellar lit-tered with sandpaper scraps which were floating in pools of water. The pools were red in colour from the sawdust that was coating the base-ment floor.

Feeling better the next morning, I went down to the cellar to turn on the water briefly. I was amazed to find the floor spotless. It had been wiped clean and dry. The pools or puddles were too large to evaporate by themselves. If they had evaporated, they would have left a residue of sawdust. In the middle of the room, next to the cupboard, sat a yellow plastic pail. It was full of water, reddish in colour. On the surface was

112

the scum of red sawdust and a bright yellow sponge.

No one had been feeling well enough to rise from his or her bed to effect the clean-up. So it remains a family mystery to this day how the water got into the pail.

Not long after we sold the house and shortly thereafter moved elsewhere in Oakville. Although the presence in the house was not a malevolent one, the house itself never really felt as if it belonged to us.

Good luck,
David

"Betty Louty"

George Gamester, a lively columnist with the *Toronto Star*, has an odd range of enthusiasms. From time to time he invites his readers to contribute to a series of theme columns.

"Tell Us Your Eerie Tales" is the theme of one of his series. Here is how Gamester began the series on 16 June 1989:

> Forget it, Rod Serling. Get lost, Vincent Price. Dry up, Edgar Allan Poe. We have all the spooky stories we need right here — thanks to *Star* readers' incredible response to our invitation to:
>> *Tell us your eerie tales.*
>> So who needs fantasy?
>> As we learn from our first $50 winner, Jo Atkins of North York, real life is strange enough ...

Here is Jo Atkins, a writer in Willowdale, Ontario, telling the amazing story of "Betty Louty."

⁂

When Elizabeth was small, "Betty Louty" appeared as an imaginary playmate. She came every afternoon for a friendly visit. We arranged the coffee table for Betty's visit: lace tea cloth, tiny cups and saucers, cream and sugar, and the inevitable cookies were part of the ritual. Elizabeth held her one-sided, polite, somewhat-comforting conversations with her unseen guest and played the sympathetic friend. Before my older child was due home, Betty Louty would depart.

"Where does Betty live?" I asked.

"A long way away," was the only answer I ever got.

No one in our family knew anyone by that name. It was unusual and we often wondered what had prompted Elizabeth to invent it. We put it down to the vivid imagination of a creative high-strung child who had suddenly found herself without her closest friend and ally ... her sister.

A few years later we all went to Jamaica for a holiday. In Kingston, a visit to the famous straw market was mandatory, as they each wanted a doll dressed colourfully in the traditional costume, balancing a basket of fruit on its head.

Our older girl chose a doll from the first stall in the market. But not Elizabeth. She moved from stall to stall but did not find a doll she wanted. No! No! was all we heard. We became a little fractious: She became more determined.

"I want that one," Elizabeth said finally, pointing most definitely in the direction of the farthest corner of the stop row of dolls.

"Take one from the bottom row," I said. "They're all the same." The heat in the market and the intractability of my daughter were getting to me.

"I want that one," she insisted, still pointing.

The old lady moved her pole along the row, first to one doll then the next. She turned to look at me.

"They are not all the same. Each one is signed by the person who made it," she said reproachfully.

"That's her!" said Elizabeth suddenly, eyes alight.

With a great deal of patience the old lady hooked the doll down for her. She patted the child on her head.

"This one is made just for you, darlin'. This lady is not makin' dolls any more. This is the last one she made. She's been waitin' here for you."

"I know she's special. I'll look after her," said Elizabeth as she hugged the doll tightly and covered her with kisses.

Throughout our holiday, that doll never left Elizabeth's side. She slept, ate, walked with her, and would prop her gently on the sand before going into the water.

"She would like to swim too, but she's afraid of the currents in the water," said our young one.

"Currants are in cake," I said jokingly. How could she possibly have known about ocean currents since she was so young and not familiar with the seashore?

It was so quiet in Elizabeth's room, I thought she must have fallen asleep, but when I peeped in I found the doll had been carefully undressed by my little girl. She had taken off all the clothes and had only the bare rag doll in her hands, cradling it gently as if it were a new-born child.

"Your bath's ready but you can't put your doll in with you. She'll get too wet," I said.

"She's afraid of water. She told me so," said Elizabeth very defensively. This game was getting to be too much for me!

"Well, let's pick up her clothes anyway," I said. "After your bath you can put her clothes back on."

As I picked up the clothes, I remembered the old lady in the Kingston market. I could not see the signature of the maker. Good saleswoman, I thought!

"I wonder who made this doll," I said.

"Betty. It's writing; I can't read it," said Elizabeth as she handed me the doll's apron.

There, on the inside band, was the maker's name ... "Betty Louty."

The imaginary playmate never appeared after that holiday in Jamaica. My daughter has her own home now but she still has the doll. For all these years she has treasured her.

It seems that "Betty Louty" finally came home.

An Apparition and a Visitor

Barbara Neyedly is the publisher of the *Toronto Voice*, a monthly community paper published for readers in the city's downtown.

She is an able and intuitive person who enjoys meeting people and sharing experiences. On 2 Aug. 1990, she responded to my request for "extraordinary experiences" by sending me two unusual experiences of her own. It is obvious that while castles, crypts, and cathedrals may be the proper dwelling place for ghosts and apparitions, poltergeists and spirits, they are also encountered in modern highrise apartment buildings and townhouse complexes.

Here are her experiences. Make of them what you will.

1.

Around 1970, I was living in a three-bedroom apartment, in the Thorncliffe Park area of Toronto, with my three children, aged ten, eleven, and thirteen.

I had taken up with a handsome Jamaican ten years my junior, and he was often at my apartment. Although from dissimilar backgrounds, at the time we shared a strong emotional bond. This emotional bond, I later came to believe, was at least partly responsible for the dramatic incidence of telepathy that took place one evening.

That night, after the children had gone to bed, my friend and I decided to have a drink of wine and then go outside for a walk around the neighbourhood. It was in late May, about eight-thirty, and it was still light outside. I went into my bedroom, at the end of a long corridor, intending to make up the bed with freshly laundered sheets before having a drink.

I remember that I was fitting the corner of the bottom sheet to the mattress corner closest to the window when it happened. My head snapped up. I saw my boyfriend leering through the outside window pane, just a few inches away — arms reaching toward me, hands curled into claws. He was in the classic "pouncing" position. His eyes were dilated, and his mouth formed a mock-menacing grin.

My screams of shock woke my daughters in the next room. They came running to see what was wrong. The figure was still at the window as I left the bedroom and hurtled myself down the long corridor.

Only later did I remember that there was no balcony outside the third-floor room, just a rough roof, hard, almost impossible to reach from our apartment balcony. The representation of my boyfriend was completely persuasive, down to the detail of the white knit shirt he was wearing that day.

When I reached the living room a few seconds later, the reality of the apparition leaped out from behind the sofa to scare me "for real." It was a carbon-copy lunge of what I had just seen at the window!

I began berating my boyfriend for frightening me through the window. It took him several moments to convince me that he had not actually been out on the roof. He laughingly protested that he had not scared me through the window.

I eventually realized it was an impossibility for him to be able to run across the roof, leap over the railing, travel across the balcony, go through the sliding glass doors, race across the room, and be there behind the sofa to scare me in the few seconds it took me to cover the hall.

But I definitely saw him there, and we spent most of the rest of the evening discussing how such a thing could possibly have happened. The only real clue I ever found was what my boyfriend told me he was thinking about around that time.

When I went to make the bed, he went into the kitchen to take the wine bottle out of the fridge. And on opening the fridge door, he had a strong thought that he should scare me. It would be a joke. He would frighten me when I returned to the living room.

That is when I think I must have suddenly seen his image at the window, doing what he thought about doing. His thought somehow communicated itself to my unconscious mind, which produced a powerful image of what he suggested, right before my startled eyes.

I don't know how it actually happened. But I believe people who are attuned emotionally, somehow, when the time is right, create the right "climate" for telepathic thought. People who have never experienced anything similar, and who also deny the existence of phenomena outside the five senses, usually tell me that I was dreaming or drunk.

No way.

I couldn't say whether the night's events had anything to do with the street number of the condominium, 1666 Queen St. E., but later I wondered about that. I did find out — much later, as well — that another resident of the townhouse complex, who lived a couple of doors away, also saw a ghost while living there.

I lived at Townhouse Number 12 from 1976, the year the condos were built, until 1986. The houses were on the tall, Elizabethan model, with multiple floors and several small flights of stairs.

It was a blustery winter night, a Saturday, in 1985, when, highly unusual for me, I fell asleep on the couch about 1:00 a.m. The couch was in the living room, which was located on the very bottom floor, facing the front entrance.

I don't now remember the reason I didn't make it up the three flights of stairs to my bedroom before conking out. I only recall being overwhelmed by a delicious drowsy sensation, so overpowering that I fell asleep, leaving several lights on. I had had a few glasses of wine with dinner, hours earlier, but I was not inebriated. In any case, booze has never, before or since, caused me to believe I saw what was not there.

I was not alone in the house. A visitor, who unlike me had made it to bed, was presumably sleeping peacefully four flights above my head.

I awoke suddenly to find all in darkness. I was surprised, as well, to find myself still on the couch. After a few moments, my attention was drawn to the carpeted staircase which lead one flight up to the kitchen. A young man appeared and began to descend the stairs a few feet away from where I was reclining, bemusedly watching. I noted a tall figure, serious demeanour, longish coat, slightly long hair. Seeing by his face that he was in his twenties, I concluded that he had been visiting my twenty-year-old tenant, Hayley, whose room was located two flights up. But I had forgotten that she was out for the evening and it was unlikely that she had given the key to anyone.

My faint greeting of "hello" was neither noted nor returned, and later I recalled that this unexpected "visitor" never once looked at me or appeared to see me. Rather, he kept looking to the right, over my head, seemingly at a distant scene, as he walked steadily past me towards the door.

Even stranger, I assumed that he would put on boots at the front door before going out into the elements. But afterwards, try as I might, I couldn't recall that he did, or that he opened the door, walking out, or shut the door behind himself, either.

Instead, simultaneously with this person's disappearance in the direction of the front door, I fell back into a deep sleep on the couch. I was reawakened only by the return of my tenant, Hayley, at 4:00 a.m. Of course, she denied having had a visitor in the house that night during her absence, and it now became obvious to my once-drowsy, now sharply awakened senses that the idea was truly far-fetched, even nonsensical. It had only been a spur-of-the-moment rationalization for coping with the fact of the young man's presence in the house.

At this point, you may be tempted to conclude that I had experienced a very vivid dream while deeply asleep. But the proof that it had been real came from Hayley's news that an electrical power failure had plunged our part of the city into darkness a few hours earlier.

This explained, of course, how I had gone to sleep with blazing lights and how I had wakened up to complete darkness, after which I saw our visitor.

My next thought was that it had been a break-in. We had had three break-ins, such occurrences being more frequent than the appearances of ghosts in the neighbourhood. But when Hayley and I checked the only possible point of entry — the sliding glass back door — we confronted an unbroken surface of sparkling, pristine snow. Not even one footprint! It was only at that moment that I realized that something without an ordinary explanation had happened!

Again, most people would write off my "haunting" as some form of vivid dream state. It's true that many of the details have escaped my memory. But I was definitely awake and I definitely saw the figure, though I was in an unusually relaxed, even languorous, state of mind at the time. I believe it was that very deep relaxation that made my mind receptive to seeing my ghost, and that it helped to lift the curtain to expose what it is that is usually obscured and what most of us glimpse only rarely or never.

Interestingly, a few years later, I had occasion to meet, once again, a couple who had lived only a few townhouses from ours at the same time we lived there. They had also moved away. We got to discussing our old abodes, the people, and the problems. I mentioned, jokingly, that on top of everything else, I had even seen a ghost there.

The wife told me that she had also seen one, but that neither she nor her husband told anyone about it. "They'd think we're crazy," she said. It turned out that one evening she had been seated alone in her dining area, two floors above the ground level, when she was more than startled to see a man, clearly dressed in black, nineteenth-century clothing. His head was topped by a tall, stovepipe hat. He stood there for a moment, and then walked right through the wall!

Before the townhouse complex had been built, there had only been an old service station in that location, about two blocks east of Coxwell Avenue on Queen. Before that, old records show a creek covering the site.

Why it is that relatively new housing units should experience ghosts, a phenomenon normally associated with old houses in which many lives have been lived, is still a puzzle to me. Maybe someday research will reveal the reason.

The Philip Phenomenon

The Philip Phenomenon is assuredly the single most fascinating development in the field of parapsychology over the last few decades. It has put Ontario on the psychical research maps.

The Toronto Society for Psychical Research was founded in 1970. Its model was the original Society for Psychical Research, established in London in 1882, and its counterpart, the American Society for Psychical Research, which was founded three years later. Some members of the Toronto SPR directed their efforts to the study of the conventions of the séance. It should be noted that these members were not mediums, although a number of them felt themselves to be mediumistic. They made no attempt to communicate with distant spirits or with the spirits of the deceased. Instead, they decided to experiment. They asked themselves the following question: Is it possible, through the use of raps — one for "yes," two for "no" — to communicate not with a spirit entity but with the *idea* of a spirit? After some months they were able to give an affirmative answer to that question: (Rap) "Yes."

The group fabricated a spirit out of whole cloth. In the time-honoured manner of the historical novelist, they created a credible character. They imagined a young Cavalier at the time of the English Civil War, named him Philip, and established him in Diddington Manor, a real country estate in Warwickshire. It was explained that Philip was born in 1624, at twenty he married the beautiful but imperious Dorothea, at thirty he fell in love with the sensuous Margo, and he died in 1654. Such are the bare bones of the authorized biography. Most intriguing is the fact that when the group began to question Philip through raps, the spirit substantiated the "cover" story and then began to embellish and revise it. New facets of his life began to emerge. Some facts were consistent with what is known of English history;

some were contrary to the historical record. The group had contacted a spirit — at times a truthful spirit, but at other times a lying spirit!

The full account of this important experiment in the history of parapsychology has been well told by Iris M. Owen, a leading participant. Owen is English-born, a social-worker, and the wife of A.R.G. (George) Owen, a former Cambridge fellow, a lecturer in mathematics, and an authority on poltergeistery. Iris M. Owen (with Margaret Sparrow) wrote *Conjuring Up Philip: An Adventure in Psychokinesis* (Toronto: Fitzhenry & Whiteside, 1976), from which the excerpt which follows is reproduced.

The Philip Experiment offers proof of nothing, but it does dramatically demonstrate the dynamics of the séance situation — with its physical and mental mediumship and its reputed "spirit-communication." This episode in parapsychological history offers promise of a better understanding of the dynamics of group interaction, of the psychical consequences of belief, if not of contact with the "spirit-world."

Members of the Toronto SPR were investigators and researchers in fields of phenomena other than that of the Philip Phenomenon, and many of the members were also active in the New Horizons Research Foundation, which was founded by George Owen at the same time as the Toronto SPR. The accomplishments of the Toronto SPR and the New Horizons Research Foundation introduced a new chapter in the textbook of parapsychology, a chapter that illuminates, if obliquely, the nature of the spirit of mankind.

⚘

It was not surprising that each member of the group became quite adept at carrying on a conversation as if with an imaginary guest. There was rarely confusion. Sometimes someone would forget that Philip could answer only yes or no, and a question would be asked that required a different type of answer. When this mistake was made Philip would invariably produce scratching noises. On one occasion, during a good session, one of the group jokingly asked Philip to give a rap under each person's hand at the table. Philip took the request literally, and each member felt a loud rap under his or her hand at the same moment in time.

Another typical meeting, which was taped and recorded, went like this.

The group met, stopping on their way to the table to eat a candy. They placed one on the table for Philip.

"Here is your candy, Philip. Would you like a song?"

(Rap) "Yes."

Andy: "What shall we sing? 'Lillibulero' and 'Greensleeves'? Perhaps he doesn't like the Lloyd George song because we sing it to the tune of 'Onward Christian Soldiers,' and that was one of the songs sung by Oliver Cromwell's Puritan army."

(Rap) "Yes."

Dorothy: "There you are, I knew he didn't like Lloyd George."

Someone else: "We can keep it to threaten him with if he won't talk to us."

To some extent this is how this particular song was used in subsequent sessions. It usually provoked a violent response in table movement. So 'Lillibulero' and 'Greensleeves' were sung, and the conversation was resumed. It was decided to change the conversation completely and to ask Philip about his personal likes and dislikes.

"Do you like horses?"

(Rap) "Yes."

"I expect you had a favourite horse?"

(Rap) "Yes."

"I bet it was a white one, was it, Philip?"

(Rap) "Yes."

"Did you have any mistresses?"

(Loud rap) "yes."

The group went on to suggest, and to elicit from Philip, that he had had a good time in London, and he was asked if he enjoyed going to the chocolate houses and meeting the ladies there. As an enthusiastic yes was elicited by this line of questioning, the group went on to tease him about his love of chocolate houses. As an historical fact, however, chocolate was not known then, and chocolate houses were not introduced into London society until more than a century after the date of Philip's "death."

"Did you get drunk sometimes?"

(Rap) "Yes."

"But not too often?"

(Rap, rap) "No."

Philip was not a drunkard, and he did not get into fights.

"Did people fight duels in your day?"

(Rap, rap) "No." When Cromwell came to power the fighting of duels was banned.

"Was life much gayer before Cromwell came to power?"

(Rap) "Yes."

As everyone started to discuss the differences between life in London during Charles' and Cromwell's rules, raps continued to come from the table as various points were agreed upon. Philip was asked if he had a position at court, and the answer was yes. But when he was asked, "Did Dorothea go to court with you?" there were knocks and scratchings, which seemed to indicate that this was a subject that Philip did not want mentioned. However, on this occasion, the various members of the group persisted in asking questions about Dorothea, assuring Philip that they were his friends, and that they needed to know all about him.

"Were you forced to marry Dorothea?" he was asked.

(Rap) "Yes."

"Did her parents force this marriage upon you? Did they need the financial help your money could give?"

(Rap) "Yes."

"Was she a cruel person?"

Rap) "Yes."

As questions and comments about Dorothea came thick and fast from the group, a picture of her emerged. She was a beautiful but cold woman, physically and mentally cruel, whom he had married to please his father and her parents, who needed the money he brought to the marriage. He had never loved her. She refused to bear him children, and they lived separate lives. Marriages of this kind were approved by the court as was the custom in those days, but it never became clear why Philip should have been prepared to enter into such a one-sided bargain; however, he did. Dorothea was the oldest in the family, she had brothers and a sister, but she was spoiled and indulged by her parents.

At this point Philip was again questioned about his religion, and he answered yes to a question as to whether he was born an Anglo-Catholic.

At this point everyone paused for some conversation and to sing songs. At most sittings there would have been much more singing and joke telling, but conditions seemed to be good on this particular night. The raps came continually, and it was evident that the group had plenty of energy.

Questioned further about Margo, Philip said, to everyone's surprise, that she had not lived in the gatehouse, but in his quarters in the house.

"Was it in the stables?"

(Rap, rap) "No."

"Perhaps they would have called them something else in this day?" someone suggested. "Perhaps she lived in the main house."

"Perhaps she lived in his quarters," Bernice speculated.

(Rap) "Yes."

So Margo had lived in the main house.

"Did you go to the theatre?"

(Rap) "Yes."

"Did you see plays by Shakespeare and Marlowe?"

(Rap) "Yes."

"Did you walk over London Bridge?"

(Rap) "Yes."

"I wonder what he would think now of London Bridge being sold to America, and being assembled somewhere out in the desert?" (This from Dorothy.) A series of scratchings was the only answer they got to this question.

"They had houses on it in this time." (This from Iris.)

(Rap) "Yes."

"Did you cross the bridge many times?"

(Rap) "Yes."

"They had a lot of illness in this time — plague, smallpox — all sorts of illness."

"Did anyone in your family die of plague?" (This was from Andy.)

(Rap) "Yes."

"I wonder who? Dorothea didn't die till after he did — after he threw himself from the battlements. Could it have been her parents?"

(Rap, rap) "No."

"Was it his parents?"

(Rap) "Yes."

When asked about Charles I's pets, Philip asserted that the king did not like horses or dogs, but that he loved cats. This is at variance with the historical facts, but the questioner was an ardent cat lover. Questioned further, Philip said he himself didn't like cats; he preferred dogs.

"Did you use dogs when hunting?"

(Rap) "Yes."

Questioned as to whether they hunted boar or deer, Philip replied yes to deer. Not only did he hunt deer, but he had deerhounds. He also kept peregrines. Asked if he used guns for hunting, the answer was yes, but when after birds he used human beaters to retrieve, not dogs. Yes was the reply.

Someone asked if he had had smallpox, and the answer was no. Dorothy followed up by suggesting — "But I beg you wished Dorothea had it?" To this question, asked half in jest, there came a series of rolling knocks. When asked directly if Dorothea ever had smallpox, the answer was no.

He was asked if he liked drinking, as he had shown an obvious preference for drinking songs, and always beat time vigorously to them. A loud rap was his reply.

And this time the reader should be convinced that in the vast majority of cases, the answers Philip gave to questions asked him were in accordance with the responses that the questioners expected to receive from him. Or, to put the matter in reverse, the questioner was usually able to elicit the answers from Philip that he expected. Rather than bore the reader with a long description of the questions and answers given, the following summary of Philip's life and times were filled in by the group. There were, however, some anomalies ...

The Root Cellar

Janet Lunn is a writer of fine books for young readers. Among her best-selling titles are *Double Spell* (1968) and *The Root Cellar* (1980). The first of these novels, appropriately, has two titles, for it is about "doubles." Canadian readers know it as *Double Spell*. American readers know it as *Twin Spell*.

The second of her novels is relevant here. A short while ago a librarian told me that Lunn based *The Root Cellar* on an actual incident that occurred in her house in Hillier, a small community which lies southeast of Trenton in the Bay of Quinte region. Hillier is located close to Consecon, the community that gave birth to the famous or infamous Fox Sisters, the foremost Spiritualists of the second half of the nineteenth century.

Now, ghosts in fictional works are products of the literary imagination, not products of powers in the spirit-world. So I wrote to Lunn to ask her if it is true that when she wrote *The Root Cellar* she was basing her work of fiction on a real-life event. She wrote back right away. I have reproduced the relevant part of her letter of reply.

Lunn ends her letter with a question. Yes, the description is helpful — and I hope it will introduce more readers to Lunn's fine books.

December 28, 1988
Dear John,

The house with the ghost is the house I live in. It is an old house, the oldest part is about 170 years, the rest newer, built in stages ending around 1890-1900. I am not one who has seen or heard the ghost (it could be ghosts, of course). Richard, my late husband, saw her on one occasion, the silhouette of a woman in a long dress and a bonnet. She came into the room that was, in former times, a parlour, leaned over as if to put something on a table then disappeared.

Dick sometimes felt a presence in the house and on one occasion heard a woman humming in the kitchen. When he went to investigate, the humming had stopped and there was no one there. We have all heard footsteps on the stairs and another room in the house unnerves all the dogs who go there.

I have no doubt that there is at least one ghost here in spite of the fact that I have not seen any myself. I do think some people are sensitive to ghosts and some aren't.

Yes, I did use Dick's ghost-seeing incident in a book. It was in *The Root Cellar* which is set in this house. In fact, the whole story turns on the incident and the ghost is one of the major characters. As for it — or any other of my books — being famous, I feel flattered, of course ... Will this description help you?

Cheers,
Janet Lunn

I Heard a Lady's Voice

The following letter was received on 14 June 1990 from Sharon Shields who is a resident of Ajax, Ontario. It was written in response to my request for "ghost stories." I am reproducing the letter in the author's own words, except for some copy editing.

The letter suggests that the author is a natural-born psychic. It may be that as a child she was contacted by the spirit which Roman Catholics and others refer to as one's "guardian angel." Anyway, the author is of Celtic background and, as everyone knows, such people are believed to be naturally psychic.

⁂

I have been told you are looking for true supernatural facts to write in your book. I must admit I had to give this a lot of thought before writing, as I feel my experiences are very sacred to me. But it is a fact that people teach people by sharing their knowledge or experience of knowledge.

I am a firm believer in the existing energies and spiritual dimensions that we live with. In fact, it has taken me from childhood to where I am now, trying to keep in tune with the spirit within. This is now my living. To try to fulfill my purpose by sharing the gifts I have been given, by helping those people who are in need of whatever assistance I can give them to direct their pathways. In fact, I have some very dear friends who dedicate themselves to helping others. The search is becoming more clear to many people who are realizing that life is not just in the natural existence of shopping malls, new cars, or big homes. We all are part of it, sometimes we get lost in it, even I have, but to realize it and recognize our spirit needs to live for our real purposes, whatever they may be is where the real fulfillment and happiness lay.

My first experience was, as I recall, when I was about six years old. We lived at the end of town in Huntsville, Ontario. My sister, a friend, and I went up the hill into the bushy area, where there was a small clearing with a big rock to the right, under a large tree. We heard a noise and a big dog came barking out from behind the tree. He didn't seem to notice me and chased after my older sister and her friend, who took off screaming, forgetting me. I was so frightened I just stood there. The dog stood at the edge of the clearing, barking, looking at them, still not seeming to notice me. I climbed up on the rock, wondering whether or not to run the other way, when I heard a lady's voice say, "Don't be afraid, Sharon, he won't harm you, he was only meant to frighten them away so I could talk to you."

I was startled, as I had not seen this woman, I had not seen her or heard her come, she was just there. She told me she had a message for me. I don't remember everything she said, but I've always remembered this: "Sharon, you have a purpose to fulfill, your path will be different from most others, so you must remember this, when you are hurt, as you will be many times, you must never be vengeful, you must forgive and turn the other cheek, because you will always be protected from great harm. You must also remember never to speak against anyone in a lie. If you must say how you feel, speak the truth, but even then it's best not to, unless it is nice, no matter how you feel or what they do to you, as it won't matter if others do this, but you can't, you won't be able to, or you will suffer until you learn, it is very important to remember this, as your purpose is of a different order." I couldn't speak for a moment.

Then I asked her who she was and where she came from. She said I would know in time. The dog had been quiet while she spoke and still never looked at me. It seemed as though everything had become still, nothing moved.

I looked at her face, but yet I don't seem to recall seeing it clearly. Her eyes were light, yet she didn't and did look into mine. Then she was gone, just gone. She came as an old woman, a cane in one hand, no, I should say like a long stick. She had an old, large-brimmed hat on, an old, large brown bag over her shoulder, and layers of old patched clothing on. I never saw anyone dressed like that, or like her, before or after.

I did make a few errors through my earlier life with my temper, when someone was being unkind or untruthful, but I did learn it always hurt me more to feel vindictive or angry. I started to very clearly see her image, and many times I have been protected before someone hurt me by warnings I received very strongly.

My friends now are good people who have travelled a lot of roads similar to mine. It was no coincidence, the time was right.

But as I grew up, many times, many things, took place, whereby I learned that there are many things that cannot always be proved, but do exist, and it is a real enlightenment to know how much we all are a part of it and how wonderful it can make our lives.

My dreams are not always normal outlets of obscure pictures and fears or tensions, but some dreams are very real and they do predict things before they happen. You have to know that these particular dreams are a way of letting your own inner consciousness guide you, warn you, or help you. They are vivid, clear, detailed dreams. Learning the difference between them is very important. To accept the fact that there are realities that do exist, to some of us stronger than others, but accepting them and knowing the difference between imagination and the fact that they exist, can benefit a person greatly.

A lot of these realizations can be looked at very scientifically.

The Radiance Technique of healing through energies that can pass through our bodies, as our bodies consists of energy, is a very ancient and real form of medicine. Not only of body, but also of mind. From intelligent cultures, as some people like to feel theirs is, to cultures that to others seem ignorant, all have worked with ancient teachings passed on to help and cure others. It seems only the pretenders get on the media and people pass by the reality of the seen facts evidenced, because they are afraid of receiving ridicule and their analytical minds will not allow them to accept what they can see.

I have from time to time in my life been connected with spiritual beings, who have given me information or who have simply shown themselves to me, not always from this time. It is unique and hard to explain.

Clairaudience, to hear voices, I have experienced. Clairsentience, to identify through the senses of smell, odours, too. Clairvoyance, to see beyond time and space as we know it in our daily frame of time and space, I have worked with. I know many good, intelligent, sane, educated people who work in normal careers as well as in all these fields, who experience and work with the spiritual essences of these connections to help others and to learn themselves.

A few times in my life, in times of crises, I have had a wolf appear in front of me, to show me that this situation or that person was dangerous and to remove him from my path. The first time this wolf appeared, it frightened me so terribly! I thought my heart would stop. Later, a few times, I wondered, why does it always come so frighteningly, but I realized I wasn't listening to my own voice inside, nor was I heeding any warnings, so I had to be shocked into listening. It was certainly effective as a warning.

The first wolf appeared when I was dating someone. I realized his moods were very changeable and he was an extremely possessive and jealous person, yet I tended to make excuses. I turned around one day and looked into this person's face. I looked into a black wolf's face, with teeth bared and burning red eyes. The fear nearly killed me. I couldn't move. Finally, I turned away, telling myself I was imagining this. I looked back, it was still there. I never spoke, but I quickly left the room.

A little time later, I tried to tell this person he had to stop seeing me. I had left it for too long. He seemed calm, understanding, and accepting, but he wanted to stay a little longer. Mistake! I felt something was different in the house, but my mind was running in too many directions to focus. The house suddenly was ice cold, a lady's voice kept calling, "Sharon, get out of this house, get out now," I was confused and not sure of what to do. She called again, "Get out of the house, he's going to kill you."

All the dogs in the neighbourhood started to bark. The house was so cold I saw my breath in the air. My two children both woke up screaming at the same time. Suddenly I couldn't move. Then I ran into their room and grabbed them. He was behind me, trying not to show the anger, saying, "Put them back to bed, they only had a nightmare, the heat will come back on."

I chose my words carefully as I moved, calmly explaining, "The heat won't work. Probably the furnace was broken, too cold. My parents were living not far away, we'll go for a while, you can come."

I hurried out, terrified inside that I might not make it, praying to God to help us. We got there, he came. My parents knew instantly something unusual had happened as they knew this was out of the ordinary, and they had not been able to sleep and had thought of me. I stayed with them until the situation was under control. Things turned out fine. But the next morning, I went back to the house and into the living-room. By the couch, under the cushion he sat in, I found a loaded gun. So thankful I am.

Believe me, knowing how so many people block out their own experiences of the supernatural (as it is called by many), and knowing how many choose to remain skeptical and ignorant of the spiritual realities that exist, it is a different area to release to the public view.

The Shapeless Ghost

I received the following letter from Fred Tiley, a resident of Bradford, Ontario. It was postmarked 24 May 1990.

Mr. Tiley wrote to me in response to my request, made in a local weekly newspaper, for real-life "ghost stories." Here, in minimally edited form, appears the text of his letter.

In subsequent correspondence I learned from Mr. Tiley that the house in question, which he bought in 1979 and sold in 1988, is still standing at No. 10 Pleasant Avenue, River Drive Park, a small community on the Holland River, north of Newmarket, Ontario.

***

I would like to relate to you my family's experience with a ghost that made his home with us. First, some background.

We bought the house from a widow lady by the name of Mrs. Gleaves. We never met her because the house was being rented when we bought it in 1979. But Mrs. Gleaves held a one-year mortgage. She renewed the mortgage for another two years, and in all that time we never got to talk to her.

After we had lived in the house for a few years, we started to get the feeling something was going into the kitchen. Now let me explain about our ghost. The only time we saw it was at night between 8:30 and 10:00. It always went into the kitchen. At different times over the years, my ex-wife and five kids and myself saw the ghost many times.

This ghost didn't really have any shape. Sometimes you would see just a whiteness. Other times you would just sense that the ghost went into the kitchen. At different times one of the family members, or myself, would say, "There goes the ghost."

To my knowledge, no one outside of our family saw the ghost. It was a friendly ghost and never upset anyone. But it did one thing. It used to turn our used tea cups upside down and put them on a small counter. This didn't happen too often. But it was proof to us that the ghost did exist.

After our mortgage was paid off, Mrs. Gleaves came by to see the house and all the work we had done on it. When we got talking, we told her about the ghost. That was when she told us that her husband died in the house and it was his habit to go into the kitchen every evening to make a cup of tea.

We sort of think the ghost was Mr. Gleaves. And the funny thing was that after Mrs. Gleaves's visit, we never saw that ghost again.

A Lady Beside the Bed

Carol Betts of Komoka, Ontario, sent me a letter about a number of strange experiences which occurred to her almost two decades ago.

Betts was born in Toronto of Irish-English ancestry. She had no strange experiences as a child.

I received her letter on 30 May 1990 and have slightly copy edited it for presentation here.

Dear Mr. Colombo:

I am writing to you in response to your letter to the editor which appeared in the *London Free Press*.

First of all, I am going to tell you I am a Christian and I was a Christian at the time of my experiences. These happened many years ago when my children were little. Lorie is now twenty-two; she was about four when the first incident took place.

At the time we lived in a small house in Strathroy, Ontario. My girls were put to bed in one room in the early evening. But girls being girls, even at their young age they would not go to sleep. So I put the oldest girl, Lorie, in my bed in my room. I then went into the kitchen to do the supper dishes. I was just about done when I looked into the bedroom (I could see into it from the kitchen) to make sure Lorie was sleeping.

There was a lady standing beside the bed looking down at Lorie. She was wearing a long white dress and had blonde, wavy hair that fell just below her shoulders. She looked over at me, then she looked down at Lorie. Then she backed up and disappeared. The only thing that was behind her was the wall.

You are probably wondering if I was afraid. No, I wasn't. I felt a sort of calm. To this day I believe this lady is Lorie's Guardian Angel.

Some time after that incident I had put the girls to bed and went to watch TV. They had been in bed for about one hour and everything was quiet. The girls' room was in full sight of the living room. I always kept their door open about two inches. I don't know what made me look over that way, but I did. I saw a hand come around the door and pull it open. I got up to see which one of the girls was out of bed and playing a trick on me. I looked in the room and both girls were in bed fast asleep.

This time I was frightened. But I never saw the lady or the hand again.

The next experience I had occurred when my mother-in-law passed away. I couldn't sleep the whole night because I kept hearing her tell me to tell Richard (her youngest son) that she was alright and not to worry about her.

I think she knew that she was going to die. The night before, she called me and talked for a long time. This was very unusual for her because it was long distance and she was on a very limited budget. She told me her job was going to be the death of her. And she died the next day, running to catch a bus after finishing a day of work. I truly believe she knew something was going to happen.

The next two experiences happened at my place of work. I work in a nursing home here in Komora. I was standing in a room talking to some friends. I had my hands behind my back, and someone or something put their hand over mine. I turned around to see who it was and there was no one there.

My face went white and my friend asked me what was wrong, so I told her what had happened. She said no one else came in the room. She was scared so we left.

The other thing that happened was while I was washing the dining room floor. (I was on housekeeping at the time.) The door opened and I saw our maintenance man walk in. He had on a two-tone brown jacket which was brand new. He walked into the kitchen. Not five minutes later the same door opened again and he walked in again.

I asked him, "How did you get out of the kitchen without me seeing you?" And he said he had just got there. But he had on the same two-tone brown jacket. His wife had just given it to him for Christmas.

I know these experiences sound strange, but they all really did happen.

I haven't seen any full-body apparitions since then, but sometimes I see things move out of the corner of my eye. Or I will hear someone call my name, especially when I am in one Woolco store in London.

That reminds me, at Easter this year, I was in Woolco looking for some Easter candy. I was talking to one of the sales ladies. We were about three feet apart. An empty Easter basket came from somewhere and landed between us on the floor. We just stood and looked at each other. There were no basket displays or people right near us. So I just told her it must be the Woolco ghost!

Please excuse my writing and spelling. It is almost midnight. But I knew if I didn't take time to write to you now, I probably never would.

I am glad to be able to share these things with you. Because, being a Christian, I am not supposed to believe in things like this. But I can't help it.

I really did experience all of these happenings.

Yours truly,
Carol Betts

The Gibson Ghost

During much of the 1970s, novelists Graeme Gibson and Margaret Atwood lived with their young daughter in an old farmhouse outside Alliston, Ontario. Their experiences were such that Gibson has reason to believe the farmhouse was and remains haunted. He described his experiences in a letter addressed to the present editor on 11 Jan. 1988.

Graeme Gibson has been an active force in the creation of the Writers' Union and the Writers' Development Trust and is also the author of a number of novels, including *Perpetual Motion* (1982), which is set in rural Ontario in the last century and tells the story of a farmer who is obsessed with the notion of constructing a perpetual-motion machine.

❧

My encounter with the following inexplicable events occurred in the farmhouse we lived in during most of the 1970s.

Built in the 1860s, the frame house had a wooden staircase, with worn bare steps, that rose from a small front hall to the back of the second and upper floor. The narrow upstairs hallway, which ran to the front of the house, had a single small window (perhaps a foot square) at the top of the stairs, from which one could see the barnyard, one of the barns, and the wooded creek bed beyond. Three doorways opened off that hall; two on the north side and one, which was our bedroom, on the south. The bedroom door was at the front of the house, or the end of the upstairs hall.

We had not been in the house six months. Margaret was away somewhere, probably giving a poetry reading. It was winter. In memory, it was a still, cold night. After turning off all the lights, I retired (as they say) just before midnight and was on the verge of sleep when I heard something downstairs. It wasn't a noise I could immediately identify. Then I heard someone in the vestibule. Almost immediately there was the sound of footsteps on our stairs. These were not the creakings or groanings that haunt old houses, but the very specific and unmistakable noise of a woman's shoes as she ascended towards the back of the house ...

Now it is important to emphasize several points. There had been no sound of a car on our curving drive, yet through my partially open window I could hear trucks half a mile away on Highway 89. Moreover, we'd recently acquired a stray Blue-tick hound who insisted upon sleeping in a pile of hay in the drive shed. Max, as we'd named him, had proved himself a reassuring addition to our menagerie by baying alarms at every provocation — both real and imagined. Yet he'd made not a whimper. To top it off, we'd had the locks changed; only Margaret and I had keys and she was miles away.

And yet there was a woman in my house wearing solid shoes. I called "Hello!" in the darkness. "Who's that?" I heard her reach the small window at the top of the stairs; then she began walking along the hall towards my bedroom door. She walked methodically, or so it seemed to me, with a kind of comfortable assurance in the dark, as if she was familiar with the house. Again I called out but there was no answer. Only the clear sound of heels on the pine floorboards.

In retrospect, I believe I remained in my bed out of puzzlement. If it had been a man's shoes I'd heard, I'd have been more immediately apprehensive, and therefore self-protective. As it was, I left it too late. She was almost to the door when it came to me with a genuine shiver (as if someone were walking on my grave?) that it was a ghost. It had to be ...

We had no bedside lamp so the only light switch was on the wall beside the door which opened towards me and was ajar. In order to turn on that light I'd have to reach past eight or ten inches of dark space that contained whatever it was that waited out there. Id' like to say that I did so, that I went over to see who or what she was. But I didn't. In some fundamental way I didn't want to know.

So I lay there while assuring myself that she could have no quarrel with me. We had not been in the house long enough. Anyway, try as I might, I could remember no instance of a so-called spirit actually harming anyone. Eventually I went to sleep.

I told Margaret, of course, but as time passed we forgot about it, as one does. Perhaps I was melodramatic in my response to the sounds of an old house. Perhaps I'd drunk more than I'd thought; perhaps, as Scrooge protested, it was merely a scrap of undigested mutton. Certainly, without confirmation, that would have been the end of it.

Almost two years later we arranged with a new-found friend to mind the house while we went north for our annual escape into the bush. We had not told her about our "ghost," nor, to my knowledge, had we told anyone she might have known. Certainly she had no recollection of the story.

On our return we discovered that our friend had been visited, not once but three times, exactly as it had happened to me. The noise in the vestibule, the sound of footsteps on the stairs, and then in the hall. The alarming difference, for her, was that she took the footsteps to be those of a man. She didn't open the door either. Instead, she threw herself against it to keep him out. But there had been no attempt to enter ...

After moving back to Toronto, we had a series of tenants before finally selling the farm. Each lasted about a year before moving on. One day, when I was visiting the second family, who were from Northern Ireland, the woman said, "Tell us about the ghost." I asked her to tell me first, whereupon she reported that her husband had been wakened by a woman who seemed to walk past him into a small room behind the bedroom.

At first he'd thought it was his wife, but immediately discovered she was still asleep beside him. Their bed was placed as ours had been, so whatever it was had apparently entered the room through the doorway from the hall. A married daughter was coming to visit, and they had put a child's crib in the back room because logically it had seemed to be a nursery of some kind. We all wondered if it was the crib that had encouraged, permitted, or whatever, the "spirit" to actually enter the bedroom.

After that there were a number of incidents that are harder to verify. She appeared at least once again to the couple. They were all convinced, for example, that the covers and pillows in the crib were moved about and some stuffed toys were rearranged.

And then, about four years later, we met, once more, a young woman who had lived in our house as a mother's helper for almost a year. She told us that she had actually seen the woman from her bedroom which opened onto the hall at the top of the stairs. She said she called out, "Hey, can I help you?" Neither young nor old, wearing a plain, vaguely archaic blue dress, the apparition seemed to pause, and then continued along the hall. There had been a great sadness about her. Our young friend hadn't said anything at the time because she feared we'd think she was nuts, or a witch, and she needed the work.

While the unconfirmed episodes give convincing substance to this story, it has been the repetition of an almost identical experience that has forced me to believe that some ghostly phenomenon really was outside my door that night ...

A Thanatological Experience

What does the conscious person experience at the moment of death? In the absence of a scientific answer to that question, folk beliefs abound. Traditionally, the dying person watches as scenes from his or her life unfold (the life review); then the spirit separates from the body and surveys it dispassionately (autoscopy); finally, there is the voyage into realms of radiance (the soul's flight).

Something approaching the traditional pattern of the near-death experience was recorded by a patient in the coronary unit of the Toronto General Hospital. The details were set down by the patient himself at the request of his two physicians who then added their own observations. They published the account under the heading "Cardiac Arrest Remembered" in the correspondence column of the *Canadian Medical Association Journal*, 22 May 1971.

The two physicians contributed the two paragraphs which appear here; in the journal, these preceded and succeeded the patient's own narrative. For present purposes the 68-year-old man has been identified as Patient X.

A 68-year-old man who previously had suffered no symptoms of coronary artery disease awoke with aching pain in the left arm. Squeezing retrosternal pain developed several hours later and persisted until his admission to hospital in the late afternoon. He was transferred without delay to the coronary unit, where his general condition was found to be satisfactory. Blood pressure was 126/78, heart sounds were normal, and there were no signs of cardiac failure. A 12-lead electrocardiogram was normal. The heart rhythm was monitored continuously and only an occasional ventricular premature beat was seen that followed the T wave by a comfortable distance. Ten hours after admission, the chest pain became worse, and the patient was given 50 mg. of meperidine. Suddenly a ventricular premature beat fell on a T wave, causing ventricular fibrillation. One of the coronary unit nurses recognized the cardiac arrest and immediately defibrillated the patient. After this there were no further serious arrhythmias, and convalescence was uneventful apart from an episode of pulmonary infarction. The ECG was normal the morning after defibrillation, and it was not until the 10th day that changes of anterior subendocardial infarction became evident. Changes in SGOT and CPK levels, however, were diagnostic of recent myocardial infarction from the first day in hospital. The patient remembered in detail the events surrounding his cardiac arrest, and the following account in his own vivid description of the experience. (The right leg mentioned was badly scarred from osteomyelitis suffered in childhood.)

It is unusual for patients to remember the events surrounding cardiac arrest. More often there is a period of amnesia of several hours duration before and after the event. This description is extremely interesting. The patient saw himself leaving his body and was able to observe it "face to face." This could be the concept of the soul leaving the body which is found in many religions. The delightful feeling of floating in space and the tranquillity, the yellow light, the rectangular shape with holes in it, associated with the wish of not wanting to be brought back again, may provide comfort and reassurance to patients suffering from coronary artery disease as well as to their relatives.

R.L. MacMillan, M.D., F.R.C.P.[C] and
K.W.G. Brown, M.D., F.R.C.P.[C]

Coronary Unit
Toronto General Hospital,
Toronto, ON

As I promised, I am setting down my experiences as I remember them when I had the cardiac arrest last May.

I find it hard to describe certain parts — I do not have words to express how vivid the experience was. The main thing that stands out is the clarity of my thoughts during the episode. They were almost exactly as I have written them and in retrospect it seems that they are fixed in my memory — more so than other things that have happened to me. It seems at times that I was having a "dual" sensation — actually experiencing certain things yet at the same time "seeing" myself during these experiences.

I had been admitted into the intensive care ward in the early evening. I remember looking at my wrist watch and it appeared to be a few minutes before 4:00 a.m. I was lying flat on my back because of the intravenous tubes and the wires to the recording machine. Just then I heaved a very, very deep sigh and my head flopped over to the right. I thought, "Why did my head flop over? — I didn't move it — I must be going to sleep." This was apparently my last conscious thought.

Then I am looking at my own body from the waist up, face to face (as though through a mirror in which I appeared to be in the lower left corner). Almost immediately I saw myself leave my body, coming out through my head and shoulders. (I did not see my lower limbs.) The "body" leaving me was not exactly a vapour form, yet it seemed somewhat transparent, for I could see my other "body" through it. Watching this I thought, "So this is what happens when you die" (although no thought of being dead presented itself to me).

Suddenly I am sitting on a very small object travelling at great speed, out and up into a dull-blue-grey sky, at a 45-degree angle. I thought, "It's lonely out here. — Where am I going to end up? — This is one journey I must take alone."

Down below to my left I saw a pure white cloudlike substance almost moving up on a line that would intersect my course. Somehow I was able to go down and take a look at it. It was perfectly rectangular in shape (about the same proportions as a regular building brick), but full of holes (like a sponge). Two thoughts came to me: "What will happen to me when it engulfs me?" and "You don't have to worry; it has all happened before and everything will be taken care of." I have no recollection of the shape catching up with me.

My next sensation was of floating in a bright, pale yellow light — a very delightful feeling. Although I was not conscious of having any lower limbs, I felt something being torn off the scars of my right leg, as if a large piece of adhesive tape had been taken off. I thought, "They have always said your body is made whole out here. I wonder if my scars are gone," but though I tried I could not seem to locate my legs. I continued to float, enjoying the most beautiful tranquil sensation. I had never experienced such a delightful sensation and have no words to describe it.

Then there were sledge-hammer blows to my left side. They created no actual pain, but jarred me so much that I had difficulty in retaining my balance (on whatever I was sitting). After a number of these blows, I began to count them and when I got to six I said (aloud I think), "What the ... are you doing to me?" and opened my eyes.

Immediately I was in control of all my faculties and recognized the doctors and nurses around me. I asked the head nurse at the foot of my bed, "What's happening?" and she replied that I'd had a bad turn. I then asked who had been kicking me, and a doctor pointed to a nurse on my left, remarking that she really had to "thump" me hard and that I would be black and blue on my left side the next day. (I don't think I was.)

Just a few comments as I think over what happened to me. I wonder if the bright yellow surroundings could have been caused by someone looking into my eyes with a bright light?

I have read about heart transplants where it is claimed the brain dies before the heart stops. In my case, my brain must have been working after my heart stopped beating for me to experience these sensations.

If death comes to a heart patient in this manner, no one has cause to worry about it. I felt no pain (other than what I had when I entered hospital), and while it was a peculiar experience it was not unpleasant. The floating part of my sensation was so strangely beautiful that I said to a doctor later that night, "If I go out again, don't bring me back — it's so beautiful out there," and at that time I meant it.

The Scarborough Poltergeist

Cindy Evanoff quite often listens to Ed Needham's phone-in pro-gramme on CFRB in Toronto. On 6 Dec. 1988 she heard Ed and the present editor discuss the supernatural and its effects on people's lives. As she had a haunted-house story of her own to tell, she phoned the station and shared her experiences with the two of us and with the pro-gramme's many listeners.

I remember thinking, as she recalled the events that took place in the house in Scarborough, Ontario, in which she and her husband then lived, here is a case that can be investigated today. I confess I was a mite disappointed when I heard that the house in question could no longer be entered and examined because it had been demolished some years ago. But what we do have is a first-person account of what it was like to share a house with a poltergeist.

Cindy Evanoff was born in Toronto in 1952. She and her husband live in Markham, Ontario, where she works as an office manager.

⚜

The following is my experience while residing with my husband in a house at 624 Birchmount Road in Scarborough, Ontario, in 1973. The house was an old, two-storey wood-frame, shingled affair nestled on a corner lot across from Pine Hill Cemetery. It was a very serene setting. Looking out the kitchen window, the view was of the cemetery's tall trees and the pretty flowers on the graves. We lived there for two years. It should be noted that the house has since been torn down, and ten new homes have been built on the property.

In 1972, my husband was renting the house and occupying it with two other bachelors who moved out in mid-1973. At that time, strange things were occurring. The mailman brought mail addressed to eight or ten different people who had, obviously, lived in the house in the past.

Prior to my moving in, my girlfriend and I — now my sister-in-law — were living together elsewhere. We did not have enough money to buy end-tables for our living-room, so one night we took two large boxes over to the house to spray-paint them in the basement. I painted them on three sides and returned the next night to pick them up. I went downstairs to fetch them and I found both of them upside-down, with the unpainted sides showing.

My husband — at that time my boyfriend — assured me that no one had been in the basement since the night before. I was always puzzled as to why these boxes had been tampered with, especially as the painted sides were not smeared. Therefore the paint had dried before they were turned over. There was always a feeling of someone being there in the basement.

On another occasion, when my husband was going down the stairs to the basement, he felt something grab his leg from behind the open staircase, and fell down the stairs. His shoulder still aches from time to time, even now, fifteen years later. That was the only occasion that "something" physically hurt someone in the house.

After I moved in, in 1973, a number of unexplained things happened. We had two cats who would not go upstairs to the two bedrooms. On a number of occasions, they would sit at the bottom of the stairs and look up and meow strangely from the bottoms of their throats, as if they were scared to death. We had a machete, which sat on the windowsill at the bottom of the staircase. Every morning, for a number of weeks, the machete was on the floor below the window. I would pick it up and put it back on the windowsill. But every morning it was back on the floor. I cannot remember what happened to it. One day it was gone.

Whenever we went out at night for the evening, we would turn on the porch light when we left. As soon as we got in the car to leave, the light would go off and then on again. One time we forgot to turn on the light. When my husband went to unlock the door to switch on the light, it turned on by itself. It was as though someone was saying, "Here, let me do it for you, just leave!"

On two occasions, as we pulled out of the driveway, we both saw a vision in the upstairs bedroom window. It was very eerie for both of us. When we were in the house, we never saw anything or anybody. On numerous occasions, when we returned home, we heard the barbells, which my husband kept in the upstairs bedroom, clanging, as though someone was lifting and lowering them. When we went to check it out, they were on the floor as though they hadn't even been touched.

On one occasion, when my husband was out with his buddies for the evening, I stayed home and went to bed early. Our bedroom was on the main floor and beside the door to the basement. I had fallen asleep but suddenly I woke up. The bedroom door was open and I could look out the doorway. I could see that the door to the basement was open. Who had opened it? We always kept it shut and even had a lock on the outside of the door. When I got up to close it, the door closed by itself before I could reach it. It was as though whoever lived there with us was trying to scare us into leaving.

Needless to say, I took off to the lounge of a nearby hotel where I knew I would find my sister-in-law. I told her what had happened. Some of our friends were sitting there and, of course, they cracked up laughing. We explained that things like this happened regularly in the house. I invited three or four of these people to come back to the house and they did. It was unbelievable. We were only in the house a couple of minutes when the barbells started to clang. You have never seen anything like it. These people literally looked like they had seen a ghost. Their faces drained and were totally white. After that they never joked about what was happening on Birchmount Road. I guess the only thing that kept us in that house and out of an apartment elsewhere was the rent of the house. It was cheaper living there than it would have been to rent an apartment.

We very rarely went down to the basement, as it was not furnished and we just kept odds and ends in storage there. But several times the light in the basement went on by itself, and we would turn it off. The next time it would be on again. We did not have wiring problems, as far as we knew. The other lights in the house did not go on and off like the basement light and the porch light.

Some time after these experiences occurred, we spent the evening in a neighbour's house. A woman was there who had lived for years down the street on Birchmount. She heard our story and told us that several years earlier a woman had lived in that house with her two children. The woman had gone crazy. Apparently she killed and dismembered her two children, threw them in the creek that ran behind the house, and then hanged herself in the upstairs closet. The closet was in the hall outside the bedroom where the barbells were located and where the cats refused to go.

By 1975 we had saved enough money to buy our own house. When we had packed up and were ready to move from Birchmount, my husband said he felt a pat on the back as he was getting into the truck. There was no one behind him. It was as though someone was saying, "Thanks for dropping in!"

148

We have a friend who is intrigued with the supernatural, etc. After talking to the management that owned the house, they agreed to let her move in. She advised us that she did not experience anything unusual. However, her daughter slept in the upstairs bedroom, where our barbells were kept. The mother said her daughter felt uneasy sleeping in that room, and many a night she would not get to sleep at all. The mother said, too, that her cat and dog, like our two cats, would not go upstairs to the second floor!

The Farmhouse Poltergeist

Here is the third and last of the reports on paranormal experiences taken from the "Psychic Survey" conducted by the Owens and Dr. Whitton for the *National Enquirer*. The informant was identified in this way: L.A.M., St. Catharines, Ontario; 28, female, housewife, ten years (schooling).

⚜

I can't remember the exact dates, but the time was between Aug. 1975 and April 1976. We had rented a house on Drummond Road in Niagara Falls, Ontario. It was an old farmhouse that had been remodelled inside. From the time we moved in, I heard noises in the upstairs hall. But as I wasn't used to a large house, I put it down to nerves.

The next morning, as I was dressing my daughter, Bridie, I happened to turn quickly toward a dresser that was near the doorway and just caught a glimpse of a little girl watching through the rails of the banister.

We had five bedrooms in the house, so a friend of ours, named John Kusma, who was in his fifties, came to board with us. My husband worked steady nights and did not like us being alone, even though we still had our boxer dog. So John being there made us all feel safer.

I hadn't said anything to John about the noises. About two weeks after he moved in, John and I were in the kitchen having coffee, when suddenly he asked me if the girls were asleep, as he could hear heavy footsteps in the hall overhead. I went to check and when I returned I assured him they were fast asleep. It was then that he told me that he had heard the footsteps ever since he had moved in.

Little did we know that the footsteps were just the start. Twice a day we found Bridie's bed stripped of its sheets and the blankets and the top mattress lying on the floor. This went on for a week. When we asked Bridie to do that for us, she didn't even know how to go about it.

John's bedroom door was always pushed open, even after he had closed it. The downstairs bathroom door, which could only be locked from the inside, was locked and my husband had to take the frame off to get at the lock mechanism.

My husband and I were watching T.V. and John was upstairs shaving when we heard him yelling, "What do you want?" When we asked him what he was yelling about, he said that he had heard a woman calling him, two or three times, and he thought that it was me. When Tim, my husband, told him that I had not said anything, John went white. He stood at the top of the stairs, staring down at us as if he didn't know whether he should stay up there or come downstairs.

My mother-in-law and a friend of hers came to see us one night and we sat in the front room. It wasn't too long before the smell of flowers, mixed with some kind of spice, drifted in around one part of the room. At times it would get stronger and then fade. This went on for about an hour or so.

Another night, my sister and John and I were in the kitchen when we heard the footsteps start upstairs. John went to the foot of the stairs to see if he could see anything. When I heard him call me twice in a loud whisper, I answered, "What?" My sister said that she also heard me being called, but that it wasn't John. I told her that it was so and that I would ask him when he came back into the kitchen. When John returned, he said that he had heard the loud whisper too, but that he had not called me.

At one o'clock in the morning, John and I were having coffee in the kitchen when we heard a child calling for her mother. I went and checked my girls, but they were sound asleep. I knew it wasn't one of mine because the child we heard had the voice of a child of about eight or nine years, and my girls were only two and five years of age at the time. Also, this child was calling Mommy and my children call me Mummy.

One morning John came running out of his room and asked Tim and me who was pounding on the walls. It sounded as if the house was being smashed down, and yet no one else heard anything.

On another occasion I was talking to my friend, Ruth, on the phone upstairs. I heard something crash in the kitchen downstairs. I went to see what it was and saw a picture that my daughter Tracey had made lying on the floor. The string on the back of the picture was still in place, and so was the nail that was on the wall.

The dog and our two cats had followed me downstairs into the kitchen but would not come back up with me. I tried to get them to come up, but the dog just whined and the cats ran and hid. About half an hour later, I was still on the phone. There was a crash that sounded like someone had taken every breakable piece of glass and dish ware in the kitchen and had thrown it against the kitchen wall. At that point I called John and we searched that house, from cellar to attic and even outside, but there was nothing broken anywhere.

A few times there was the sound of doors opening and closing, followed by muffled conversation between a man and a woman, but you could never make out what they were saying.

One night I was reading in bed when I felt something come into my room. If you have ever felt something totally evil, then you will have some idea of what I felt. It seemed to hold me down for about ten minutes. When it finally left, I ran to John's door and asked if I could sit there for a while. It was two hours before I could go back into my room.

Then for about two weeks things seemed to quieten down. Just before we moved out of the old farmhouse, the footsteps started again, and the bedroom door kept opening.

We moved at the end of April, before our lease was up.

The Apparition of the Cat

During the course of a radio interview, which was conducted by Jeff Howatt of CHUM-FM in Toronto, I discussed a handful of the unusual events and experiences that are dealt with at greater length in my book *Mysterious Canada*. I extended an invitation to listeners — and readers — who had unusual experiences of their own to communicate with me.

One listener who took up the invitation was T.J. Muckle, M.D., F.R.C.P.(C.), Director of Laboratories, Chedoke Division, Chedoke-McMaster Hospitals, Hamilton, Ontario. Dr. Muckle phoned me and identified himself. He politely inquired if I *really* wanted more accounts of strange experiences. He had in mind the fact that as I had already published a book about the paranormal I might no longer be interested in collecting such accounts. I assured him that I was busy amassing material for future books in the field, and that I would love to hear his story, especially as his medical training required that he be precise and objective, indeed clinical, in recording events.

Dr. Muckle related the events described below. I asked him if he would be willing to prepare a detailed account for publication. He agreed to do so, and indeed did so in his letter dated 20 Dec. 1988. Here is his account of the apparition — or "apparition" — of a family pet.

In the summer of 1976, I took my wife and three girl children to Camp Oconto on Eagle Lake, northwest of Kingston, for a vacation (for them) and a working holiday (for me). I was the "camp doctor."

In the middle of the afternoon, several days later, I was sitting in an easy chair, reading a book on the verandah of our small bungalow. The chair was sideways-on, so that in the corner of my eye I could see the living-room through the open door. Quite suddenly, but at the same time with no sense of dramatic suddenness, I could see our pet cat walking slowly across the room, apparently quite unconcerned, calmly looking straight ahead. It took me a couple of seconds to realize that she was walking along a foot and half or so above the floor level. She ambled across to the other side of the room and, just short of the far wall, disappeared — not quite instantly, but within a fraction of a second.

This "apparition" had been present, I suppose, for about fifteen seconds. I would like to emphasize, however, that there was nothing about what I saw to suggest any form of apparition. The cat was normal in every detail, completely opaque and moving in her accustomed fashion. She was not surrounded by any dark aura, or glow, and I have to say that in every way, apart from being a foot and a half off the floor, she appeared absolutely normal. At the time of the "apparition" I had no sense of dread, or fear, no sensation of cold or heat, or any other unusual sensation whatsoever.

My first thought, within a second or so of her appearing, was the following: How did she manage to travel all the way from Hamilton? Then I realized that she was, in fact, a foot and a half off the floor, and it couldn't be her. By this time she was about one-third of the way across the room, and for the remainder of her walk I just watched her with my mind blank. My sense of blankness persisted for maybe a minute or so after she had disappeared. Then I began to "re-run the tapes," and take a closer look at the living-room to see if, by any faint chance, it could have been some sort of optical illusion and that a cat very like ours had in fact been walking on something which I hadn't perceived. However, I couldn't find anything to substantiate this.

I called two of my children from nearby to tell them what I had seen and to give me a hand to see if we could find any cat anywhere in or near the bungalow, just in case I was losing my mind. We couldn't. During this exercise I began to wonder not whether or how I had seen this, but why. Immediately, of course, I was reminded of having read of similar sightings and that the associations were usually bad. Half an hour later, telling my wife and my other children of the occurrence, the only strong impression I had of the whole event was a feeling of the absolute reality of this "apparition."

The above is strange enough in itself, but the real impact came about two and a half hours later, when we went into supper and I was told that there had been a telephone message for me at the Camp Telephone Office from our neighbours in Hamilton. I went across and, on the way, the uneasy suspicion that something bad had indeed happened recurred. I telephoned our neighbour, and she told me that our cat had been run over by a car about three hours before, which was pretty near the time I saw the "apparition." She also added that the cat had not been killed instantly but had lived for a few minutes after being hit. I immediately wondered whether I would have seen the apparition had the cat died instantly — the implication I trust is obvious.

This is the only experience that I have had that I would really call paranormal, although I have had other experiences such as "some places give me the creeps," and on two occasions I have been overwhelmed by a fainting sensation when somebody nearby was, unbeknown to me, in the process of fainting. Please feel free to use this experience as you wish.

Grandmother's Ghost

Byron McKim sent me the following account on 18 Oct. 1991. It tells of poltergeist-like effects that took place in Mississauga, Ontario.

Mr. McKim lives in that city, which lies west of Toronto. He heard me on the Toronto pop-rock radio station Q-107 when I was discussing ghosts and spirits, poltergeists and apparitions. After the show he phoned me and promised to send me an account of some experiences he shared with his sister Lynnette. Almost six months later the account arrived in the mail.

꙰

The experiences I'm about to relate to you revolve around my sister Lynnette. She seems to have a special sensitivity to the Other Side. Through touch and sense she knows other people's feelings.

Our grandmother died in our home when my sister was about fourteen years of age and I was nine years old. Grandma had come to live with us about three years earlier. She shared a room with my sister. During this time the two of them became very close. They talked to one another each night about different subjects regarding each other.

One evening Grandma was babysitting us, as she had done on numerous occasions in the past, and arguing with us about going to bed. As she left to turn back to bed, both Lynnette and I heard this crash in the bedoom. After arguing about who should go and check on Grandma, I eventually "won" by short straw and young age to investigate.

There lay Grandmother on the floor, breathing with a very heavy and low sound.

"Grandma, are you okay?" I called from the hall, but she didn't answer. "Grandma, are you okay?" I called out again inside the room, but again she didn't answer.

I ran back to my sister and told her that Grandma had fallen on the floor and wouldn't answer. Lynnette told me to go over to the Ferrises, our neighbours, for help, while she phoned Mom and Dad.

When our neighbour Sandy Ferris came, he went to Grandma's room. She had already passed away. Sandy picked her up and laid her out on the bed.

After that, my sister continued to sleep in the same room. She did so without any incidents *that I'm aware of* until she moved out to go to college in Sarnia and study to be a nurse.

Several years later Mother and Father built a new house and we were preparing to move out of the old family home. At the same time my sister graduated and got married. As we moved out, my sister and her husband moved into the old home.

Shortly after the move, my sister and her husband were expecting their first child. Once Devon was born, things began to happen in the house. The first thing that occurred were the sounds of laughter and crying coming from the room my sister had shared with Grandmother. The room was being used only for storage. Then came the sounds of footsteps in the night.

My sister would go to the kitchen to warm a bottle of milk for Devon, and there it would be, sitting on the counter, already heated. Diapers began to appear when they were needed, as well as soothers, food, toys, etc. My sister never found this unusual. She always said it was Grandma.

Then came the time when my sister and her husband thought it best to leave the family home for a larger house because they were expecting their second child. On the day of the move, Lynnette began packing and putting things in the old bedroom that she had shared with Grandma. She would leave the room to get more boxes. When she came back, all the boxes would be unpacked. She would then repack them and leave. When she returned again, they would be all unpacked again. My sister said that this happened several times, until she decided to have a long talk with Grandma, to explain to her the reason why they had to leave. After that she had no problems.

After they moved, she rented the family home to friends of ours. In time they had a child who was born and raised in the house. Now, between the time my sister had lived in the house and our friends had begun renting it, more than eight years passed.

I approached the couple and casually asked them if anything strange had happened to them in the house, especially around their child who was not eight years old. Suddenly Chris, the husband, opened his eyes wide and stared at me. He spoke sharply, "How did you know? We've never said anything about it to anyone!"

I told him that the disturbances were caused by our grandmother and that they were not to worry. I proceeded to tell him the whole story.

Two years later, my sister sold the property to the owners of the factory directly behind the house. The new owners tore the house down and never built anything else on the land.

That was thirteen years ago. To this day my sister and I ask ourselves, "Where has Grandmother gone?"

Ghosts During Bereavement

Does a newly bereaved patient as a matter of course experience hallucinations about the dead person?

It seems that hallucinations of this sort are common. "Our experience in five recent cases of bereavement has been that the bereaved person frequently has hallucinatory experiences," noted two researchers at the Sunnybrook Medical Centre. They added, "Four out of five of our patients admitted to these phenomena."

"Ghosts: Their Appearance during Bereavement" is the title of the report prepared by Janice Smith, B.N., and Earl V. Dunn, M.D., and published in the *Canadian Family Physician*, Oct. 1977. At the time Ms. Smith was a public health nurse with the City of Toronto with a part-time assignment at the Family Practice Unit, and Dr. Dunn was a staff member of the Family Practice Unit, Sunnybrook Hospital, Toronto.

They noted that such experiences are normal, not abnormal. "Hallucinatory experiences are common, normal phenomena during widowhood. These phenomena tend to indicate good prognosis and should be actively inquired about. If present they should be used for the reassurance and comfort of the bereaved person." They went on to describe the experience in more detail:

> Common phenomena during this period are various hallucinatory experiences. These experiences may be tactile, visual, olfactory or may merely create a "sense of presence." They can be frightening to the bereaved person and usually the person involved feels uncomfortable in expressing and revealing these experiences to others. These events, however, are usually a

positive experience and when recognized can be used beneficially to help the person through the mourning period, if they are dealt with in a positive manner.

The authors reported on two cases, reproduced here in their entirety. Their accounts shed light on some of the visions regularly reported in the literature of the unexplained.

Case Reports

Case 1.

Mrs. P. was 69 years old when her husband died. He had a long illness and finally died from intractable heart failure due to long-standing rheumatic heart disease. Death had been discussed with both husband and wife. Mr. P. had insisted that he was going to die sitting in his favourite rocking chair at home. Mrs. P. was ambivalent in the desire to grant this wish. In fact, he died in hospital about 12 hours after falling and injuring himself trying to move himself from his bed to this particular rocking chair. Mr. P. did not die directly of these minor injuries.

Mrs. P. was at his bedside in hospital when he died. There were no children and no relatives. Neither Mr. nor Mrs. P. had strong religious beliefs and the funeral was very quiet and private. There was no service and no friends were invited to the funeral parlour. Shortly after his death Mrs. P. began to see glimpses of her husband in his rocking chair and to hear sounds of him moving in the house. The smell of his shaving lotion and their dog's low growling were also evidence of his presence to Mrs. P. The ghost was friendly but very restless because he had not satisfactorily passed on. The ghost had to "die in his chair." In her visits with the physician and public health nurse, Mrs. P. talked freely about the hallucination experience, was comfortable with the experience and had considerable insight into the reason why her husband's ghost might be restless and unhappy — his goal to die at home had not been fulfilled.

Over a period of six months Mrs. P. followed a usual bereavement period, living alone and functioning adequately. Mrs. P. was seen approximately monthly by her family physician and the public health nurse. Discussions about the ghost were frequent between Mrs. P. and both her physician and the public health nurse. Constant assurances of her good care and her wise judgments in his long-term management helped to alleviate the guilt she felt. The hallucinatory experiences were a positive part of her bereavement and were used to reinforce acceptable and appropriate reactions to her life situation. Mrs. P. still occasionally is aware of her husband's presence more than one year after his death. The ghost is no longer restless.

Case 2.

Mrs. I. was aged 64 when her husband died. Mr. I. had also had a long illness following a stroke about five years before his death. He had never completely recovered and continued to have considerable disability until the time of his death very soon after another massive cerebrovascular accident. Mrs. I. was still working and had the support of a large and close family. Both Mr. and Mrs. I. had strong, firm religious beliefs. About one month after his death Mrs. I. began to have hallucinatory experiences, occasionally of the visual type, but mostly auditory.

These were frightening to her. She thought she might be "going crazy" and was afraid to mention this to anyone, especially to her family. When asked indirectly by her physician Mrs. I. admitted to these experiences, was relieved to talk about them and found the discussion of her experiences beneficial. About six weeks later she was no longer having hallucinatory experiences and she had had no further experiences for over six months.

The Ghost in the Attic

The memoir which follows is a highly detailed account of a haunting. The reader of Michele L. Marshall's letter will revel in the family detail. What is missing is any sense of the identity of the ghost, its relationship with the trapdoor that leads to the attic, and its purpose in haunting this house. Yet the account is so immediate! Mrs. Marshall is currently a resident of Spencerville, Ontario.

May 25, 1990
Dear Mr. Colombo:

My twin sons are outside on their fourwheelers so I have some time to write to you without having to explain this letter. What I'm about to tell you few people know except for my children and their father.

I am thirty-nine years old, I work in a factory, and I have a home in the country. I am the mother of four children — two are gone and two are at home. This experience happened to me many years ago, but it comes back to me in my mind quite often.

In December of 1978 my husband and I bought a brick home in Prescott, Ontario. We moved in shortly after Christmas. It was an average home. It has three bedrooms and was actually built by someone in my husband's family about one hundred years ago. I found this out after I started searching for answers.

At the time we moved in, the children were all pretty small. My daughter had one bedroom, the three boys another, and my husband and I the third. In my daughter's bedroom there was a closet and in this closet a set of steep stairs which lead up to the attic. When we moved in I went up the stairs and with my husband's help we lifted the trapdoor. It weighed, I'd say, about fifty pounds, and it had to be pushed straight up and over to get into the attic. To my disconcern, the attic was filled with old junk. I never really got back up there. It was dark. There was no light or electricity. And I told the children to never go up the stairs. They couldn't lift the trapdoor anyway.

About two months after we moved in, I was upstairs in my daughter's room cleaning up. My daughter used the stairs to the attic to store her shoes and boots and some discarded stuffed animals and stuff. I opened her closet to put something away. It was so cold! I looked up the stairs. It was as dark as ever because there was no electric light in her closet. The trapdoor was wide open. So I moved her things away and climbed up the stairs and pulled the door back down. I was so mad! Here it was in the middle of winter and those damn kids had opened that door. I didn't know how they had done it, but they were gonna get it when they got home from school.

Now, the twins were about a year and a half old, so I blamed the two older kids, who at the time were eight and six years old. Well, it slipped my mind, with my busy life, and I never did ask them about it.

A couple of weeks went by and I was in my daughter's room again, cleaning up, and I found it so cold. I thought, maybe the window could use some chalking. But her closet door was ajar and I went over to close it and it seemed like a wind was coming from the closet. So I opened it up and looked up the stairs. Well, that stupid door was open again! This was it! Those kids were getting it tonight! So when they came home from school, I lit into them, telling them about the cost of heat. This was happening during the oil embargo, and we couldn't afford to heat an uninsulated attic!

Well, they swore they had never opened that door. I looked at their faces and I could tell they were scared. So when my husband came home from work, I asked him if he had been up in the attic and he said he hadn't. I mentioned to him that I had to shut the trapdoor twice since we had moved in.

Not long after that, in the spring, we bought a bloodhound, a beautiful dog whose name was Bones because he was just skin and bones when we bought him. Well, Bones slept on a rug in our bedroom right beside me. Sometimes he would get up and check out all the kids, then come back, sniff me, lay back down.

In the heat of August it was so hot we had an air conditioner upstairs. I went into my daughter's room and threw some stuff in her closet and just automatically looked up. Sure enough that trapdoor was open again! I was so mad. Here I was trying to cool the house down and someone had left that door open, letting in all that hot air from the attic! So I went up and closed it. I remember hurting my back doing so because the trapdoor was so heavy. Well, I went out to find the kids and they said they never went near the attic. I'd had enough, so when my husband came home, I had him nail that door shut. He used those big four or five-inch nails. Those little brats wouldn't get in there anymore!

At the time my husband and I owned a restaurant-motel and we were spending a lot of time at work. Needless to say, we weren't getting a lot of sleep, especially as the children were so young. Now, what I'm about to tell you now just sent chills through me ... even after all these years!

One evening my husband and I went to bed about 1:00 a.m. As usual, Bones was beside me. Well, he kept getting up and going out into the hall. So I got up and asked, "Is something wrong, Bones?" I thought one of the kids had fallen out of bed and was on the floor, so I checked all the children. They were fine. So I said, "You gotta go outside?" I started down the stairs, but he just lay down. So I went back to bed, but Bones stayed out in the hall. I said, "Come here, Bones. I'll pet you for a while." I could do this while I lay in bed. But he wouldn't come back into the bedroom. Eventually I fell asleep.

A little while later I heard my dresser drawer next to my bed being opened. I thought it was the dog. I opened my eyes and there was *this guy* going through my underwear. He was bent over and when I started to say something, he held his finger to his lips to tell me to be quiet. He was smiling. Slowly he removed his hand from my underwear, closed the drawer, stood up, turned, and walked out of the bedroom.

I lay there, stiff, my heart pounding, a tear coming to my eye. Was I going crazy? I got up about five minutes later. But it seemed like eternity before I could move. Bones was downstairs. Now he never went downstairs at night. I checked the children. All were fine. Okay, what should I do? I needed sleep. I was exhausted. I went back to bed, moved real close to my husband, hugged him, and slowly went to sleep.

At this point I have to tell you what *this guy* looked like. He was about twenty-two with blond, curly hair. He had the prettiest blue eyes. I'd never seen eyes so blue as his. He had beautiful teeth. He wore a striped blue-and-red shirt and he had sneakers on and jeans. I will never forget what he looked like or what he wore. Never.

The next day, when I was alone with my husband, I told him about the ghost I had seen. I thought he would laugh at me or tell me I was crazy. He just said, "We really need to take some time off from work." He asked if I felt threatened by the ghost. "No," I said, "it was like he was talking to me but his lips never moved." We talked about half an hour, and then we went to work.

Three days later I was upstairs cleaning up and went into my daughter's closet. You guessed it. That trapdoor was open again. How could that be? It was nailed shut. I went up and closed the trap door. There were no nails! None. Not even a single nail-hole. I shook, I was so scared. But I didn't say anything to the kids. I went to our local library, got all sorts of books about ghosts.

What to do? Are they bad? Will they harm my children? I couldn't tell anyone about what was happening. I was afraid they wouldn't believe me, and it's such a small town. It would be all over town in no time. I kept it to myself. But I told my husband about the trapdoor to the attic. He went up and drove about fifty nails into the door. He said no one would ever get in or out of that trapdoor again!

I wouldn't undress in my bedroom because I felt someone was watching me and laughing. I dressed and undressed quickly in the bathroom. Bones wouldn't sleep upstairs anymore. He slept at the bottom of the staircase. The kids asked why Bones wouldn't come upstairs anymore. I just said he probably was more comfortable downstairs because it was cooler.

About five days went by. One day my husband and I came home from work about 11:00 p.m. We hadn't cashed up. We were very tired. Then our bartender called and said there was quite a bit of money in the till and did we want him to put the money somewhere. My husband said no, he would drive back and pick the money up. He told me to go to bed, he'd be home soon. I undressed in the bathroom but wouldn't go to bed without him. I was afraid and called the restaurant and asked him how long he was going to be because I couldn't go to bed without him. He said he'd be home in twenty minutes. I turned on all the lights in the house. The kids were asleep, and I sat on the couch in the living room. I turned on the stereo real low so I wouldn't wake anyone.

I heard someone coming down the stairs. I thought it was one of the twins. I looked up and there "he" was again. He was leaning over the banister, smiling at me. He slowly walked down the stairs, never taking his eyes off me. When he got to the bottom of the stairs, he disappeared.

I slowly got up, went to the phone, and called my husband. I said, "Whatever you're doing, it doesn't matter, just come home right now! I need you! Hear? Right now!" He was home in seven minutes, and I collapsed in his arms. I said, "I can't take it anymore. We have to move. I'm afraid." He argued. He said we would talk about it in the morning.

I stayed home the next day and read those books from the library. The consensus was that ghosts will not harm you. They are trapped,

trapped because of dying too soon, before they could finish something. Either that or they were murdered.

I went to the people we bought the house from and asked them questions without telling them anything. Had anything ever happened while they were living in the house? No, they said. Any problems with the attic door? No."Who owned the house before you did?" They listed the previous owners and I went through the list. No one died while living in the house. No one was ever murdered in it. Dead end.

Okay, try this. In one of the books it said that if you asked the ghost to leave you alone because he was upsetting you and scaring you, he would go away. Okay, I'll try that.

About a week went by. I was in a hurry to change my clothes and I was undressing in my bedroom. I knew he was behind me. I could feel his eyes on me. I didn't turn around. I started to cry but I said, "Please, you're scaring me. I can't live here anymore if you are here too. I hold nothing against you, but I'm not strong enough to take this. So would you please leave?"

I was shaking. My heart was pounding. I heard a faint sigh, "Yes, I'm sorry." And that was the last I saw of him or the trapdoor opening.

Seven months later we sold the house to a young couple. After we moved to another house, I told the children about the ghost. They were fascinated, but I know they would have been scared had I told them about it while we lived there.

A couple of years later the children went "trick or treating" to that house and told the young couple living there that they had seen a ghost. They laughed and thought the kids were trying to scare them. If only they really knew the truth!

I have shared this with you because I want the world to know that, yes, there *really* are ghosts. They do exist. I will never forget my experience. My children believe me and they have an open mind compared with mine at their age.

What bothers me today, so many years later, is why he was so happy. I thought ghosts were supposed to be sad. Why was he always smiling? Why did he make me feel like he meant me no harm? Why was he in that house? If I went back there, would I see him again? If I had stayed, would he have talked to me?

Sincerely,
Michele L. Marshall

Ghost of Grandmother

Sharon Steele is a resident of Chatham. She has a musical bent. She saw my request for "extraordinary experiences" in the pages of the *London Free Press*. She wrote to me and assessed that my interest in the paranormal was serious, so she sent me this account of half a lifetime punctuated with odd and inexplicable experiences.

Mrs. Steele's account is dated 6 June 1990, and it is reproduced here in the form in which it was written with only routine copy editing. After reading the account, one is left with questions. Is Mrs. Steele a genuinely psychic person? Does she attract to herself, does she "collect," such experiences? Is there someone or something in her past that refuses to go away? Is there a middle-aged woman, a witch, a spectre, someone or something that plays the piano and sings "Ave Maria"? Has she seen the last of this spirit?

※◎◎※

Even as a child, I was aware of unexplainable phenomena, as I had two grandmothers who not only seemed to have a "sixth sense," but who actually "spoke" to people who weren't there. Some would say such activity was attributable to senility or to being "not wrapped too tight." But, around our house, it didn't seem strange at all!

I remember stories my parents used to relate about their respective mothers' abilities. My maternal grandmother was known for her unconventional conversations with people from the Other Realm, while my paternal grandmother had the extraordinary power of "seeing" things as they happened. In one instance, my father related how, at the age of about twenty, he was involved in a motorcycle accident and hurt his nose. It was subsequently bandaged at the hospital. Upon arriving home, being quite late, he quietly entered the house through

167

the door into the room in which his parents slept. (I should clarify that this happened in Jamaica quite some time ago, and with eight children, each room in the house was used to its fullest extent.)

As he was passing by the bed, his mother called out, "What has happened to your nose?" This wouldn't ordinarily seem odd, except that her back was to him at the time and it was so dark that he had been feeling his way around. When he explained he was fine, just a minor accident, she replied, "I know. I saw it."

On another occasion, when my father was younger, he had an even younger brother who came down with a case of spinal meningitis, which, at that time, was difficult to diagnose and impossible to treat. When he became ill in the morning, he was taken to the local hospital, quite some distance away. Later in the day, his mother, who had been ironing in the kitchen, suddenly and quietly put the iron down and announced, "Roland has just passed." The family knew better than to question the statement. It was about four o'clock. Sometime after six that evening, the knock on the door came. (There was no telephone.) A policeman on his bicycle had arrived with a message from the hospital. Their son Roland had passed away at four o'clock that afternoon. No one was surprised.

After hearing these stories about our family, it really didn't seem strange when I saw my first ghost. I was about thirteen. I had come home from school for lunch and was in the living-room waiting for my girlfriend to pick me up, when out of the corner of my eye, I saw movement. I swung my head around and saw someone dressed in a mauve robe heading for the basement stairs. The person's back was to me, but I assumed it was my cousin, who lived with us. I assumed she was home from work because she had been ill. I called her name, and getting no answer, I figured she hadn't heard me, so I got up and walked to the doorway of the stairwell and called again. Still no response, so I headed down the stairs. I reached the basement and called again. Silence. I searched that basement for five minutes and found no one. Whoever it had been had simply disappeared.

When I mentioned that incident in later years, I discovered I was not alone in my sighting. Apparently just about everyone who lived in the house had seen or heard this person!

Home, until I was fifteen, was Rexdale, Ontario, but, just after turning sixteen, we pulled up stakes and moved to Oakville. Things got interesting about a year after we moved in. At this point, I should tell you that, until the age of thirteen, I had studied piano with the Royal Conservatory of Music in Toronto, and played frequently, mostly classical pieces by Chopin, Beethoven, and company.

One morning, at breakfast, I was accosted by one of my sisters. "What were you doing playing the piano at three in the morning? Don't you know people are trying to sleep at that hour?" I guess I must have looked blank because she said, "Wasn't it you?" I shook my head and we continued to look at each other, wondering if anyone else had heard anything. The weird part of it was, my bedroom door was right across from the piano and I hadn't heard anything. And I thought I was a light sleeper! It wasn't long before just about everyone in the house had heard the music. My father tried to explain it away as crossed radio wires or an avid radio listener, but we knew better.

My younger sister's girlfriend received quite a surprise one afternoon. She used to come to our house at lunch-time every school day and wait for my sister to come so they could eat together. One day my sister arrived to find her friend practically cringing in the chair by the fireplace in the family room. She was as white as a sheet. My sister breezed into the room and, not known for her tact, exclaimed, "Hi! My God, you look like you've just seen a ghost!" Well, it seems her girlfriend had been treated to a concert of Mendelssohn. She had thought I was home from college and yelled out to me. When I didn't answer and the playing continued, she assumed I didn't hear her, so she went to the basement door. The instant she opened the door, the playing stopped. There wasn't a soul in sight. I was getting a little weary of taking the blame for this character. But in a way, I was pleased. This person could really play!

In a more recent vein, about ten years ago, my husband and I moved from Toronto to Chatham. We rented a house in a newer neighbourhood and subsequently bought the house four years later. During that time, we were subjected to a few incidents, some of which weren't so pleasant. I started finding things in the oddest places. My purse was in the refrigerator one day. A few weeks later, I found my watch in the cupboard under the sink. I thought I was losing it. Then, about a month later, my husband dropped me off at the dentist and returned home. When he came in the door, he said he heard a ticking sound like a clock, but the only clock that close by was a cuckoo clock that we had hung in the hallway for decoration only. The stupid thing had quit on us the day we put it up after the move from Toronto. It had worked beautifully until then.

Well, guess what decided to work after a couple of years of doing nothing? Not only that, but upon closer inspection, he found it was set to the correct time! When I arrived home, I couldn't believe what I was hearing. It even cuckooed! For four days it ran. Then it quit again and it was on to bigger things!

One evening, I had gone to bed earlier than usual and my husband had stayed downstairs to watch the eleven o'clock news, as is our usual habit. He came upstairs around eleven-thirty or thereafter and proceeded to come into the room and touch my shoulder. I woke up, startled. He was calling me and I answered, "What's the matter?" He asked me if I had been singing. (I sang with a couple of choirs and did some solo work at the time.) I asked him what on earth he was talking about. It would seem our ghost liked to sing — "Ave Maria."

Shortly thereafter, she either turned nasty or someone else came into the picture. I had two sons at the time, three and two years old. They slept in the same room. For almost three weeks, every night at about ten o'clock, they would wake up in unison and begin to scream. This was definitely out of character for them, and I asked the older one why he was screaming. This was done out of earshot of the younger one. He replied that there was "a witch" in his room and she was on fire. When the younger one was asked, he said (in his own language), "Bad mon'ter. Burn me, Mummy," and started to cry. This went on, as I said, for about three weeks, and then stopped.

Finally, not long after that, it was afternoon and the kids and I were eating lunch in the kitchen, when the two-year-old pointed to the kitchen door and said, "Who dat, Mummy?" I looked around just in time to see a figure fading away, almost like a mist dissipating. It was a woman; she had been middle-aged, short, wavy hair, dressed in a house dress that was worn back in the days of "Father Knows Best." She seemed to have been smiling.

From that day, we haven't had any problems. But, every time something the least bit weird happens, we look at each other and say jokingly, "She's ba-a-ck ... !"

The Ghost in Bed

Michaeleen Berger, a resident of Paris, Ontario, saw my letter requesting "ghost stories" in the *Brant News*, and sent me the following letter. I am reproducing it as she wrote it.

It is interesting to note the fact that experiences of this sort seem to occur at dawn and at dusk, often in surroundings new to the observer, when the conscious mind is either waking from deep sleep or falling into deep sleep. Psychologists refer to such perceptions or misperceptions as hypnagogic or hypnopompic experiences. Parapsychologists suggest that such experiences occur to the mind because it is in an altered state and hence accessible to other realities.

June 6, 1990
Dear John:

I've always wanted to write a Dear John letter ... (sorry, couldn't help it!).

I read your letter in the *Brant News* and thought you might be interested in my experience. It happened to me once. It never happened to me before or after.

My husband and I bought an old house and the night we moved in I had this experience. My husband worked the night shift from 11:00 p.m. to 7:00 a.m. I worked around the house till about two o'clock, emptying boxes, etc.

When I went to bed, I fell asleep right away. I half awoke when I felt my husband getting into bed early that morning. I was still very tired so I rolled over in bed to face him and put my hand up to his face to give him a pat on the cheek.

My hand encountered his nose. My fingers went along the bridge of his nose, and I remember thinking, "That's not Rod's nose ..." Rod has worn glasses all his life, and when he takes them off they leave a mark on the bridge of his nose.

My fingers went up and down this nose, and it felt too long and it had a sharp ridge to it. I sat up in bed, really frightened, and turned to see who was in bed beside me.

The man was about fifty years old with a receding hairline. His hair was salt and pepper and cut real short. He was lying there and smiling at me.

I jumped out of bed and said, "Who are you?" He just lay there and smiled. (We didn't have our phone in yet, or I'd have called the police.) I ran to the bathroom and locked the door. I thought, "Well, he can't stay the rest of the night. I've got to get rid of him somehow."

So armed with a can of Lysol, I went back into the bedroom, but he wasn't there. I looked under the bed, for that was the only place he could hide. (We didn't even have any closets built yet.)

The man had just disappeared! Then I thought, "Maybe I'm dreaming this." I pinched myself hard — and it hurt like blazes. But the shock didn't seem to wake me up, so to speak, so I just couldn't be sleepwalking!

An hour later, after I'd had a cup of tea and calmed myself down, I said to myself that I was probably overtired and that I had dreamed the whole thing.

I went back to the bedroom and got into bed. As I was pulling the covers up, I looked over at the other pillow. There was a dent in it, as if a person's head had lain there ...

Michaeleen Berger

Blue Boy

October signals the fullness of the fall season. It also warns of the advent of Halloween.

To prepare for the thirty-first of the month, with all its winds and whispers of witches and warlocks, Barbara Neyedly and the other editors of the *Toronto Voice*, the city's lively inner-city monthly tabloid, asked those readers who had experienced the unexplained to send in their best true-life ghost stories. Then they asked me, as a regular columnist, to rank them and publish the eeriest. Here is one of the eeriest that appeared in the Oct. 1991 issue. It was contributed by a regular reader, Neal Landon. As for the identity of the Blue Boy ...

Whenever I hear people use the expression "looked as though he'd seen a ghost," it is usually to describe a look of blind terror, witlessness, and a wearer who seems capable of doing little more than retreating into shock. But having actually seen a ghost and compared my reactions, I conclude that the phrase is not particularly apt.

In the final years of my marriage, my wife and I lived in Scarborough, interred by our financial situation in an ugly cinder block of a structure that provided every one of its sixteen floors with bugs, rodents, cold rusty water from every tap, and a basement generator as dependable as the postal system. I never brought up the fact there was a ghost in my dwelling at tenant meetings or mentioned it to my wife.

The ghost looked to me to be that of a small boy, perhaps six to eight years old. He had unruly, medium-length hair and there was always a quick and merry look in his eyes. He smiled whenever he was spied upon playing his hide-and-seek games. Then he would vanish. He had Caucasian features although his skin was blue. His clothes and, for that matter, everything about him was enveloped in a fluorescent turquoise aura. He never uttered a word or stayed more than a few seconds in one place.

I wrote off the first four visits as inventions of fatigue, a hallucination caused by a faulty bulb blinking, or the passing headlights from a car outside. Those times he just raced past me, a blue blur on the periphery of my vision, vaguely identifiable but nothing to lose sleep over.

One night the glow caught my eye for the fifth time. I turned suddenly and there he was, exactly as I have described him. Right before my eyes he ran away from me, growing smaller and smaller, like a figure receding into the horizon until he was gone. It was too small an apartment. His actions had been confined to the same spot where he had been standing. It reminded me of a television set being turned off. Was I scared? I was more relieved than anything. I finally had a clear picture of what had been disturbing me, I thought, as I remembered the earlier instances.

Now, it's hard to rationalize a ghost, but compared to other creatures of the night, or rats, or bugs, a ghost is not difficult to accept. Over the next half year, he showed himself to me a total of three more times. Those visits went along the same lines as the fifth, so there's not much point in going into them now. One thing: I'd crouch to his level.

One night I was in the bathroom with the door open, when I heard my wife in the kitchen say, in a sweetly admonishing voice, "What are you doing here?" I knew she wasn't talking to our son because from where I was I would have seen his bedroom door open. He had been asleep for an hour. Hearing a sudden rush of air into my wife's lungs gave me a better idea of whom she was addressing. I saw her go charging through the apartment wearing an expression Clint Eastwood would have been comfortable with.

We checked in on the kid's room and, satisfied that everything was safe, returned to the kitchen. I assured her I had seen no movement of any kind around that door. When I pressed her for details, she shut right up and viewed me with suspicion. I confessed to seeing weird sights but would give her no details of my own. Her interest aroused, we agreed to a trade. Without saying a word we would write down a description of our visions and read each other's.

As it turned out, that had been her fourth and final sighting of the ghost. We talked about seeing him, about what it meant, what could be causing it, and what we could do about it until, after ten minutes, we exhausted our capacity to converse without repeating what we already knew, which amounted to very little. We simply never mentioned it again.

It wasn't like we wanted to go out of our way looking for trouble. We had enough problems with the real world as it was.

A year later the wife and I broke up. It wasn't the fault of the ghost. I never even saw him again and haven't thought much about the whole experience in the interim. Naw, what happened with me and the wife was, well, actually I'm rather hard-pressed to come up with a cut-and-dried explanation for you.

So what else is new, eh?

A Scarborough Poltergeist

Dan Carter is a Torontonian who heard me being interviewed by Bill Carroll, host of "Barometer," the popular early-afternoon programme on radio station Q-107. Phoning me at my home later that day, he shared with me the story of a spate of poltergeist-like disturbances that he and other members of his family experienced in an apartment in Scarborough, Ontario. (For the record, the apartment is No. 704, 3 Glamorgan Avenue.)

What Dan Carter described could be called the effects created by a poltergeist, a "noisy ghost." A poltergeist is known by its effects, not by its appearance, although at the end of this account "something" does appear. Dan Carter accepted my invitation to write out a sequential account of his experiences. I received it on 17 April 1990 and here, in a minimally edited form, it is.

✦

A series of events made our lives rather interesting over a period of six to eight months.

On October 1st, my brother and I rented an apartment in Scarborough, on Kennedy Road, near Highway 401. From the time we moved in, odd things would happen. They occurred during our absences from the apartment. E.g., I would come home from work and find all the doors inside the apartment closed, the doors to the bedroom and bathroom, etc. Sometimes lights would be on when I entered and then a short time later they would go off by themselves. My brother and I kept blaming each other for these occurrences.

The linen closet at the end of the hall was extremely cold. We used to keep milk in it as it was colder than the fridge.

We were the first tenants in this apartment for it was a new building.

176

Sometimes my fiancée, who worked right across the street, would come to the apartment for lunch. One day when we were out, she came over and found the hall light on and every tap in the place on full blast. Thinking it odd, she shut the taps off — the kitchen tap, the taps in the bathroom sink, the tub and shower taps, etc. That evening she asked us why we had left them on.

One night my fiancée and I were watching t.v. in the living-room. There was a loud crash in the kitchen. From the kitchen a cigarette butt flew through the air at great speed and smashed into the back of the front door of the apartment, leaving a black mark from its ash on the top part of the door. I would guess the distance to be about ten or twelve feet. When I went into the kitchen to clean up the mess, I found that nothing was disturbed.

Sometimes bedroom doors would close, either one at a time or all at once, with great force. One time I came home early from work. As I got off the elevator, I heard music playing, very loud music. As I approached the apartment, I discovered the music was coming from inside the apartment. To be sure, I checked the apartments next to mine, above and below, by placing my ear to their doors. The music was definitely coming from my apartment. It occurred to me that my brother had come home from work early and was playing music. I was going to give him a blast for playing the music so loud. When I opened the door to the apartment, everything went dead quiet. My brother was not at home. The only stereo in the apartment was located in his room. It was not on.

When I got married, my wife, my brother, and I stayed in the apartment. Once she and her girlfriend were preparing to hold a Tupperware party and were cleaning up. When they were doing the dishes, they placed the glasses upside down on the drain board. The glasses kept flipping right side up. They did not fall over, but went up in the air, turned over, and landed right side up. This event was witnessed by three people. They phoned me and said, "Come home now. We will meet you in the lobby." When I got there fifteen minutes later, the girls were in the lobby, white and hysterical. To make matters worse — when they took the elevator from the seventh floor down to the lobby, the elevator went back up to the seventh floor, stopped there, came back down, stopped, and nobody got off.

The Tupperware party was held that evening. All the people who entered the apartment that night reported the same thing occurring. Their watches stopped. If they stepped outside the apartment and into the hall, their watches would go again. Re-entering, they would stop again.

We finally decided that there was something else that was living there with us. We also knew that it was out and about because you could hear the breaking of glass. It sounded like expensive crystal. Suddenly the room would get extremely cold, as cold as the linen closet. We believe it lived in the closet.

At night, when you were in bed but not yet asleep, you could hear the chains on the living room lamps clang against the stems of the lamps. Going out to check on these noises, you could hear them more clearly. But as soon as you entered the living room, they would stop. All the while the windows were closed.

Sometimes, at night, my wife would wake me up and say, "Someone is walking down the hall." Listening, I would tell her it was my brother and he was playing a joke on us. Getting out of bed and listening by the door, I heard something walk past, stepping with one foot and dragging with the other, walking towards the linen closet. Opening the door very gently, and jumping out to surprise my brother, I was surprised to find no one there. My brother's door closed tightly. It was warped. You had to body-slam it to close it tight.

In March of 1974, I received a call informing me my grandmother had died. My mother and father flew up from Miami for the funeral. My father stayed with his family, my mother stayed with us. We told my mother not to worry about the odd noises. Apartments are noisy places,

The next morning, my mother informed us she was leaving. When we asked her why, she told us she was lying on the sofa, almost asleep, when she heard glass break in the dining room. Suddenly the room got extremely cold. Reaching for a blanket, something touched her on the shoulder, as if to say, "It's okay. It's only me." She said it was a very warm, loving touch. But she never forgot it.

That night, she decided to prove to herself that something did, indeed, live with us. My mother stood a cigarette on its end on top of the t.v. set. Sitting on the sofa with my brother, his girlfriend, she spoke: "If there is anything in this room, prove it to me by knocking my cigarette down." The cigarette fell down. My mother then stood the cigarette up again and said, "A kid can do that. I want you to really prove it." The cigarette then flew across the room, as if someone had swatted it. My mother was convinced.

Somehow word got out about our place, and people would come to the door asking, "Is this the apartment with the ghost? Can we see it? Would you like to sublet it?"

The last thing I remember of "the ghost" was this: I was asleep when all of a sudden it was cold in the bedroom, so cold that I woke up shivering. I looked toward the doorway. It was wide open and a dark shadow entered the room. I felt frozen and could hardly move. The only thing I could do was close my eyes and shiver. Then the room warmed up and it, whatever it was, was gone.

These events took place sixteen years ago. If you need further information, call me or my wife Debbie.

Spirits of
Niagara-on-the-Lake

Najla Mady is a professional psychic. She was born in Rouyn, Québec, but since the 1950s has made her home in the Niagara Peninsula, latterly in St. Catharines. People in the area know her well, for she has her own weekly cable-TV show called *A Psychic Hour with Najla*. It was on this show that she predicted the assassination of Egyptian President Anwar Sadat the day before the fatal shooting.

Najla Mady is the author of the booklet *Simply Psychic* (1984) and the book *Boo!! Ghosts I Have(n't) Loved as Encountered by Najla Mady* (1993) published by NC Press Limited of Toronto. In her books she recounts in a lively manner the experiences she has had with people and with "disturbances." The excerpts focus on the spirits of the historic town of Niagara-on-the-Lake.

⁂

I am always drawn to where a spirit is. If there is a spirit in a house, I will walk right to the spot where it manifests itself.

An extremely unusual case occurred in Niagara-on-the-Lake at the home of a friend of mine. Patricia called me and said, "For a long time something's been going on in my house, but now it's bothering my son David. He's not sleeping at night. He sees something in his bedroom. I have seen it too. Will you come? My older children have seen children playing in the house as well, but they're not bothered. The one in his room is troubling David, however."

When I arrived I discovered six or seven spirits living in that house. But one was much more complex and hostile than all the others.

I told Patricia and Michael, her companion, to follow me, to observe what was happening. When I am concentrating I am not always aware of all the things going on around me. Again, I asked them not to tell me what had occurred in the home; I would learn about it as I proceeded through the house.

I immediately walked through the living-room and up the stairs to David's bedroom. There I started to describe what had been happening. There had been apparitions at night from an ambiguous spirit. In a way, the spirit was friendly and trying to play with David, but in another way the spirit was trying to frighten him. I felt the spirit was a person who had never had the chance to be a child during his own life-time — that his own life had been cut short and that he was envious and resentful of David's youth.

When I entered the bedroom, the air turned cold, the bedspread and drapes started to move, and an extremely cold current of air enveloped me. Digging my heels into the floor, I stood firm as the spirit moved through me. The air around me started to warm, so I felt I had put the spirit to rest. This process took about ten minutes.

As we started to go back downstairs, I realized I had only partially completed my work, for I began to pick up another spirit in another part of the house. I felt friction. Then, all of a sudden, Michael, Patricia, and I could feel a force behind us on the stairs, pushing us all down, as if to hurry us out of the way.

What followed next was one of the worst experiences I've ever had. If ever I was frightened, this was the time.

The pushing concerned me, but I was so exhausted I needed to rest, so I walked towards the chesterfield in the family-room and lay down.I listened as Michael and Patricia described what had occurred. They quietly described with incredulity things moving on the wall behind me, the air turning cold, and the hem of my dress swishing back and forth. Suddenly I bolted up and said, "Patricia, I must go into your living-room. Something is there!

They followed as I walked straight to the corner, where a large plant stood. It was there that I started to feel the most stubborn, hostile force I had ever felt. The plant was shrouded in a most bitter, angry field of negative energy. Never before had I experienced so much force.

The spirit had transferred itself into a living, growing thing. I didn't feel anything evil, merely angry. The air around the plant began to turn ice cold, colder than anything I had ever experienced before, and I thought, "Oh, my God, I don't know if I can do this." It was so strong!

I took a very stern stance and said I was going to absorb that spirit no matter what. Now I was beginning to get angry myself — to think the spirit was so stubborn, so hostile, and so determined to stay and continue to bother the children!

I stood directly in front of the plant. The feeling inside of me was extremely heavy, yet I felt I was starting to absorb the spirit. It started to lift, but there was something wrong this time.

For the first time ever, I didn't feel it was lifting on its way to rest. It was lifting because it was so much stronger than I was. (I even felt it might "escape" me entirely.) So I just stood there, as firmly and as defiantly as I could, and willed it to me.

Then I started to feel it. The hem of my skirt began swaying back and forth, and my one foot began to move involuntarily, inching away from its place beside my other foot, putting me off balance, distracting me. With all my strength, I concentrated my will to remove the force that was now concentrated around my ankle. I stood still, arms raised, fighting for every bit of energy I could muster to combat its force. It was my will against the spirit's will.

As I stood there, concentrating on the plant itself, I saw it!

At first it was just a shimmer of its leaves. Then, as if relenting, one by one its leaves began to droop and shrivel. As this happened, I began to feel lightness and warmth around me.

I had absorbed the spirit. The spirit had "died" and, with it, the plant.

By this time I could barely walk, I was so weak; Patricia and Michael helped me into the living-room where I lay down. Then they both noticed a most startling thing. There, on my ankle, were white indentations — thumbprints where something had grabbed me and tried to knock me off my feet. Michael rubbed my ankle until it returned to normal.

I told them to bury the plant as soon as possible, which they did. I learned later from Patricia that at one time a young boy had lived in their house and had died of leukemia at nine years of age. Although Patricia speaks freely about the episode, she is concerned about the young boy's parents who still live in Niagara-on-the-Lake and remain grief-stricken by their son's tragic death. For that reason she doesn't speak very often about the occurrence in her home on that day. Her children have not been troubled, so there is no reason to ever mention it again.

I am an instrument, a conductor, through which a disturbed spirit may find release and eventual rest. It doesn't stay contained in me. I absorb it and then release it. It is as if such spirits don't know their way to "the other side," and I show them the way, which direction to take, which channel to enter.

I don't question this ability of mine. I only know I am able to do it, and when it concerns the well-being of children, I thank God I have it. Otherwise, the disturbances would go on indefinitely.

◈

One of my favourite encounters with the spirit world happened in the historic town of Niagara-on-the-Lake, Ontario. I met Captain Swayze when asked by the host of a local television programme to go on a live ghost hunt for a show that she was producing. I was to walk through a few reputedly haunted establishments and relate to the television camera what I was psychically picking up.

The flimsiest of reasons will take me to my favourite little town. This seemed so much more substantial than a flimsy reason, and I readily agreed.

Away from the busy streets and throngs of visitors to the quaint little town of Niagara-on-the-Lake, sits the Angel Inn, circa 1771. Few tourists converging on this historic town are aware of the activities created by the spirits inhabiting the little inn.

Florence Le Doux, the past owner, has shared her more than seventy-year life with Captain Swayze, who was a British Army officer during the War of 1812. Her great-grandfather first met Swayze, as Florence lovingly refers to the captain, when he bought the inn in 1823.

Obviously a gentleman, the officer introduced himself by name to Mrs. Le Doux's great-grandfather. After the passing of some time, he felt he wanted to know more about Captain Swayze. He wrote relatives of his who lived in England, asking them to research the Swayze family tree.

The results were most fruitful. The co-operative family sent along personal information, including a portrait of Captain Swayze. He had been a talented artist in his lifetime. He was a sculptor, a painter, and was masterful at playing the piano. The self-portrait showed him to be quite a handsome man. It hung at the inn on a wall for all to admire. It was a wall I didn't like; it upset me to stand close to it.

The crew and I must have presented an unusual sight to its ghostly inhabitants as we noisily entered, carting in everything we'd need to record my psychic reactions while we wandered throughout the inn. The crew had to rush and set up their equipment because, immediately upon entering the premises, I began to pick up its historical inhabitants, including a few situations.

My instincts directed me to the far left corner of the building. While approaching the area, I felt overcome by a sense of suffering. The feeling intensified as I drew closer. Suddenly, I realized that what I was

183

picking up was coming not from the room, but from below the floorboards on which I was standing.

I felt pain, unnatural pain, caused by torture. Beatings, broken bones, starvation, bloodshed — I felt it all. I also felt the small area wasn't a part of the rest of the inn. It was different somehow.

My eyes were drawn to a portrait of George Washington hanging on the wall above this particular area. The thought that flew through my mind was it definitely shouldn't be there. I also noticed a portrait of a British officer. As I gazed at the painting I saw the silhouette of two more officers. This told me that all three had suffered the same torturous fate.

I expressed my thoughts and feelings to the camera before moving onto other areas of the building. I was drawn to one particular bedroom upstairs. I learned later that this was the room Florence had been born in. I turned to a hotel employee and remarked that this was truly a very busy room. I could hear fife and drum music, soldiers were marching, and there were beautifully dressed young ladies and gentlemen in army uniforms strolling arm in arm.

The employee agreed, saying that she and many others had heard the music and sensed more than one presence emanating from the room. I reluctantly left the lovely little room and the historical years of the early 1800s.

It was now time for me to meet Florence Le Doux and discuss the events I felt had happened in the inn. Florence loves her family — family of ghosts, that is. She has enjoyed the company of the handsome captain.

She told us that he has been her constant companion, guardian and friend ever since she can recall. They have had wonderful chats over the years, and he has also been her teacher. She informed us with pride that he taught her to paint, sculpt and play the piano.

Pointing to a portrait of Swayze, she told us that she painted it while his hands guided hers. A well-executed bust of the talented ghost sits proudly on display. Florence tell us Swayze actually molded it using her hands and grey clay she picked up from nearby Fort Mississauga. He told her what type of clay to use and where she'd find it. Florence often treated patrons of the Angel Inn to an impromptu piano serenade. She happily told us that it was Swayze who taught her to play the instrument.

The love and affection she has for this spirited ghost is beautiful to behold. Her faced softened into a lovely smile as she related to us years of memorable experiences she has shared with Captain Swayze.

She never opposed discussing her colourful ghostly guests with patrons of the inn. Heaven knows, she's had to explain them often enough! The spirits are not discreet and entered the bedrooms of overnight guests. Florence recalls that about eighty ladies have complained of a man in red uniform standing behind them in the public washroom. His unwelcome visits were reflected in the washroom's mirror. She became adept at calming jittery tourists and employees alike.

Florence and a visiting psychic were deep in discussion of the ghostly captors happening at the inn when a waiter overhearing them disclaimed any belief in the paranormal. The psychic challenged Swayze not to let himself be talked about in such a manner, demanding that the captain show proof of his presence to the waiter. A heavy mug flew from its shelf across the room and hit an oak support beam, leaving a dent that is still seen today. The mug, on its way to hitting the beam, brushed against the waiter's hand causing it to bleed. The shaken waiter, after he calmed down and was bandaged, admitted that he now believed in ghosts.

As I listened to Florence recounting the ghostly occurrences at the Angel Inn, it became clear to me why I felt General George Washington's portrait shouldn't be hung at the inn. Swayze and his spirited cohorts wouldn't appreciate being reminded of their American captor.

She also pointed out the reason I felt so terribly disturbed as I stood in the small area I first entered. It was the original building built in 1771 and had been used as a prison to house British soldiers captured by the Americans. The cellar beneath it had housed a cell used to confine and, eventually, torture Captain Swayze to death. The building, as it stands today, was built around the original one. This explains why I felt it didn't belong with the rest of it.

Florence has since moved from the inn, and Swayze has followed her to her new home, where he has made himself known to her two-year-old granddaughter.

The Haunted Farmhouse

Is it houses that are haunted, or people?

Certainly some places seem to be haunted. Certainly some men and women are haunted ... haunted by their experiences in old houses, especially old farmhouses, like the one that may be found on Bow Park Farm Road on the outskirts of Brantford, Ontario.

Patricia Greathead works in a retirement home, and her husband is an employee of Uniroyal. They now reside in a non-haunted house with their family in Brantford. Mrs. Greathead wrote the letter that follows on 26 May 1986.

After seeing your letter in the *Brantford Expositor,* I decided I would tell you of one of my strange experiences. The most vivid experience that happened to me occurred four or five years ago, when our family was looking for a house just outside the city of Brantford.

My husband, my younger son, and I were taken by a realtor to look at a farmhouse. The farm was located off a country road and had a lot of acreage. The farmhouse was two storeys in height and empty at the time of our inspection.

As soon as I entered the front door a feeling of *crawliness,* a *prickly sensation,* came over me. At the time I didn't give it a second thought. We looked around the downstairs and then proceeded to mount the stairs. I was very reluctant to follow the others up the stairs, but I didn't let on. For a few seconds it felt as if my feet were glued to the very stairs. The prickly sensation grew stronger and I felt a *chill* in the air. I really did feel strange, but I mounted the stairs and with the others went into a bedroom to look around, all the while trying to act calm and collected.

All of a sudden I thought, "Something terrible has happened here."

I couldn't wait to get out of that house. I quickly left. As soon as I was outside, the sensations themselves vanished, though I still felt creepy or weird. But I didn't say a thing to anyone.

When we got back to our own house, my younger son turned to me and said, "That house was spooky!" He must have felt something too. I told him how I had felt. My husband laughed and said we were both nuts. I didn't realize how weird my son felt or how shaken up he was from the experience until a few minutes later. He went out to start his car. It backed up, smacking into our neighbour's car. No one was hurt and there was no damage, but I shook inside for a good hour after that.

My older son came home and wanted to know what house we had seen and what we had thought of it. When we told him where the farmhouse was located, I was really shaken by his reply. He said, "That house you went to see on Bow Park Farm Road is haunted! Didn't you know that? Everyone else does!"

Well, we didn't know that it was haunted. We had never heard about it before. Apparently there had been a triple murder committed in the house forty-five or so years ago. It was a lover's triangle or something like that. I learned from a friend that whoever had lived in that house since then had experienced bad luck, or had been driven out by some tragedy or other while living there. I wondered if the realtor who took us there knew of this story.

I also learned that a red, driverless truck had been periodically spotted in the vicinity of the house. I didn't get the particulars of the truck or the murders. Just out of curiosity I have meant to follow up the details, but I have not got around to it. One visit to the farmhouse was enough for me. I didn't want to go back. I have always wanted to forget the experience, but it's still on my mind.

Ghost of an Elderly Woman

The following letter was written in response to one of my requests for "ghost stories." The request appeared in the *Keswick Banner Era*. The response was sent to me by Mrs. Velma Grace who is a resident of Keswick, Ontario. It would be interesting to know if the current occupants of this house of visions have any strange visions or experiences to report.

July 7, 1990
Dear Sir:

In answer to your letter requesting information on ghosts, I'm not much of a writer but will do my best and you can take it from there.

My husband and I moved into the back half of a 10-room house. My son and daughter-in-law had the front half, on Leslie Street just north of the Newmarket boundary. This 2-story house was over 100 years old, with 2-inch thick and 2-foot wide lumber going from the main floor to the roof where the uprights were 4-by-4's with 4-by-4 supports put in from the left bottom corner to the right top corner. It had been a farmhouse. There is still a farm behind it. The house is set well back in off the road. We renovated the place and lived there.

My first experience was awakening to see a halo-like light with an elderly woman with long gray hair almost to her waist standing in a doorway. I rose up and she disappeared.

I cannot remember how long it was until I was awakened again. This time there was the light and a man, a woman, and a child of about 10, also in the same doorway. They were there and they disappeared when I rose up, the same as my first encounter.

We lived there 2 years, and 5 times after that I was awakened by this same woman standing beside my bed putting a shroud over me. I raised my arms, and each time I pushed the shroud away, she would disappear. This upset me so that I would wake up screaming and my husband would come to me and try to console me. I used a Bible plus I wore a necklace with a cross. I also spoke to a woman that offered to come and exorcise the house.

My daughter-in-law would hear music playing when there was no one home but herself. She would also find things moved from where she had put them. On advice from Dr. Dennison of Newmarket, we sold the house as it was too much of a strain on me.

This went on from about 1982 to 1984. The house is at 17740 Leslie Street. I don't know whether this will help you or not.

Yours truly,
Velma Grace

P.S. I was 62 and it made me a nervous wreck.

The Shuter Street Poltergeist

Isabel Germiquet prepared this detailed report of the poltergeist-like disturbances that she has experienced over the five or so years while living in her own apartment. For the record, the apartment is located in the building at 295 Shuter Street in downtown Toronto. She prepared this report at my request on 19 December 1988. She had contacted me after learning that I was on the lookout for accounts of hauntings, strange sightings, etc. The report was keyboarded and printed by Mrs. Germiquet's son on an Apple computer. I have minimally edited it for publication here. It takes a hardy soul to endure such disturbances!

≈≈◈≈≈

I moved into the one-bedroom apartment in which I am now living on August 13th, 1983. As I was moving from a large, two-bedroom apartment, I had too much furniture. So I hung my clothes in the closet in the bedroom, and I put away my things in dresser drawers there, but at first I didn't actually sleep in the bedroom. I could hardly reach the bed for all the furniture and things. Whenever I worked my way through the bedroom to get a change of clothing, I could hear a male voice groaning from within the closet.

During the weeks that I couldn't use the bed, the door was kept closed because the bedroom was such a mess of furniture. In spite of this, I found that the door was frequently open. This happened many times a day, and I knew that I had not left it open. One particular day, when the door was shut, I tried to push it open, but it felt like someone was holding the door tightly shut. Suddenly it gave way, and I stumbled into the room. This was just the beginning. The following is a list of the phenomena that occurred in my apartment over the last five years, and continue to occur to this day.

Aug.- Oct. 1983. The day after I moved in, I began to hear tapping noises in the bedroom whenever I entered it. These noises spread over the entire apartment. Then snorting sounds came from the oven and spread all over the apartment. The first night that I slept in the bedroom, all the coat-hangers in the closet started to rattle for no apparent reason. Snorting came from inside the closet. These sounds continued on a nightly basis. Occasionally growling noises came from behind the television set.

Dec. 1983 - Jan. 1984. My granddaughter and grandson moved from Vancouver to Toronto. They spent a considerable amount of time in my apartment and experienced some of the following phenomena. We were touched on the arms and had our hair tweaked. We heard snoring sounds from the oven and the rattling of the oven-racks. My daughter suggested taking pictures of the open oven. The film showed faces and figures. About this time I was hugged by an invisible presence. On Christmas Day, rapping was heard on the headboard of my bed, and my daughter, sleeping over that night, was struck in the back. Banging was also heard on the inside of the closet door.

My daughter and I saw a male shadow moving out of the dining-room. There were no males present in the apartment at the time. The next night, on the advice of the Psychic Centre, we decided it was wise to sleep at my daughter's apartment on Wellesley Street. When leaving my place, we heard footsteps behind us, as we walked down the corridor to the elevator. We turned and looked, but no one was there. While we were at my daughter's, some plastic bags began to rustle, as if someone was moving them.

During this month I read the book *Supernature* by Lyall Watson. It said a man in Sweden was getting spirit-voices on his tape recorder. I decided to borrow a tape recorder from my son. We turned it on and recorded a voice saying, "Strange one, Jimmy. Find me, Jimmy. Jimmy, find me if you can."

April 1984. My daughter moved from Wellesley Street to an apartment in a building next to mine. One night, she left my place at 7:30 p.m. Just after she left, my apartment door opened and closed by itself. At 9:00 p.m., my daughter telephoned to tell me she could hear a man humming in her apartment. At midnight I could hear him humming in my apartment. On one occasion, I heard the sound of someone flicking the light-shade. When I looked up, the light-shade was vibrating.

May 1984. I found an enormous hand-print on the kitchen cupboard. A mysterious formation of moisture appeared on the wall without explanation. I called 100 Huntley Street, and a minister came to my apartment. After the minister left, the bottom of the drapes over the sliding balcony door were flung about one or two feet above the level of the floor, and I heard growling and scratching, as if an animal was trying to escape.

July 1984. My eight-year-old daughter and I saw many quarter-moon shapes of light moving about the living-room. Later that month I saw two flashes, orange-like flames shooting across the walls. The flames were about 16" by 4" in size. At the time all the doors, windows, and drapes were closed. Also during this month, I sat on the sofa reading and heard a male voice whistling a tune a few feet away.

Aug. 1985. My granddaughter, aged nine, was alone with me one day when I put on the tape recorder. I recorded a male voice that said, "Go out on the 29th. Look up, Trudy. Don't worry, everyone is coming back — your dad, Ethel, friends." My nickname is Trudy, and my dad and Ethel have been dead for thirty-five to forty years. Another time, when I was alone, I heard a noise. I turned on the tape recorder and a different male voice said, "Come, child ... find thy rest ... ending from thee."

Sept. 1985. While taping, I recorded a woman speaking Italian. I asked three different people to translate the words for me. They all said the woman was telling me to read the books in my library. Later that month, my granddaughter was sitting on the floor watching TV. We heard the noises that generally accompany the phenomenon. Then we both heard a childlike voice saying aloud what sounded like "boak ... boak." We decided that the male voice was saying, "Book ... book."

As I was wrapping gifts, I heard the rustle of a Simpsons bag on my sewing machine. I turned and saw a large handprint form on the surface of the bag. As I watched, the handprint on the bag relaxed. On closer examination, I could see the sharp indentations left by the fingernails. A variety of unexplained smells occasionally occurred in the apartment — everything from perfume to rotten meat. On investigation, they did not appear to be coming from air ducts or from other apartments.

Feb. 1986. One day I saw three golden balls of light in the living-room. They were moving around about a foot from the floor.

Aug. 1986. My youngest son was staying over for a few days. One night, while he was listening to music on the tape recorder in the bedroom, I heard the buttons on the machine being pushed, one after the other. I was about to ask him what he was doing, when he shouted for me to hurry into the room. He was very upset and he told me that something he couldn't see was pushing the buttons on his tape recorder. It was now turned off. I turned on the tape recorder and watched as something turned it off again. I could feel a presence in the room, and I shouted at it in anger to go away. There was a swooshing sound and a sharp banging on the inside of the closet door. Thereafter the tape recorder operated normally.

Oct. 1986. One day my son was visiting me and we had a quarrel and I called him a stinker. He left, and a few minutes later I heard a lot of tapping sounds, so I turned on the tape recorder. I recorded a woman's voice saying, "Let stink out the door ... walk in the bare." I wondered if the voice was telling me not to let my son come back.

Jan. 1987. One night my granddaughter was visiting. She wasn't feeling well and went to bed about 9:00 p.m. About five minutes later she started screaming, "Nanny, Nanny, help me! Get me out of here!" When I got to her, she was hysterical. But she told me what had happened. She had turned out the light and pulled up the covers, with the top part folded to about the middle of her chest. Suddenly the covers were yanked down to the bottom of the bed. I looked and I could see the spot where they had been grabbed.

Feb. 1988. I was sitting in the living-room and I saw a bright flash of light in the kitchen area. As I watched, it flashed repeatedly in the direction of the apartment door. The flashes looked like balls of light. They made a whoomp sound, as if they were hitting something. Suddenly the balls of light started to make a sudden, ninety-degree turn and rush straight toward me. They seemed to flatten out a few feet from me, and make the whoomp sound as if they were hitting something there. This continued until seven o'clock the next morning.

One kind or another of the above phenomena has occurred continually in this apartment over the past five years. There has never been a break of more than three weeks between occurrences. Usually there is an occurrence every night.

The Feeling of a Presence

I received the following letters from Mrs. H. Nagy of Welland, Ontario. The first arrived on 1 June 1990; the second was dated June 6 of the same year.

In the first letter Mrs. Nagy described the nature of some peculiar events and experiences that had occurred to her six years earlier and that had left an indelible mark on her memory. In that letter she alluded to "a bizarre culmination of happenings" which she did not describe. So I wrote to her asking for more information.

In the second letter she elaborated. It must have been a hard letter to write, but it makes fascinating reading. Far from being "a whirlwind of memories," the account in the letter is a vivid description of the possession of the living by the dead.

Both letters are reproduced here in slightly edited form.

1.

I am writing in response to your advertisement in our local newspaper, the *Welland Guardian*.

In 1984 my mother-in-law passed away because of cancer. It was a long, painful time for her and we were with her when she passed over.

About four months later, "occurrences" started happening to me. There are too many to list here, but in general they include shaking chairs, the presence of a "white cloud" (which was also witnessed by my two-year-old daughter), and what I called "the feeling." This was an unpleasant "smothering" of my body. I had trouble breathing, and felt very confined, almost like I was being hugged by a bear. This feeling would last only a minute and then the "apparition" would appear.

I documented every time an "occurrence" would happen to me, and there seemed to be no rhyme or reason as to when it would happen. I was scared and very curious as to who or what this was and why it was happening only to me and not to my husband. I talked to many people about this, and the ones who didn't think me crazy thought it was because I was a bit more "sensitive" than my husband. It was a very hard time for my family and I was always on edge because I never knew when it would happen.

It all ended in a bizarre culmination of happenings that were truly unbelievable, and I hesitate even now to put them in writing. I have talked to many people who, I thought, would believe me, and even they thought I was crazy.

But to sum it up, I told the apparition to leave and it did. During this culmination, I was brought to believe that the spirit was that of my mother-in-law. I will go into details if you are interested.

Let it be known that during this time I was tested by psychiatrists and by medical doctors for epilepsy, and there was nothing wrong with me physically or mentally.

2.

Your letter asking me for more details has started a whirlwind of memories for me.

One of the major things I remember is that I was almost always alone whenever anything strange would happen. This makes it very difficult for people to believe in what you are saying.

I remember how my family and I had just begun our dinner, and while I was sitting in my chair, it began to shake. Hard. The shaking lasted only seconds, then stopped.

I said to my husband, "What was that?"

He said, "What was what?"

I asked him if he felt anything and he said no. I passed it off.

Moments later it happened again, and this time it was harder and longer. I jumped up and yelled, "There it is again!"

I went and sat on the couch, and looked at the window, and that is when I saw what looked to be a translucent white moon hanging above my window. Moments later it was gone. No one saw it but me.

Days later my daughter pointed to the wall above the hutch and said, "Look, Mommy, moon." It was the same thing I saw.

This went on for some time, and every time before it would happen and the "moon" would appear, I would get the feeling of being smothered. Finally ... after months of it appearing only to me, in front of the TV, while drying my hair, and once right next to me on the chair where I was sitting ... I had had enough. I called a friend and asked her what she thought I should do. She asked me if I had tried just telling it to go away. So simple, I had never thought of it.

The next time that it happened, I was, of course, alone. The feeling of a presence was the strongest it had ever been, and instead of getting scared, I got angry. I had had enough of all of this. I yelled, "Who are you?"

The moment I did, my right arm went completely numb. No feeling from the shoulder down. Now this was the arm my mother-in-law had had amputated, due to cancer, so I concluded it was her spirit.

I said, "Okay, now I know who you are, now tell me what you want." My arms flew up in the air, my head went back, and I couldn't move. Now I was terrified. I began to cry. I screamed, "Go away, you're ruining my life!"

Then it stopped. Just stopped. The feeling slowly disappeared, and I never saw the "moon" again.

To this day I still don't know why it happened. I'm still not sure if it was my mother-in-law's spirit. But to console myself, I tell myself it was her, and she was trying to tell me, in the only way she could, that she's okay."

Bertha's Spirit

The words "haunted house" spring to mind. Also the words "haunted people."

Perhaps the inhabitants of certain houses are haunted. Could it be that the occupants of these houses are specially sensitive to the spirit of place? Perhaps it is that they are sensitive to the spirits of the place.

These are some of the questions raised by the following letter which was written by Joan Y. Clodd of Oakville, Ontario.

May 26, 1990
Dear Mr. Colombo:

I saw your letter in *Oakville Today* and thought you might be interested in my experience.

My father had passed away and I was breaking up his house, preparing to rent it. The house was built in 1925 and had been moved from one side of the creek in Oakville to the other.

Anyway, my cousin, mother-in-law, and myself had worked all day of April 10, 1984, packing and cleaning. Later on that evening, we had come back to my new home, when I realized I had left our kettle at my dad's.

It was about 8:00 p.m. I drove up, still with my mother-in-law and my ten-year-old daughter. I opened the door and reached for the light switch. I immediately felt unwanted and very fearful. However, I carried on in. My daughter went in and began looking for her dolls.

The light would not work in the basement where the dolls were. My mother-in-law scurried in, lifted something, and scurried out again. All the while I was feeling "Get out! Get out!" My daughter began to cry and called out for help. The dolls were lost in darkness. I shone a light for her and she was also fearful. She ran out and I was left alone in the deserted house.

I knew it was not my dad because the energy was very angry and did not want to be disturbed. I was frozen for a few moments. Then I ran out too.

When we pulled away in the car, my mother-in-law asked if I had felt "something." Now, this lady does not "feel things." In fact, she does not give any credibility to anything "spooky." When I told her I had felt "something," we compared notes and found similar fears. I went back the next morning and felt nothing at all.

About six months later I had a reading done by a medium who did not know me or anything about me. She said a woman called Bertha was saying sorry for being aggressive with me at my dad's house and did not mean to frighten me. I was pleased and amazed all at once. You see, I never really met a real spirit before, although I have been interested for years. In fact, I was sorry I had run away. I should have tried to speak to her.

The tenants of the house never complained, so I don't know if Bertha only made herself known to us.

I hope you find this of interest.

Yours truly,
Joan Y. Clodd

P.S. I must tell you I have dealt with spirits for years as I was a practising psychic and I have never run into a negative energy before. I think that was what made me fearful. All the spirits I had dealt with were lost or helpful. I have also cleaned out houses where spirits were trapped and encountered no fear.

I tend to channel without being aware and this becomes difficult for me. I hope you can use my experience for your work. I have read some of your work with interest.

J.Y.C.

The Spirit of Amity

Readers with jaded tastes who prefer their accounts of haunted houses to be as scary and gory as the Amityville Horror are well advised to skip the next account. The residence in North Bay that is described in this letter is haunted (to the degree that the word applies in this instance) not by a ghoul but by a spirit of love and approval!

This account is based on a letter sent to the present editor and dated 15 May 1987. The author, Norma Metz, was born in Washington, D.C. She spent ten years with a French-Canadian, Roman Catholic missionary community in Montreal and she is a graduate of the University of Ottawa, having majored in English literature. Metz, a freelance writer, settled in North Bay where she wrote about the uniqueness of her home in a column for the *North Bay Nugget* on 7 February 1987.

Shortly after writing the letter upon which this account is based, Metz moved out of the house into a smaller one. That move was made with a degree of regret.

※◎※

I was always afraid to be alone. As a child I would sometimes be so petrified when hearing some unexplained noise that I'd freeze, unable to move for the longest time. My imagination ran wild. It still does. However, now I have developed more rationalizing power.

When my friend Ruby and I first visited this three-storey house at 918 Algonquin Avenue in North Bay — prior to buying it in the spring of 1985 — I was standing outside looking up towards the roof. The third-floor dormer has two windows. The house stands so tall that these windows appeared to be eyes peering down, almost daring me ... to do what I don't know, just daring me. I thought they were attic windows, but when we toured the house I discovered they were the windows of the third floor. There was still an attic above that! My apprehension grew and secretly I prayed that I'd never be left alone in the house.

We moved in on May 17. During the first month, we renovated the third floor, which already consisted of two bedrooms and a very large room that the previous owners used for entertaining and dancing. We converted this entire third floor into a three-bedroom apartment, complete with bathroom, kitchen, and living room.

The incident occurred while in the midst of this construction. I was awakened in the middle of that night by the sound of strong winds outside. Suddenly I heard a strange sound coming from the third floor and focused my attention on it, trying, through my drowsiness, to imagine what it could be. A ball? Maybe a golfball or a very large marble being rolled across the hardwood floor? The noise would stop, start again, rhythmical and continual.

Now at that time we had a cat named Smokie. I thought perhaps that we had left the door to the third floor open and that she was up there playing with something. But the noise was too steady, too regular. Besides, when I sat up, Smokie was still lying on my bed! With head and ears perked up, she was looking out towards the hallway. She must have heard the noise too. Naturally I froze right then and there!

Finally, with all the courage I could muster, I got out of bed and woke Ruby. She's always so brave. I knew she would investigate, hopefully without me. However, out of curiosity, I did venture up to the third floor with her and found the door to the attic was ajar. One of the windows was open and the wind was blowing through the apartment. We turned on all the lights. I told Ruby about the sound of a ball rolling on the floor but we didn't find anything resembling a ball. And Ruby, always so brave and perhaps sleepy, didn't seem too concerned. We went back to bed. I never heard the noise again.

The next day, in broad daylight, I looked over every inch of the third floor and found nothing that even came close to being a golf ball, a marble, or a rolling stone! Ruby concluded, "It was just the door blowing in the wind." But does a door blowing in the wind sound like something rolling across the floor? As I said I never heard that noise again and strangely enough, after that night, I was never afraid of being alone in the house.

I do believe there was a presence letting me know it was there. But why only me? (And my cat?) Why not Ruby?

Sometimes I like *not* knowing all the answers to such mysteries. When I do think about that incident and others similar to it, I can devise all sorts of stories. As I said, I do have quite an imagination! For sure though, I'll continue to believe in spirits. (I don't like the word "ghost.") I believe in a spirit of goodness, a spirit of evil, one of love, and one of hate, but whether such spirits can produce sound effects, I don't know.

I believe that a good, loving spirit permeates that house on Algonquin Avenue. When people ask me about my "ghost," I say it must be the spirit of the man who built the house. I think D.J. Morland, Sr., its original owner, built it in 1926 with a great deal of love for his family, that he still keeps watch over it, and that maybe, on that night two years ago, he was letting us know he approved of the manner in which we were maintaining his house and of the improvements we were making on the third floor.

Whatever the explanation may be, my "friendly ghost" was calm and non-violent. And that's the way I like my life.

But it'll remain a mystery to me why he chose to roll a ball of some sort across the floor just to announce his presence. Could it be he was practising his golf putts?

I discovered more information about D.J. Morland, Sr., after that incident. He, all his sons, and all their sons, were and still are avid, renowned, prize-winning golfers!

The Vision of a Crime

Is it possible for someone who is living today to "tune in" to the events of the distant past and witness them now as they must have unfolded decades ago or even centuries ago? Mediums and psychics claim to have this power — this ability to be "sensitive" to the past. They maintain that far from being "dead," the past is very much "alive." From time to time there are disturbing reports from other people — individuals not known for their mediumistic gifts or abilities or talents or predilections — who supply some out-of-the-way evidence that they have accidentally "tuned in" to the past. A good instance of this type of sensitivity is the remarkable experience of Allen Goldenthal, B.Sc., D.V.M.

Dr. Goldenthal is a veterinarian with the City of Scarborough as well as the owner-operator of the Birchmount-Steeles Animal Clinic in that city. His account comes from a letter written to the present editor and dated 9 June 1987. It gives one pause ....

❦

I read with interest your request in the Sunday *Sun* for people with any insight into psychic phenomena to share this information with you.

If I had seen this request a year ago, I would have ignored it completely, as I was made to feel apprehensive about revealing some of the strange, unnatural events that have occurred to me over the years. In the past I shared these stories only with the closest of my friends, and even some of them were quite skeptical about them. Regardless of that, one event left me more relaxed and free to talk of my psychic experiences.

In January of 1987, I was driving north up Warden Avenue towards Highway Seven. Suddenly, up ahead, on the west side of the road, a southbound car pulled over. It was an old car, lime to faded green in colour. The driver of the car was a man. A woman got out of the car, pulling a child behind her. The woman was about six feet tall. She had a build that was almost masculine. She wore a long black dress and a high collar. The dress went down to her ankles. She had silver-platinum hair, a high-up hairdo, done in a fifties style.

At first I thought she was taking the child into the field to pee. But then I noticed the child struggling and trying to pull away. The child's hair was cut short, almost in what they used to call a Prince Valiant hairstyle. I placed the child between four and six years of age.

Then the woman started dragging the child across the road to the field on the east side. I could hear the child yelling for help, even though my windows were up. At one point she paused in the centre of the road and looked directly at me. Even though I was in the north-bound lane doing seventy kilometres, I did not seem to be getting any closer to her. It began to bother me that the cars in the southbound lane were passing by this scene as if nothing was happening.

When I came alongside the parked car, the man in the driver's seat turned to face me. He was Greek or Italian in appearance, with an oblong head, full moustache, and balding pate. His eyes were dark and cold.

Finally I had driven past the scene. I was about fifty yards down the road when the strangeness of everything suddenly dawned on me. I turned the car around and stopped. There was no one there and no longer any car. Then the name of the car — BelAir or Belmont — suddenly hit me. I don't know why, because I am not at all familiar with these automobiles.

The next day I related what had happened to me to some friends and inquired of them what I should do. Their reply was that if I had witnessed a crime I could expect to read about it in the papers in a day or so and then I could give my information to the police. Obviously nothing had happened, or at least nothing had appeared in the newspapers, so I stored the scene in my mind. I could no longer sleep well at night, however, as I was troubled by the events I had witnessed.

It dawned on me that what I had witnessed might have occurred in the past, long ago. Nevertheless I refused to tell anyone else about the vision, even though it weighed heavily on my mind. There is a certain amount of fear connected with talking about such things. As a public servant, I have to consider what my clients' reactions would be if I talked about such things. So I kept quiet about it for four months. By April I knew that I would no longer be at peace with myself unless I investigated the matter more fully. So I resolved to act.

One of my clients was a constable with 41 Division, as I remember. I asked him to do me a favour and investigate the first vision for me. I told him I believed that it took place in the time period between 1956 and 1960, that some crime or other was committed farther into the field on the east side, and that I believed the child was a boy between four and six years old.

Constable Adams did some inquiring for me and got back to me a few days later. He had created quite a stir because the oldest officer in York Region had only had twenty-five years of service on the Force. But the officer did recall coming onto the Force with an unsolved murder in the files. My client protected my interests by not telling him why he was interested in this case and where he had received his information about it until he had talked to me.

The facts of the case are these. On Jan. 9th, 1955, young Judy Carter was abducted from her Toronto home on Sherbourne Street and taken to Warden and Highway Seven where she was murdered. She was six years old. Her body was found on Jan. 11th beside the creek that at one time flowed past Warden which, at that time, was only a concession road. Somehow I had witnessed a crime that had occurred four months before I was even born! The chief of police for York who investigated the crime was Harvey Carps and he retired without ever closing the case. Constable Adams informed Metro Homicide that I was willing to talk about the case I had seen. He told me that they would call me in the future for what information I could give. But that was some time ago. I'm still waiting, but at least I can sleep at night.

Supernatural Occurrences

Tracy Austin heard me discussing paranormal phenomena on the Toronto rock station Q-107. Later that day she phoned me to tell me about a series of seemingly inexplicable events and experiences that she and some of her friends had been having in an older house in Toronto. I was intrigued and urged her to describe them in writing. Some months elapsed before she contacted me again and sent me what is, in effect, a log that conveys a sense of what has been happening to her.

I received the typed, log-like account on 8 January 1991. It is reproduced here in a slightly edited form. The author added to the log the following handwritten note which sounds somewhat mysterious: "P.S. More to add to these realistic happenings of supernatural occurrences."

My name is Tracy Austin. I'm sending you a list of supernatural occurrences that some of my friends and I have experienced.

Winter 1989

- Strange odour (stench) rises from the basement and lasts approximately fifteen minutes, disappearing as though it had never been there.
- Garbage in small bags pulled from a larger green bag (located under the basement stairs) and its contents spread out on the laundry-room floor leading to the stairs. It had been picked through (as though someone was looking for something).
- The second time, a small garbage bag was moved from one side of the basement's living-room floor to the middle of the floor and ripped open. Once again garbage was spread out

leading to the stairs. Garbage was sorted through — someone was looking for something. (The garbage never contained perishables, mainly cigarette butts, paper, beer cans, etc. The garbage was never thrown about in such a messy manner.)

- Earlier that evening, Joy and her boyfriend were in the second-floor bedroom. They heard a clattering noise and footsteps in the hallway. Joy went to check it out and the noise stopped — no one was there.

- A week later, at approximately 3:00 a.m., my boyfriend, who was living in the basement apartment at the time, heard someone walking around the main floor above him and went to see who it was. The footsteps ran up the stairs to the second floor and stopped halfway — no one was there. He returned to the basement and within five minutes the footsteps started again. He ran upstairs once again. Footsteps ran halfway upstairs and stopped — no one there.

- The following week, my boyfriend lying on the couch in the basement, hands behind his head, felt a light brush of hands — no one there.

- Within one week, Stephanie (Joy's daughter) lying on the couch on the main floor feels cold hands touching hers — no one there.

- My boyfriend would not sleep in the bedroom in the basement — it felt too uneasy. I would sleep there (with the lights on). One evening, I was awakened by a clapping noise to see a white flash above me.

- My boyfriend in the basement, Stephanie on the couch on the main floor, I went to the store and was gone approximately fifteen minutes. When I returned, you could hear someone walking around upstairs, going from room to room, rattling doorknobs, opening and closing each door in turn. Stephanie told me the disturbance started right after I left, stopped for a bit, then started up when I returned — also, no one was upstairs.

- My boyfriend ran up from the basement. We shouted upstairs to get no answer. The three of us proceeded upstairs, checked every room and closet — no one was there.

- One evening, a few weeks later, I was in the basement lying on the couch. The phone cord hanging from the coffee-table, which was right in front of me, started to wiggle. Then a bag, which was on the second shelf of the coffee-table, moved slightly — I didn't feel a breeze, I didn't feel frightened. I would like to state that there are no windows — so there is no breeze and the only way one can get in is by the doors upstairs — or the main door to the basement.

Summer 1989

- By this time my boyfriend had moved out and I wasn't in the place as often. My girlfriends and I were holding a girl-party one evening. I was in the kitchen preparing food — the butter dish suddenly flipped over.
- While the party was in progress, a guest watched a book slide off the shelf, as though someone was pushing it off — but no one was near.

Winter 1990

- Joy had moved her bedroom into the basement. One evening, Joy and her boyfriend were lying in bed, when he felt a cold hand touch his shoulder.
- A few days later, Joy, lying in bed, saw a white flash coming towards her in a striking position.
- A picture of Joy's deceased brother flew off the TV — no one near.
- Stephanie, lying in the upstairs bedroom, heard her name being called out — no one there.
- Stephanie, a week later, when no one else is home, hears the warning, "Be careful."
- The last occurrence (to date) happened on Saturday, April 14, 1990. Joy and her boyfriend were sleeping in the basement. They hear someone downstairs. Both see someone near the bed but neither bothers to call out — they are half asleep. The next day they asked the family that was living downstairs about the night before — but no one had been down there.

The points of occurrences that I have written down are true experiences. Not one has been made up.

Vision of a Large White Persian Cat

"I read, with interest, your letter in the local newspaper for stories of parapsychological happenings and think you might be interested in what I have to say."

So wrote Brenda P. Baltensperger, a resident of Goderich, Ontario, in her letter to me, dated 12 June 1990. She was responding to my open letter carried by the *London Free Press*.

I am reproducing Mrs. Baltensperger's letter because it is uncommonly interesting. How does one account for such events or experiences?

Mrs. Baltensperger ended her letter, which refers to her husband Peter, in this fashion: "I hope this is the sort of thing you're looking for. If you'd like to visit us any time, you're welcome. I can't promise any results, though, as they are unpredictable."

The next time I am in the vicinity of Goderich, I plan to pay a visit to the Baltensperger residence — but not if it's a stormy night!

In the fall of 1989, Peter and I moved into a turn-of-the-century house in Goderich. We have two cats that seemed quite content with their new home. They would accompany me to bed where I would read for an hour before going to sleep.

One evening, while Peter was away in Toronto for a few days, I went to bed around ten o'clock, as usual, to read. About ten-thirty, a storm erupted, mildly at first, and then grew in strength. I heard a low growl from Max, the cat sitting beside me. When I looked up, his hair was standing up along his back. He was wild-eyed. I assumed it was the storm and looked over to the foot of the bed where Jenny, the other cat, had been curled up asleep. She was staring wide-eyed and had crouched back as far as she could in the corner of the bed.

Suddenly, I was aware of a large white Persian cat padding across the bed towards me, its tail straight up in welcome. My first reaction was, "How the hell did that get into the house?" I knew that I had locked both doors and there was no access through the windows. About arm's-length distance, the cat disappeared. It looked as solid as one of my own cats. The storm dissipated, but the cats remained agitated, so I let them sleep with me for the night.

A few months later, early spring, I was watching television. Max was curled up asleep on the chesterfield across from me, and Jenny, likewise, beside me. The wind picked up and howled around the house. Suddenly, Max stood up, hair bristling, and stared towards the open door of the sitting room. Jenny whimpered and nestled as close and low as she could to me.

Through the open door, I could see, on the small landing at the top of the stairs, the white Persian cat. It trotted down the stairs, and as it stepped into the hallway, about four feet from where I was sitting, it disappeared.

This last appearance has been repeated twice since then, the last time about two weeks ago, when we had a really vicious storm. Unfortunately, Peter has yet to see the white Persian cat.

I have done a little research on parapsychology. (Peter and I were planning to write a book on the subject when we lived in St. Catharines.) I am convinced that the effect is a magnetic impression due to the possible magnetic lines running through our property.

I have inquired in the neighbourhood if any previous owners of the house had a white Persian cat, but no one remembers anything. If it had only been my own impression, I would have said I was hallucinating, but the cats certainly did react to something.

The couple who live in an 1897 house across the road from us also have a "ghost." They, and visitors to the house, have heard someone walking about the upstairs hallway at night. Also, Verne, who has been quite ill, has awakened at night to find a tall, severe woman in a dark-coloured Victorian dress standing over her bed. A friend of hers, who is some sort of psychic, can't bear to be in the house. She says she senses a presence that is ominous and overbearing. I told them to write to you also, but I don't know whether they will or not.

Believing in Ghosts

Daniel David Moses is a Delaware Indian who was born on the Six Nations Reserve near Brantford, Ontario. He has worked at the Harbourfront cultural complex in Toronto, and he is a member of the Committee to Re-Establish the Trickster, a Native group active in preserving traditional lore and learning. He is a published poet and the author of the theatrical play *Coyote City*. Indeed, dramatic script-writing is what the following article is all about.

"Spooky" is the preface to an essay of the same name which goes into detail concerning the writing of Moses's play *Coyote City*. The memoir appeared in the Toronto literary tabloid *What,* Dec. 1989.

Spooky? Yes. That's the word.

Spooky.

It was last year, May, and we were rehearsing my play, *Coyote City,* soon to open at the Native Canadian Centre of Toronto. And it must have been a Tuesday well into the rehearsal period, a first day back to work after our Sunday and Monday off. And one of the actresses came to me and told me that over the weekend she had gone home to the reserve and to Longhouse and that afterwards she had had a vision and that it was because of my play.

Rings of fire burning dry fields of grain is the image I remember, but I could be mistaken. I wasn't giving her vision my entire attention. Part of my mind was of course already at the table inside the rehearsal hall, wondering how we would get the car and bus scene to work. Another was focussing on my actress's face, on her wide and beautiful eyes, her excitement. And one part of my mind was standing still, thrilled and pleased to be privy to these personal experiences of the supernatural.

Which of course meant that one further part of my mind was in panic, retreat, covering its ears, not wanting any more of this spooky stuff. My actress's story was only the most recent in a series of spiritual experiences that the more traditionally minded members of my cast and crew had been bringing to rehearsal, bringing to the play, to *Coyote City* and of course to me.

Coyote City can be described most simply as a ghost story. It's structured as a journey and a chase from a reserve into a city. Its impetus is the love Lena, a young woman, has for a young man she doesn't know is dead. The play begins with a monologue from the young man, the character Johnny, whom we, the audience, only later discover is already a ghost.

In developing the story for the play, the subtext, the world that the words should imply from the stage or the page, I was surprised to find that I was afraid to make that simple decision. My progress came to a halt as I tried to develop a psychological explanation, tried to say that the character Johnny was a figment of Lena's imagination, that she was mad. In my fear, I had stumbled into Romantic cliché and it was getting me nowhere.

Why was I afraid to simply decide that the ghost was as much a character as the rest? My intuition told me I had to make that proverbial imaginative leap if the play was to work. I had to believe in the ghost as much as I did in the girl or her mother if I was to do justice to the story, the play and the audience.

I have seen girls. I have seen mothers. I have a mother. They're part of my existence and easy to believe in. But I have never seen a ghost. And I don't mean a ghost like my character Johnny or Casper or like in *Ghostbusters* or the Holy Ghost. And I don't mean, at least at this point in my story, a ghost in a dream. I mean wide-awake experience of a spirit, what those so-called scientists working at the fringes of our knowledge have labelled paranormal.

I grew up on a farm on the Six Nations lands along the Grand River near Brantford in southern Ontario. I grew up nominally Anglican in a community of various Christian sects and of the Longhouse, the Iroquoian traditional religious and political system. These form the largely unarticulated base of my understanding of the world.

I grew up hearing on occasion ghost stories rooted in that community, stories I only paid small attention to, because I was being educated to have — let's call it — a western mind, to balance being a good Judaeo-Christian with being scientific. Ghost stories may be thrilling and amusing, art may be thrilling and amusing and sometimes prestigious, but we only really believe in what we can see with our own eyes and measure with our own hands.

How could I possibly believe in a character, write a character who was a ghost? We're advised to write about what we know and at that point I was quite sure I didn't know anyone who was, well, dead.

What I did at the time was sidestep the existential issue. I had to have the ghost or the play would be dead. That I knew. What I did was try to use my so-called western mind. I argued with myself: Art is, after all, artificial and not a question of believing but of doing. So go ahead and do the ghost. Construct it. What's metaphor for, after all? This death stuff is only symbolic. Come on, you coward. It's only a story, only words.

Only words.

The Sticky Man

Donna Schillaci, a mother who lives in Oakville, Ontario, saw a letter from me in a local newspaper, inviting readers to send me their true-life "ghost stories."

Ms. Schillaci had a scary experience to relate, one that involved not only herself but also her young son Adam. She sent me one account of "the sticky man" on 5 June 1900 and then, on 22 June 1900, a second, fuller account. It is the second account that is being reproduced here.

One cannot help but wonder: Is there a "sticky man" in the basement of her house? Is the spirit there still, biding time until the appropriate moment when it will reappear ... ?

June 22, 1990
Dear Mr. Colombo:

As I'm writing this letter to you I can't help but wonder if anyone could possibly understand or even believe what both my small son Adam and I experienced. But I guess that's what you want to hear about.

About a year and a half ago, when Adam was almost two years old, we moved into an older house. I think the house was between eighty and ninety years old. I never felt anything unusual about the house when we first moved in, but as time went on I felt a heaviness about the walls. I ignored the feeling.

Then one day, while in the basement, I felt the heaviness again. It was stronger this time. I noticed the furnace room door was more open than usual. Perhaps in vacuuming I had bumped into it. I couldn't remember.

And then I saw it — its form transparent so I could see the bricks of the wall through it. What caught my eye most of all was the figure's face. It was male. His eyes were leering and devilishly playful. He seemed to be challenging me — and in a frightening way.

I ran back upstairs as fast as I could. I tried to pretend I had imagined it all. It was hard. The bathroom, the shower, the tub were all down there in the basement, and when I went down there, I had to feel comfortable.

Thereafter, as best as possible, I tried to keep the furnace room door closed. Some days I felt something in there, other days nothing. Gradually I began to forget about it all.

Then one day, while I was showering in the basement, Adam screamed from outside the shower curtains. It was a horrible scream, one I had never heard from him before. I shakingly opened the curtain and asked him what was wrong. He screamed, "Mommie, a sticky man on the wall!"

I quickly climbed out of the tub, looked around, and tried as best as I could to see something where he pointed with his tiny finger. There was nothing there. He kept saying, "Sticky man, sticky man!" Instead of asking Adam too many questions, I knelt beside him and told him it was all pretend. He calmed down.

The first time this happened my explanation was enough. Yet it happened two more times. And always it was a "sticky man" he saw. Early one evening Adam was dancing in the kitchen. He got strangely delirious with joy and laughter. With both arms waving to the music he loudly cried out, "Sticky man is coming upstairs!"

Frightened, I yelled out powerfully for the "sticky man" to go back downstairs and to leave us alone. I ranted, raged, and repeatedly stamped my feet at the edge of the basement steps. I stated it wasn't fair. He was frightening a little child. I never let on he was scaring the skin off my face, too.

From that evening on, we were no longer bothered by his appearances. And if I did "feel" him around, I bravely and confidently spoke out. My commands were simple. Go away. Sometimes my tone would soften and I would pray for this poor soul to find its way back to God because I instinctively sensed he was lost. But I always made it very clear — I didn't want him around.

I try not to talk to Adam about his experiences. I have to admit I'd love to know how much he does remember. Six months ago he asked if Mommy remembered the "sticky man." A jolt of panic sped up my spine. I looked sadly into his clear hazel eyes, quickly nodded "yes," and changed the subject. I don't want him to be afraid of life, and I don't want him believing in ghosts. I'm firm about that. Yet it's too late.

He's constantly zapping ghosts with an imaginary gun. Maybe he's lucky: he hasn't associated "sticky man" with ghosts. I really don't know.

As for myself, I still feel my stomach turn whenever I talk about it. No matter how much courage I mustered up in facing it, there was always fear not far behind. But I have to admit I'm stronger for having stood up to a ... can I say it? ... a ghost!

Sincerely,
Donna Schillaci

$\mathscr{D}uel$ of the $\mathscr{S}pirits$

This is a short account of an unusual experience that took place in the living room in an apartment in the Cambridge area of Ontario. The account was written by a housewife who prefers to remain anonymous. She has artistic ability, is a musician, and has illustrated what she saw. Her original drawing is between eight and nine inches in size.

This account of her experience is reproduced from the handwritten text included in the *Report of the Cambridge U.F.O. Research Group*, Issue No. 37, Aug. 1991. The editor of the Report is Bonnie Wheeler, to whom thanks are due for preserving this account and for allowing it to be reprinted here in a slightly edited form.

Date: March, 1990
Time: 11:30 a.m.

While vacuuming the dining area of my apartment, I suddenly felt pressure exerted on both of my shoulders — pushing me backwards — trying to trip me and make me fall over the canister of the vacuum cleaner which was directly behind me.

I *hollered*, "Stop it!" and the pressure stopped.

I didn't see anything, just felt pressure.

So I turned the vacuum off and went and sat down in a chair at one end of the living room. Something caught my eye at the other end of the living room — a round object, slowly rising. (I saw it when it was level with the keys of my organ.) It was not spinning, just gracefully rising. It went right through the Tiffany hanging lamp and out the corner of the living room. It was a charcoal colour, had a slight space at the top between two bone-like partitions. One bone was larger than the other — looked something like a blade bone of a blade roast. The

216

perimeter looked feathery and light. I had no fear of this orb — rather a feeling of security.

I've concluded that there were two spirits there — one wishing me harm, and the orb defending me against that harm.

Enclosed is a rough sketch — the object was about a third again as large.

I do not wish to partake in any meetings, etc., regarding this phenomenon. I feel it was a very personal encounter. Perhaps the "good spirit" even went "out on a limb" to protect me — maybe — who knows?

A Ghost Called Matthew

I was the guest of Bill Carroll on the radio show "Toronto Talks" on 8 Feb. 1994. The show is heard on AM 640 and Q107 and has a wide listenership. Bill and I talked with seven listeners. We could have talked with seventy listeners, as the switchboard was lit up with incoming calls like a Christmas tree!

About a week later I received the following letter from Jim Young, of Barrie, Ontario. At the time of the incidents described in this account, Jim was working as a data processing operations manager and Shirley was a lab secretary in Barrie. Then they moved to Eganville and then back to Barrie. The account speaks for itself. And it speaks volumes!

February 10, 1994
Dear Mr. Colombo:

Yesterday I tuned into the Bill Carroll show and was disappointed to discover I had missed the first part of the show featuring you as the guest. The topic, as you know, was ghosts and poltergeists. This is the reason why I am writing to you.

I am submitting our "ghost experiences" to you for your evaluation and possible inclusion in your new book about ghosts in Ontario.

It started here in Barrie in 1990, shortly after my wife Shirley and I purchased a home on Wilson Court. In the beginning, of course, we were unprepared. We didn't make any connection between what was occurring and we didn't anticipate future incidents. So we didn't make careful notes as to the dates or the order of the events. They are described here the way they happened, though not necessarily in chronological order.

At our house on Wilson Court, when we were in the master bedroom or the main bathroom, we would often hear music. It was usually a little louder in the bathroom, which was in the middle of the house. It did not have an outside wall. The music wasn't clearly distinguishable, but sounded like the faint signal of a modern radio station or stereo without any commentary. On a couple of occasions we tried to trace the source of the music by going outside or opening windows to see if a neighbour was playing music loudly nearby, but we could hear nothing, even though we could hear the music inside these rooms before and after checking outside.

We used the middle bedroom in our house as a small study in which I had my computer set up. One evening the lights and power went out in that room. After checking the panel box, we discovered no switches had been tripped. Even more peculiar was the fact that the TV in our bedroom, which was on the same circuit as the computer, would still work. I mentioned this to my brother-in-law who is an electrician and he suggested there might be a short somewhere that should be checked out. We didn't follow up on his recommendation. After a couple of weeks the power mysteriously returned to the room, and we had no further problems with the power for the rest of our stay in that house.

The "spookiest" event, however, happened one night when I was not home. I was working on a special project at work that required me to stay there all night. In the middle of the night, Shirley was awakened when she felt someone leaning on her pillow and pulling her hair. At first she thought I had come home early, but when she turned to look, there was no one there. Shirley immediately called me at work to tell me what had happened, as it had given her quite a scare. When she spoke to me, Shirley told me that she had a creepy feeling that someone or something was there.

In 1992 we moved to a small home near Eganville where most of our "ghostly" experiences have happened. Shirley had a ceramic doll in the shape of a little girl who was lying on her side praying. Its mate had been broken by her abusive common-law husband in her previous relationship. On two different days, we returned home to find the doll on the shelf turned 180 degrees and facing the wall. The first time this happened I assumed she had turned the doll, perhaps while dusting it, and Shirley had assumed that I had done it for some reason or other. When we talked to each other about it, however, we both confessed that we had not touched the doll. The only explanation we could come up with was that it had been done by the ferrets. During one of their runs out of their cage they might have disturbed the doll. We couldn't really comprehend this happening, as there were several other figurines on the same shelf, none of which had been moved. Anyone who has ferrets would quickly realize that, clumsy in their investigations, some of the other figurines would certainly have been moved if not knocked off this narrow shelf.

The second time this happened, however, we noticed the dust on the glass shelf on which it sat had not been disturbed and the outline of its proper position was clearly visible. We were now certain it was not the ferrets, as we had checked the shelf frequently, particularly after their last run, so they could not have moved the doll without disturbing the dust.

Shortly after we moved into this house, we painted the back doors and door jam. As it was summer, we left the inside door open at all times, except at night. On the way out one day, I noticed deep scratch marks on the inside of the jam that had recently been painted. The scratches were inside the two doors and therefore could not have been caused by an animal from outside. At that time we had not only the two pet ferrets but also a cocker spaniel puppy. It would have been impossible for any of them to have caused these scratches, as they were far too deep for even the puppy to have caused them. He just simply didn't have the weight or strength to dig that deeply into the wood. Furthermore, the scratches were probably too high for even the puppy to have reached. In fact, there are scratch marks on the door that our puppy did make, which are hardly visible on the paint. There is absolutely no comparison of these two scratch marks. We have not repaired the door jam, and the scratch marks remain there to this day.

Around this time, one of our two canaries died, for no apparent reason. I buried him in a shallow grave in the backyard. A couple of weeks later, his mate also died, and I decided it would be appropriate to bury them together. I returned to the spot where I had buried the first canary to discover he was lying on top of his grave, although there was no evidence the ground had been dug up or disturbed since I had dug his grave there. Although it was starting to decay, the bird did not appear to be mutilated, as it would have been had a wild animal or neighbour's cat or dog dug it up. It would have eaten the dead bird or carried it off.

I have a bad habit of often being excessively neat and organized, to the point where I will face the canned goods in our cupboards or the beer in our refrigerator. One morning I noticed the loose change that I had left on our dresser a couple of days earlier, neatly lined up in rows of pennies, dimes, and nickels. It was something that would not be out of character for me. However, I had not done this. In fact, if I *had* lined them up, I would have placed them in neat piles, as opposed to laying them out side by side as they were. When I asked Shirley why *she* lined the coins up, she told me she had noticed them but thought I had done it.

On the top shelf in our bedroom clothes closet, we keep a box of massage oils that I use to give Shirley back rubs. Upon noticing one of the bottles sitting on Shirley's dresser, I assumed she was hinting that it had been a while since I had given her a back rub. However, when I confronted Shirley about this, again she had assumed it was *I* who had got the oil out.

By now we realized that we had a presence in our house. We affectionately named our ghost "Matthew" for no particular reason other than that it was a name that just popped into my head.

As I slept in one morning, I woke to hear my name whispered very clearly in my ear. I had been awake earlier and knew Shirley was already up, but I had gone back to sleep. I assumed Shirley had come back into the room but I rolled over to find myself alone. I immediately got up and went to the far end of the house where Shirley was and discovered she had not been even close to that end of the house since she had risen some time earlier.

I began on occasion to see Matthew as small "wisps" of white light floating across the rooms. Most often, these sightings were made from the corner of my eye and disappeared as I snapped my head around for a better look. One night, however, as I lay awake in bed, I clearly saw Matthew float past the clothes closet. Our house was isolated in the country where it is very dark at night. No cars were travelling down the road at the time and there was no light source that I could find that would have caused a reflection. Matthew did not appear to look like I would have imagined a "ghost" should look like, based on what I had read up to that time. However, a short while ago, I saw a television program about some people who had captured some ghosts on video. Their ghosts were very similar to Matthew, with the exception that theirs moved very quickly. There were a number of them and they were slightly larger than Matthew.

Our cocker spaniel, during this time, would often walk around the house with his nose in the air, as if following some aroma around the room.

In the bathroom, I once heard scratching coming from some spot nearby. The ferrets' cage was right beside the bathroom, so I first thought they were awake and making the noise. When I left the bathroom, however, I discovered both ferrets sound asleep. Yet the scratching continued. I didn't mention this to Shirley at the time because I was afraid we might have unwanted rodents in the crawl space, although before that time, and any time since, I have never found a trace of anything other than insects in the crawl space, a space that is well sealed with a concrete foundation and close-fitting doors.

Shirley has often felt a tugging on the covers at the bottom corner of the bed on her side of the house and occasionally still does. (Although we have since moved to Barrie, we continue to visit the house in Eganville whenever we can.)

In July of 1993, we moved back to Barrie to a basement apartment, where we are presently living. This Christmas past, we had a few candy canes hanging from various places, including a cardboard box which is temporarily serving as a filing cabinet for me. Shirley got up one morning to discover a candy cane, the only one different from all the others, lying in the middle of the floor. We no longer have our dog, and the ferrets are locked in their cage and only allowed out for supervised periods during the day.

About a month following this incident, I got up one morning and found one of Shirley's negligees, which usually hangs on a hook in the bedroom, lying in the middle of the living-room floor, not far from where Shirley had found the candy cane.

I discussed this with a friend once, who told me that ghosts didn't normally follow people from house to house. Another friend, however, asked, "Who makes up the rules for ghosts? Can't they do just about anything they want?"

I am not suggesting that there is no logical explanation for some of these occurrences. Furthermore, they may or may not be related to each other. I have merely made a note of them for interest's sake.

If you have any questions about these incidents, please don't hesitate to contact me at any time. Should you wish to include them in your new book, please feel free to do so.

Sincerely,
Jim Young

George or Helen

Janet Warfield is the pseudonym I have given the writer of this letter, and Central Oshawa is the generalized location of her house with its resident spook. Whether it is called George or Helen, the spook is a specialist in the production of effects that seem silly and mischievous. Perhaps the spook is best described as a poltergeist.

I took part in a phone-in programme on the subject of ghosts. Janet Warfield heard the show and later phoned me and described these occurrences. I urged her to describe them in detail in a letter.

Here is that letter.

March 3, 1994
Dear Mr. Colombo:

Further to our telephone conservation of February 21st, 1994, I have made note of the occurrences of oddities that have taken place at our residence in Central Oshawa.

As I stated, we moved into the house in June of 1992, and after approximately three weeks, in the early morning hours, we were awakened by the sound of dishes tinkling. We immediately called out, "Who's there?" and rushed downstairs. We checked both doors, which were soundly locked. After checking the main floor and basement level, we noticed the buffet door in the dining room was open and the dishes which had been stacked inside on the bottom shelf (including plates, glasses and vases) were sitting on the floor, placed as they had been in the buffet. My husband and I both expressed our surprise, returned the dishes to the buffet and returned to bed.

The next occurrence was 6-8 weeks later at, I believe, approximately 11:00 p.m. during a week night. I was ironing in the basement while watching TV. My husband was in bed, two levels up, at the time. The remote control for the television was on the desk close to the edge of same but not hanging over. The remote control *turned over*, and fell off the desk and when it hit the floor, button side down, the TV shut off. I immediately pulled the plug on the iron and raced up to bed. Many, many times over the years we have dropped the remote control on the floor button side down, but never has the TV shut off.

After this point in time, while entertaining friends and discussing these incidents, their children nicknamed our mysterious being George. Later, however, noticing the interest George displayed in the dishes in the buffet, and based on a dream that I had that I was talking to the ghost, I insisted it be called Helen.

My dream occurred while we were at our cottage in the late summer of 1992. I could see myself sitting at the table talking to a young woman of thirty or so who was dressed in long skirts and an apron, and I recall she had brilliant blue eyes. She stated her name was Helen. She said she met her husband during the Civil War when she nursed his wounds, and following the war they wed and came to Canada to settle. She stated her husband was killed in a freak accident while building their homestead. Following the death of her husband, she left to return to her home state, got lost and never reached home. She asked me if she could stay with us. I replied yes and then woke up. I found myself sitting on the edge of the bed. I immediately woke my husband and told him about the dream.

We have never performed a search of the title of our property, other than the usual forty-year search undertaken when we purchased the house and property, so we have no idea of the status of the land prior to the time the modern house was built.

Several things have happened between about September 1992 and June 1993, which I will list below:

1. There was a loud knocking on the closet door in the basement, heard by my husband and immediately reported to me. We checked and found nothing in the closet that could have fallen and produced a knocking noise. Later that same evening, loud knocking on the closet door was again heard, but by me this time. My husband and I joked that we had accidentally locked George in the closet and he was trying to get out.

2. My father-in-law stayed overnight, sleeping on the pullout in the basement. He was awakened in the night by a voice. The voice was very low and he was unable to ascertain whether it was a male or a female voice he heard talking. He insisted he was awake at the time. He said that the stereo was on at the time so he didn't bother to listen carefully to the words being spoken. He added that the stereo was on because the red power light was on, but the power light is always on. Upon checking, we ascertained that the stereo was not on.

3. One morning, at approximately 4:45 a.m., when I was in the bathroom getting ready to go to work, I distinctly heard the sound of someone next to me scratching an arm or a leg. That sound and the thought that something or someone was standing next to me made me

feel rather uneasy.

4. One evening in the Winter of 1993, we arrived home from work and discovered that the toilet-paper roll was partially unrolled. It had unrolled across the bathroom floor and out into the upstairs hallway. On another evening in May of the same year, I believe it was, we arrived home from work to find that the Kleenex box in the upstairs bathroom had been emptied (it was only half full at the time) and clumps of two or three tissues were lying around the bathroom and hallway. It appeared that they had been scrunched up in a person's hand.

5. On Mother's Day, 1993, we were visited by my parents, and we discussed the fact that nothing had happened since early Spring of 1993. The following Tuesday, we arrived home from work and that was when we discovered the Kleenex box had been emptied. That same night, my husband got up early in the morning to go to the bathroom. Sitting on the toilet one can peek around the corner and see into our bedroom. When we had moved in, we tore out the wall between the two adjoining bedrooms in order to enlarge the master bedroom, thereby leaving a trench in the walls and the floor all the way around the room. As the floor was not yet covered in and was somewhat hazardous, my husband had turned on the light in the bedroom. The switch is located near the door. While sitting on the toilet, he noticed that the bedroom light had gone out. He asked me why I had shut it off and I informed him he could see I was in bed and hadn't gotten up to shut the light off. He stated the bulbs must have burned out or they were loose, but when we checked the switch, we found it had been turned to the off position. We joked about George having done it. In the morning, when the alarm went off at 5:30 a.m., we didn't immediately jump out of bed, as is usual, but instead, lay there for a while. After seven or eight minutes, the light turned on by itself, at which point we got up and stated something to the effect, "Knock it off, George, we're getting up."

6. A couple of times, while watching TV in the basement and doing laundry at the same time, the door between the laundry room and the family room has shut by itself, as if to say, "Shut the door, I can't hear the television." This has not happened recently.

7. The last occurrence took place on the evening of December 25th, 1993. My sister-in-law was scraping food off the plates into the garbage, when she heard a "growling" sound coming from the corner where the stove is located. When she looked around upon hearing the sound, the upper cupboard door just to the left of the stove was in the process of closing, at which point I walked into the kitchen. She men-

tioned the noise to me and said she hadn't touched the cupboard door, which had obviously opened prior to her seeing it closing.

To date, all remains quiet. We often joke that we eagerly await the next occurrence.

For resale reasons, etc., I would appreciate it if you did not mention our names or address in the book, should you choose to include these details. Our location in Oshawa is best described as Central Oshawa.

We shall await your response.

Yours truly,
Janet Warfield

Ghost of the Great Dane

Beverley Ann Akers lives in Midland, Ontario. She did not hear me when I was talking about ghosts on Radio Station AM 640 with Bill Carroll, but a friend of hers did and told her I had a sympathetic ear. In any case, Beverley contacted me and told me that her house is haunted by "man's best friend." Her ghost dog, Pony, is apparently Beverley's best friend. I convinced Beverley she should type up her story, and so she did. Here is her letter with the "atrocious" spelling corrected! (The spelling wasn't as atrocious as all that!)

Mar. 1 / 94
Dear John:

I'm sorry that I haven't gotten this letter off to you sooner. Usually when I procrastinate there is a reason, as you will see when you read the ending to this story. At any rate, here is the "spirit" story you asked me to send along.

I bought the house in which I am now living on Fitton Street in Midland, Ontario, mainly because I had a good feeling about it. After settling in, I found that if I looked back at the front window, as I drove away from the house, I would have the sense that someone was looking out the window. There was no one I could really see, just a sense that someone was there, looking out.

In January 1993, I was sitting, late at night, at the dining-room table, talking to one of my boarders. I looked into the kitchen and saw a brown mist cross in front of the fridge. I decided I was tired, and so I went to bed without giving it another thought.

It was at about this time that my Burmese cat, Psycho, began to act strangely. He would suddenly wake up from his sleep, put his ears back, and in a roundabout way make his way to the basement. He would often stay there for two to three hours. This is totally out of character for him.

One evening I happened to be home alone, watching a good movie on TV. I made a quick dash to the washroom and left the door open. What can I say? It was a good movie, and I didn't want to miss any of the dialogue! I looked out the door and down the hallway in time to see a brown mist come up the basement stairs, turn right, and go into the kitchen.

While I was trying to shove my heart back down my throat, I noticed Psycho making his dash downstairs. My initial thought was that I was not really home alone.

My son Adam came to visit over the Easter weekend. One night he stayed up to watch a movie. When I got up in the morning, the coat closet and front doors were wide open. Since no one else was home, I did the motherly thing and scolded him for leaving the doors open. He explained that, at approximately 3:00 a.m., the closet opened, as if someone were standing there. I suggested that the cat might have been in the closet, but Adam said that the cat had been in the basement when he came in from the garage after having a cigarette. (No one smokes in the house.) Who or what had opened the closet door?

Friends suggested that I use a pendulum and ask questions that could be answered yes or no. Imagine me, a skeptic about pendulums, actually using one. The pendulum answered the questions I put to it: No, whatever it was wasn't here to scare me; no, it didn't come with the house; yes, it did follow me here; yes, it did open the closet door ....

Well, that did it for me! I put the pendulum away.

A month after this, I learned that the boarders in the house would be leaving. The idea of being all alone in the house, especially at night, with a cowardly cat and an unnamed spirit, was too much for me. I decided to address the spirit.

I explained to it that I knew it meant well and that it hadn't hurt me. But I asked it if it could leave me alone for a while, at least until I got used to being alone in the house.

Well, it left, and I immediately felt guilty. Nothing strange has happened since then.

John, this is a follow up, as a result of my procrastination. So help me, it's true.

On February 27, I went to a health-awareness day held in Barrie. There were various displays for alternative therapies. At the suggestion of friends and because I am fascinated with UFOs and such things, I approached a gentleman from Toronto who was there who specializes in crystal and sound therapy. (Sound therapy is really something new; I guess I'm getting better at not bursting out in laughter at some of the New Age things I see.)

At any rate, I explained to the gentleman what I hoped he could help me accomplish in the fifteen minutes he allotted to me for a reading. When he finished, he very quietly asked me if, as a child, I had ever had a large dog, and if I had, what its colour was. He sensed that this dog was around me. You could have knocked me off the chair with a feather. He repeated three or four times that the dog didn't know it was dead.

Pony was the name of the Great Dane I had had as a small child. Pony was brindle in colour and bigger than I was. He was my protector and no stranger could come near me when Pony was around. My parents gave him to friends who owned a farm. Not long afterwards, he ran out onto the road and was killed.

When I got home on Sunday, I went through the house, calling him, apologizing for not understanding the situation. I told him that he could stay if he wished, but not to scare the other animals. At the risk of becoming certifiable, I again resorted to the pendulum. If animal spirits can make pendulums move, then Pony is here in the house, has been here, and doesn't want to leave.

When I went to bed, I settled down to read. I had to fight with the cat for my spot on the bed. The cat was sleeping when he suddenly sat up, walked to the edge of the bed, and stood there for about three minutes, staring down at the floor. Then he resettled and went back to sleep. My only assumption is that the cat sensed that the spirit was back and was lying beside my bed.

I know this sounds unbelievable and I sometimes wonder why these things happen to me, but I do swear it's all true. I am sorry that I am so long-winded, but that's the way I am — ask my friends.

I also apologize for the atrocious typing (this is my second corrected version). Use what you need out of all this and good luck!

One thing I do know is that I have my hands full with the complete food chain I have residing in my house: lizard / turtle / canary / cockatiel / cat / one live dog / and one dead dog's spirit.

Lord, help the next teen who thinks he wants to bring home another part of the food chain!

Sincerely yours,
Beverley Ann Akers

Hunting Henry's Ghost

Some people's faces light up at the mention of the word "ghosts." Other people's faces grow dim at the suggestion of spirits and spectres.

Kathryn Newman's face lights up when she hears the word "ghosts." She is a freelance journalist. She contacted me for any information I might have about ghosts in Toronto, especially those that might inhabit buildings in the city's west end.

As it happened, I was able to draw her attention to some reports of ghosts and hauntings in that quarter, one of the older parts of Metropolitan Toronto. She was able to use some of them in her survey of "local haunts." It appeared in the Oct. 1993 community newspaper the *Villager* and was called "Looking for Ghosts? They're Right in Your Backyard."

In her account she mentioned the haunting of the Royal Canadian Legion's Hall on Royal York Road below the Queensway. It is believed that the ghost of a young soldier, named Henry, is trapped in the hundred-year-old building.

Kathryn was plainly attracted to the idea of Henry, so she decided to devote one night of her life to seeking him out. She did so and described the experience in a second, personal story which she called "A First-hand Encounter with Henry's Ghost." It first appeared in the *Oakville Journal Record*, 31 Oct. 1979.

Here is the personal story.

May your face light up reading it!

❧❧❦❧❧

Ghosts have always been a part of my life.

As a young child I would sit at my grandmother's knee and listen to her weave stories of haunted spectres and eerie happenings. At the end of each story, she would tell me that when you are dealing with ghosts, you have to be ready for the unexpected.

As a freelance writer, I have learned to expect the unexpected. However, no amount of stories, training, or experience could have ever prepared me for spending a night in "the haunted Legion Hall" on Royal York Road.

Originally the structure was built, and named Eden Court, by Edward Stock. The Stock family was one of the first families of settlers to populate the area which is now considered part of the Bloor West Village in the west end of Toronto. In its heyday the building was an attractive house with a sprawling porch, verandah and beautiful gardens.

There is a shadier side to the Stock House. During the 1930s it was used as a gambling hall and meeting place for the criminal element. Gangster Abe Orpen owned the building, and when it was renovated in 1966, bullet holes were found in the doors.

When Harry MacIsaac, the assistant Stewart at the Legion informed me that permission had been granted for me to spend the night looking for the ghost of Henry, I almost jumped right out of my skin. The veterans and staff at the Legion had named the ghost Henry after a boarder who at one time resided in the attic.

I immediately recognized that I needed someone to accompany me on my adventure. It would have to be a person who could verify any ghostly phenomena and not jump to conclusions. My first and only choice was Sylvia Peda. She had a background in journalism, and we had worked together on many stories. Armed with notepads, a tape recorder, pens, talcum powder, and a flashlight with new batteries, we stepped through the legion door into the unknown.

Bill Lazenby, president of Branch 217 Legion Hall, escorted us through the building and up onto the third floor. This was the floor that had the reputation of being the most haunted.

"There is something I should tell you. The light switch is at the end of the hall, and you have to walk down in darkness to turn it on. The only escape is by the main staircase. If you are cornered, you have had it."

Thankfully, the president turned on the switch for us and wished us luck. We were on our own.

Sylvia smiled one of the sly smiles that she is most famous for. With a gleam in her eye, she reminded me that we would probably be found with our heads at the bottom of the stairs, our faces frozen in hideous expressions of terror.

Despite Sylvia's bizarre sense of humour, I was glad that she was with me. I would not want to be in this place alone. Besides, when the atmosphere became too weird for my liking, I could always send Sylvia into the darkness to switch on the light.

We had to decide whether we wanted to conduct our investigations in the dark. After much discussion, we both decided that it might be wiser to leave the light on for the time being. While we were debating the issue of the light, we both became aware of a noticeable chill. It became intensely cold, and then Henry turned out the light. We tore down the stairs sensing Henry at our heels. It was then that I realized that I had left some of my equipment upstairs.

The second floor is set up as an entertainment area. Small tables are scattered along the side of the large room. At the back is a stage. We felt comfortable there. We convinced ourselves that we were safe and that nothing could happen on this floor. We relaxed.

We needed to gather our thoughts. "There is so much history here," Sylvia commented.

"Yes," I responded. "But it's more than that. When you think of what could have happened here with the gambling. Hey, maybe Henry's still up there in the wall," I chuckled uneasily.

There is a fine line between fantasy and reality. It was important to try to restrain my imagination. We needed facts, and we both knew it was time to go back upstairs and face Henry head on.

With courage and determination, we marched up the stairs. A ghostly green glow shone in the hall, and the doorway to the third floor was cloaked in darkness. Somewhere between the second and the third floor, I lost my courage. But it was my turn to brave the hall and turn the light on. I tried not to notice the room getting colder. I switched on the light and then I heard footsteps and thumping right behind me.

Sylvia sprinkled talcum powder on the floor, and we ran for our lives. This time I remembered my equipment. A cold breeze passed by us in the entrance on the second floor. We stood for a few seconds, trying to determine its direction, and then we returned to the safety of our table in the entertainment area.

Traditionally, the witching hour is the time when spirits are said to be most active. As the clock on the second floor ticked towards midnight, I wondered just how much more activity I could endure in one night.

For the next half hour we listened to the building creak and moan. Cold breezes invaded our space. Unusual noises and whispers were heard coming from the second-floor bar. I experienced itching on my hands and feet. It felt like I had been exposed to fiberglass.

Sylvia became so cold that she was forced to put her winter jacket on. Then, at 12:30 a.m., she was touched on the head by an unseen entity. It took her several seconds to recover from her encounter with the ghost.

We began to discuss our next move, and just as we were about to enter the stairway hall, the toilet on the third floor flushed by itself. Sylvia and I grabbed hold of each other's arms for support. We held our breath. "I didn't know ghosts went to the bathroom," Sylvia commented.

The hours ticked away. We began to discuss our departure. We had seen enough ghostly phenomena to last a lifetime, and we both sensed it was time to go. It was important to leave the building the way we found it. That meant all the lights in the building needed to be shut off.

For the last time we climbed the stairs to the third floor. I felt the ghost's presence ahead of me. I was not nervous. In fact, I sensed a sadness. Sylvia did not sense the same thing. Her sense was one of a spectre who was lost, caught between worlds.

White powder footsteps had formed in the talcum which we had sprinkled on the floor. The steps started on one side of the room, travelled in one direction, and stopped suddenly. I flipped the light off, and darted through the hallway, and down the stairs. I did not look back.

One by one we turned off lights until we reached the rear door of the second floor. That was the way out. I felt relieved to be outside the building. It was good to feel the cold fresh air. I turned, and waved goodbye to the upper back windows of the building. I knew somehow that Henry was watching us leave.

As I drove the car to the front of the building, I decided to stop to take a few pictures. Sylvia and I climbed out. I was fiddling with my camera, when a circular flash of blue light shone from behind the centre curtained window on the third floor. Several seconds later the curtains on the second floor parted ever so slightly.

Upon reflection, Sylvia and I both believe that this was Henry's way of saying goodbye. One thing is for certain. Whoever Henry is, he gave us an experience neither of us will ever forget.

Trick or treat.

Short Circuit

By tradition, ghosts and spirits of the departed are associated with phantom footsteps, cold spots, creepy feelings, and other related phenomena. They are not widely associated with electromagnetic effects. Yet if the presence of a ghost can produce the sound of a footfall or a sudden drop in temperature, it should certainly be able to snap the thin filament of an electric lightbulb or upset the delicate operation of a facsimile machine.

Are there fifty lightbulbs in your house? If so, how often do the bulbs burn out? You will ponder such questions after reading Jack Kapica's account of odd and unusual experiences in the wake of the passing of a friend and tenant. The author of the account, a native of Montreal, is a long-time Toronto resident. He is a writer for the *Globe and Mail*, having served as its book editor and its religion columnist. He and his wife, the writer Eve Drobot, live in the Riverdale area of the city.

⚜

Losing Paul was more than losing a friend. It wasn't until he died that we realized we had lost a member of the family.

We had shared a home for seventeen years. We met when he was recovering from his second busted marriage, and he said he just wanted to learn how to live alone. No problem, I said, I wasn't looking for company, just someone to help carry the cost.

And so we worked out an arrangement. We shared a house and the entrance to the house, but Paul's rooms were discreet, as was his schedule. He worked as an editor at a newspaper, and started at three in the afternoon, and returned only after closing down the bars in the wee hours. When the front door slammed, we knew it had to be 1:35 a.m., which represented bar-closing hour plus a five-minute cab ride.

We never socialized actively. Sometimes, days would pass when we didn't see him, and we could tell he was at home only because the mail had been sorted. It wasn't until my wife found him stretched out on his bed, dead of a mercifully sudden heart attack at the age of fifty-three, that I realized he was like the brother you see twice a year, at Thanksgiving and Christmas, and whose company you enjoy so much you swear you've got to do this more often. But somehow you never do.

That awful day, we had to wait for several hours in the company of two policemen for the coroner to come by to declare that everything was as it appeared. Well, everything indeed was as it appeared to everyone but the cat, who over the years had developed a special relationship with Paul. He came up to Paul's room, jumped upon his bed, and curled up against his already cold body and began to purr.

Like many single men, Paul had simplified everything in his life, from his wardrobe (jeans) to his furniture (black leather) to his passions (the Blue Jays) to his diet (peanut butter, beer, and cigarettes). It was the diet that killed him two games into the 1993 American League Championship Series.

Over the years Paul often commented on how much he enjoyed our living arrangement. He even welcomed the arrival of my daughter who for the first five years of her life refused to sleep, and put up an all-night racket that anyone else would have found irritating. It was a "natural" sound, Paul said, and he liked it. She grew up calling him "Uncle" Paul.

His single-guy professional lifestyle allowed him to put a respectable amount of money in the bank, and friends were always suggesting he do something with it, such as invest in real estate. So on several occasions, he said, "Maybe I should buy a house of my own."

The thought of losing Paul to another house was very saddening. But my wife and I would always counter, "Oh, Paul, how would you manage? You can't even change a light bulb."

That was a terrible mistake.

Because shortly after Paul died, the light bulbs in the house started to blow.

In a house with something like fifty lights, a bulb is bound to burn out reasonably often. So when one of the three-bulb dining-room fixture lights burned out, I thought nothing of it. But the next day, the second one blew. Then the third went on the third day.

Then the fax machine went into permanent "receive" mode, as though someone were trying to send us a fax, but nothing was coming out. My wife brought it to the Mitsubishi people, who pronounced it healthy, and sent it home with a recommendation to discuss it with the phone company. A phone company repairman replaced all the wires leading to the fax, declared them in perfect running order, and recommended we talk to an electrician. The electrician plugged the fax into a different electrical outlet, and it worked.

But, my wife protested, it worked for more than a year in the old outlet. What happened?

He considered the old outlet. "Beats me," he said. "Maybe it's haunted."

In fact, my wife said, the fax machine had stopped working only when ... only when ... ah, well, when Paul died.

In the meantime, I had replaced two lights in the master bedroom, one in my daughter's room, the swing arm over the computer, both vanities in the bathroom, both carriage lamps at the front door, the tri-light in the study, two potlights in the basement, and the hanging one in the kitchen, which is such a bitch to change because of the glass bowl and the three set-screws holding it on to a swinging chain.

Just to add a menacing note, the microwave oven ceased working in the middle of a casserole, and the videotape recorder refused to record the Mighty Morphin' Power Rangers, which our daughter announced was going too far.

All in about four weeks. The situation had moved from coincidence to freakish unlikelihood.

One night, my wife, my daughter, and I lit a candle, held hands in a circle around it, and had a little chat with Paul.

We tried, as best we could, to explain that we all loved him dearly. He was not to worry, because the Blue Jays had won both the ALCS as well as the World Series. He was perfectly welcome in our home even if he was in no state to help with the rent. And we were terribly sorry we had ever teased him about the light bulbs, so could he give our wiring a break, please?

Our daughter was convinced her parents had taken leave of their senses, but played along anyway. And a good thing too — that very night, lights started to burn out at a rate much more statistically acceptable. I can't tell you what statistically acceptable means, but anyone who has lived in a home for a long time just knows the life rhythm of its light bulbs.

The cat, however, was having none of it. He moved into Paul's room to await Paul's return.

Soon after, we started to plan a Christmas vacation, and contacted a woman called Diana, who is a genius at organizing other people's lives. She had helped us stage a reception at our house for Paul's friends and relatives after the funeral. We wanted Diana to take care of the house while we were away.

"Do I actually have to sleep there?" she asked.

Well, no, not if it's a problem, we said, but why?

"Because I don't want to stay over if Paul's going to be there."

I beg your pardon?

"I mean, he was there at his funeral party. I saw him there."

You sure it wasn't his brother? They look awfully alike.

"No, I know Paul, and it was Paul."

Okay, so it was Paul. And what was he doing?

"Oh, just walking around. He was picking up things and looking at them, then putting them down. He looked all right."

Okay, no sleepovers. Just make sure the cat is fed and the plants watered.

A little later, I was talking on the phone to the information officer of the Anglican Church of Canada, when the other line rang. It was Diana, finalizing our arrangements for the holiday, and seeking more assurances that the electrical phenomena had stopped. As far as I could tell, they had, I said. And you still don't need to sleep over.

Back on the phone with the Anglicans, I told the information officer about that conversation, and about Paul and the light bulbs. I mentioned the VCR and the microwave too.

"Uh," he said, "we, ah, have some people here who could help you get rid of that sort of thing, if you want .... "

Had it come to that, then? Bell, book, and candle? Were we going to hurl the wrath of heaven at Paul? I mean, were we going to petition the Almighty to cast our former tenant into eternal eviction just for trashing light bulbs?

"Jeez, no," I said. "Thanks, but no. It would be just devastating to the cat."

"Oh," he said. "I understand."

I'm not sure he did.

The Most Beautiful Woman in the World

Robert Hoshowsky is a freelance writer who lives in Toronto. "The Most Beautiful Woman in the World" is an amazing ghost story. It has all the qualities of imaginative fiction, yet the author maintains that it is a complete and accurate depiction of what he saw early one morning when he went out jogging in North Toronto. It first appeared in the October 1992 issue of the community weekly *Midtown Voice* — the Halloween issue.

A long time ago, before it became fashionable, I was a jogger. Not just a block or two, but five, ten, even fifteen miles each and every night. Initially, I was joined by friends. The three of us huffed and wheezed our way through the labyrinth of streets and alleyways known as North Toronto a couple of hours after dinner, long after the sun had dipped below the horizon and the food in our stomachs had settled enough so we wouldn't puke. With our lungs straining for the next breath, we savoured every second of our run with youthful enthusiasm.

After a while, however, one friend after another dropped off and sought other pursuits. Tyler discovered the joys of poker, and became forever lost to gambling away his pocket change after class. Dwight formed a heavy metal band, and pretended to bite the heads off stuffed parakeets in the high-school auditorium during lunch. Since I had no musical abilities whatsoever, I kept running, alone.

One night, feeling especially adventuresome, I decided to try twenty miles. No stopping, not for pain or traffic lights. This was in August, and there are surprisingly few people awake at three in the morning.

Dressed in a ratty old muscle shirt and shorts that looked like they'd been washed ten thousand times, I was ready. And, up until the time I saw her, I was having a pretty good run. She was about half a mile away, on the other side of the street. I rubbed the sweat from my eyes and kept on running. At first, I thought she was a disheveled housewife, wandering around looking for her cat. That is, until I noticed a few little things.

Her bare feet weren't touching the ground.

I stopped so suddenly that I nearly fell flat on my face. The "house-coat" she was wearing was a nightgown, a very old-fashioned one, adorned with a high lace collar and white material that reached to her ankles. Her hair was loose, and hung around her slender shoulders in thick black ropes.

What shocked me the most was her body. It was translucent, not like anything I had seen before. With every passing second, sections of her appeared and disappeared at the same time. She seemed just as astonished to see me as I did her, looking at me like I was intruding on her territory. Yet she was striking, with firm, high cheekbones and a lovely oval face. She couldn't have been more than thirty.

Her entire appearance suggested nobility, as if she had just drifted off the canvas of a Pre-Raphaelite painting. Long, slender hands, the supple neck of a swan, and enormous dark eyes which seemed to occupy most of her exquisite face. I fell in love with her in an instant, despite the fact she was a ghost. Never before have I wished so hard for one thing: for this woman to be truly alive, with warm human flesh and the breath of the living, not the wind of the dead. By the way she was dressed, she had been that way for at least a hundred years.

As I walked towards her, I felt my knees turn to water and stopped, not out of fright but of fear — of myself. We stood on opposite sides of the road staring at one another for an eternity, a supernatural breeze blowing the nightgown around her naked form. She was trapped, a prisoner caught in the never-world between life and death; a place I could not enter, and a land she could never leave.

I turned and ran, stopping only when I reached the top of the hill. The instant I turned to look at her, she swirled around, her body slowly disappearing into the darkness. The look of sadness hadn't left her eyes, and won't until the day I am dead, when we can meet again, not as strangers, but lovers.

She was, and forever will be, the most beautiful woman I never met.